Between Christian and Jew

THE MIDDLE AGES SERIES

Ruth Mazo Karras, Series Editor
Edward Peters, Founding Editor

A complete list of books in the series is available from the publisher.

Between Christian and Jew

CONVERSION AND INQUISITION
IN THE CROWN OF ARAGON, 1250–1391

Paola Tartakoff

PENN

UNIVERSITY OF PENNSYLVANIA PRESS

PHILADELPHIA

Published by
University of Pennsylvania Press
Philadelphia, Pennsylvania 19104-4112
www.upenn.edu/pennpress

Printed in the United States of America on acid-free paper
10 9 8 7 6 5 4 3 2 1

Library of Congress Cataloging-in-Publication Data
Tartakoff, Paola.
    Between Christian and Jew : conversion and inquisition
in the crown of Aragon, 1250–1391 / Paola Tartakoff. —
1st ed.
        p. cm. — (The Middle Ages series)
    Includes bibliographical references and index.
    ISBN 978-0-8122-4421-2 (hardcover : alk. paper)
    1. Jews—Spain—Aragon—History—To 1500.
2. Christian converts from Judaism—Spain—
Aragon—History—To 1500. 3. Judaism—Relations—
Christianity—History—To 1500. 4. Christianity and
other religions—Judaism—History—To 1500. 5. Aragon
(Spain)—Ethnic relations. I. Title.
DS135.S75A787 2012
305.892'40465509023—dc23
                                              2011049639

For Daniel

Contents

PART III. BY THE FIRE

Note on Names, Money, Terminology,
and Transliterations

In the pages that follow, I have sought to preserve a sense of the linguistic diversity of the medieval Crown of Aragon. Thus, I have used the Catalan forms of names of people from and towns in Catalonia and Valencia (Pere, for example, instead of the English Peter, the Castilian Pedro, or the Latin Petrus) and the Castilian forms of names of people from and towns in Aragon (Esteban, for example, instead of Steven, Esteve, or Stephanus). For the sake of consistency, however, I have used the Catalan titles of the rulers of the Crown of Aragon (referring to King Peter the Ceremonious as Pere III, for example, and not as the Aragonese Pedro IV or the Valencian Pere II). For the sake of clarity, I have used the most commonly cited forms of the names of well-known individuals, such as the convert Pablo Christiani. In addition, to reduce confusion stemming from the variable orthography of medieval sources—although at the cost of obscuring data of interest to readers concerned with historical linguistics—I have regularized the spelling of toponyms in accordance with modern orthography (referring to Sant Pere de Riudebitlles, for example, instead of Sant Pere de Riudebirles). I have regularized the spelling of Hebrew names, as well, using the forms that most frequently appear in documents (spelling the English name Joseph always as Jucef, for example, instead of sometimes as Juceff or Josep).

The Crown of Aragon was home to three distinct coinages, all based on silver: sous of Barcelona (the currency in Catalonia), sous of Jaca (the currency in Aragon), and sous of Valencia, or reials (the currency in Valencia). All three used the Carolingian ratio of one lliura (or pound or libra) to twenty sous (or shillings or solidi), and one sou to twelve diners (or pennies or denarii). The relative values of these three currencies were constantly in flux. Gold coins circulated as well, and two types of these figure in this book. Morabetins were struck after 1172. In 1293, one morabetin was worth nine Barcelona sous. The florin of Aragon was first minted by command of King Pere III in 1346. In 1365, one florin was worth eleven Barcelona sous.

On account of the limitations of my sources and the thrust of my analysis, I have used the noun "conversion" and the verb "to convert" primarily to refer to an official change of a person's religious affiliation, and not to denote interior transformations. In addition, with an eye toward the complexity of converts' identities, I have made an effort to use the noun "apostate" and the verb "to apostatize" when discussing an individual in relation to the faith and community that he or she formally left behind and the noun "convert" and the verb "to convert" when discussing an individual in relation to the faith and community that he or she formally joined. Upon first introducing a convert, when possible, I provide his or her Jewish and Christian names. In subsequent references, I usually use only the Christian name.

I have transliterated Hebrew terms in accordance with the standards of the journal *Jewish Social Studies*, with several exceptions. I have preserved the conventional spellings of terms that commonly appear in an English context. I have not marked the Hebrew letter *ayin* with an apostrophe, and I have transliterated the Hebrew letter *het* as *h* instead of *ch*.

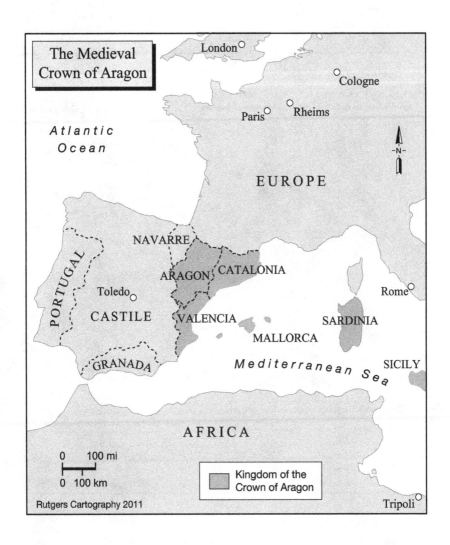

The Medieval Crown of Aragon

Atlantic Ocean

London

Cologne

Paris Rheims

EUROPE

-N-

NAVARRE

PORTUGAL

ARAGON CATALONIA

Toledo

CASTILE VALENCIA

Rome

SARDINIA

MALLORCA

GRANADA

Mediterranean Sea

SICILY

AFRICA

0   100 mi

0   100 km

Kingdom of the
Crown of Aragon

Rutgers Cartography 2011

Tripoli

Selected Jewish Communities
in the Medieval Crown of Aragon

FRANCE

NAVARRE

CATALONIA

Anduze

Manosque

Montpellier

Marseille

Toulouse

Pamiers

Narbonne

Montclús

Egea   Huesca

Tauste

Zaragoza

Puigcerdá   Elne   Perpignan

Berga   Ripoll   Besalú

Solsona   Castellón de Ampurias

Cervera   Vic   Pals

Calatayud   Ricla   Pina   Tárrega   Manresa   Peratallada

Daroca   Valls   Girona

ARAGON   Barcelona

Tarragona   Vilafranca del Penedès

Teruel   Montblanc

CASTILE

Valencia   Morvedre

Játiva   Alcira

VALENCIA

GRANADA

Palma   MINORCA

MALLORCA

IBIZA

Mediterranean Sea

-N-

0   100 mi

0   100 km

Medieval Crown of Aragon

Rutgers Cartography 2011

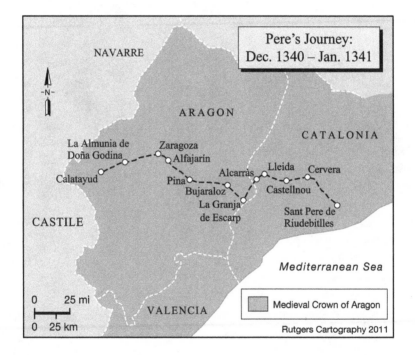

Introduction

Writing about Muslim converts to Christianity in thirteenth-century Valencia, the great historian of the medieval Mediterranean, Robert I. Burns, noted that converts were "a by-product of the main dispute, a kind of displaced person, whose story and status illumine the larger scene."[1] The same could be said of Jewish converts to Christianity who lived in the Crown of Aragon during the century that preceded the massacres and forced conversions of 1391.[2] Their lives lay bare the intensity of mutual hostility between Christians and Jews across a period whose first decades in particular have been celebrated as a time of interreligious harmony.[3]

In the medieval Crown of Aragon, the situation of Jewish converts was, in some ways, paradoxical. Christians were enamored of the idea of winning over Jewish souls, and some Jews were eager to bring apostates back to Judaism. Yet many Christians were disdainful of actual Jewish converts, both on account of converts' dubious motivations in seeking baptism and also because of converts' ties—real and merely perceived—to Judaism, and most Jews repudiated apostates as traitors and sinners who had been polluted by baptism and life among Christians. Sometimes courted by Christians and Jews, yet usually ultimately rejected by both societies, many converts became wandering beggars, some made a living by tormenting Jews, and others took great risks to return to Judaism.

The present work explores these dynamics with special attention to the activities of medieval, or papal, inquisitors, the forerunners of the personnel of the notorious Spanish Inquisition, which was established in 1478. In so doing, it argues that, decades before Jewish conversion became a mass phenomenon in Iberia, and over a century before Jewish converts were inquisitors' primary targets, Jewish converts were a focus of tensions between Christians and Jews.

Their experiences thus reflect and shed light on deep undercurrents of mutual antagonism.

The Case of Pere

The story of a convert from the Aragonese town of Calatayud whose Jewish name was Alatzar (Eleazar) forms the backbone of this book. Alatzar was the son of a Jew named Isaach Camariel, and he seems to have been of humble origins. He and his father frequently dined at the home of a Jewish cobbler, and he once worked as a messenger for a wealthy Jewish family. In mid-December 1340, Alatzar was baptized, hundreds of kilometers from home, in the Catalan town of Sant Pere de Riudebitlles, taking the name Pere (Peter). We do not know how old he was or why he decided to convert.[4]

Pere might never have appeared in written records had it not been for a dramatic turn of events. On January 5, 1341, less than three weeks after his baptism, he returned to Calatayud and narrowly escaped death at the stake. Flames were lapping at his feet, in fact, when the local Dominican prior and the commissary of the bishop of Tarazona—having heard that a Jewish convert was being burned—rushed to the scene, ordered that he be freed from the fire, and had him brought to the Dominican monastery of Calatayud, Sant Pere Mártir. There, Pere told a hastily assembled inquisitorial tribunal that a group of Jews had convinced him to court death at the stake. These Jews had done so, Pere explained, by telling him that in order to save his soul he would have to renounce Christianity before the local *justicia*—the magistrate in charge of administering justice—thereby incur the death penalty and die as a Jewish martyr. Pere added that the Jews also told him that they previously had convinced a convert whose Jewish name was Abadia (Obadiah) to do this. Abadia had burned to death, and his soul was now "safe with God." According to the inquisitorial scribe and notary who was present at Pere's interrogation, the Christian townspeople of Calatayud confirmed that seven years earlier Abadia had "had himself burned because he had gone over to the Catholic faith."[5]

Pere's accusations were corroborated in detail by two Jewish eyewitnesses, and they sparked a series of trials that unfolded over the course of twenty months, passed through the hands of inquisitors in Aragon, Valencia, and Catalonia, came to the attention of King Pere III, and concluded in Barcelona under the supervision of fra Bernat de Puigcercós, the inquisitor of all the territories of the Crown of Aragon. Pere was sentenced to prison for life, and so were two of the Jews whom Pere blamed for his actions—the prominent Janto (Shem Tov) Almuli of La Almunia de Doña Godina and his wife, Jamila. A third Jew—the illustrious Jucef de Quatorze of Calatayud—was turned over to the secular arm to burn at the stake.[6]

Pere's case is extraordinary in several respects. First, Jews and converts were uncommon defendants for medieval inquisitions, which began to operate in the 1230s in order to eradicate Christian heresies, such as Catharism.[7] Moreover, Jews were technically off limits to medieval inquisitions as, unlike converts, they did not belong to the Christian fold. Indeed, the records of the trials of Janto and Jamila Almuli and Jucef de Quatorze not only include some of the earliest known inquisitorial trial transcripts of any kind from the Crown of Aragon, but they are especially unusual as complete records of inquisitorial proceedings against Jews.[8] As such, they raise broad questions about the relationships between medieval inquisitors, converts, and Jews. How commonly did medieval inquisitors prosecute Jews and converts? With what offenses were Jews and converts usually charged? How did these trials unfold? What impact did inquisitorial prosecution have on Jews and converts? How did the prosecution of Jews and converts affect inquisitors and Christian society?

Historians have begun to explore these questions in general terms.[9] The dossiers of the Almulis and Jucef de Quatorze grant unprecedented insight, however, into daily interactions between Jews, converts, and inquisitors. They allow us to trace the arc of a complex case in detail, and they preserve the unedited ruminations of a medieval inquisitor on the prosecution of Jews. Moreover, in conjunction with additional sources—including royal, papal, and episcopal records and inquisitorial manuals—they illuminate how the inquisitorial prosecution of Jews was intended to punish Jews for perceived attacks against Christians and the Christian faith, and they demonstrate the symbolic importance of Jewish conversions for the medieval church.

Pere's case is remarkable also insofar as it highlights the existence of Jewish converts to Christianity in Iberia prior to 1391. With the exception of occasional victims of Christian violence and several converts who became prominent anti-Jewish polemicists—such as Peter Alfonsi (formerly Moses Sefaradi), Pablo Christiani (formerly Saul of Montpellier), and Alfonso de Valladolid (formerly Abner of Burgos)—Iberian Jewish converts who lived before 1391 have lurked below the scholarly radar.[10] Pere and Abadia were not alone, however, in journeying from Judaism to Christianity when they did. Nearly two hundred Jewish converts emerge from the pages of royal, papal, and episcopal correspondence, inquisitorial records, and rabbinic *responsa* composed between 1243 and 1391. Moreover, additional converts undoubtedly have been lost to history. Baptismal records were not yet systematically kept during this period. Episcopal documents of the kind that most frequently mention converts were not produced until the first quarter of the fourteenth century, at the earliest. Finally, wars, natural disasters, and poor storage conditions have destroyed enormous quantities of archival material.

Although fragmentary, extant sources establish that Jewish converts constituted a significant presence in Jewish and Christian communal life in the Crown of Aragon. Jewish apostates often tore apart Jewish families when they went over to Christianity, and they threatened Jewish communal security by denouncing Jews to Christian authorities and drawing inquisitorial attention to the Jews with whom they interacted. Repentant apostates' efforts to return to Judaism sowed strife among Jews and often sparked inquisitorial investigations. Converts who were itinerant beggars became a familiar presence among Christians, and those who worked as Christian preachers drew Jewish and Christian audiences. Highly visible, converts galvanized tensions between Christians and Jews at the same time as they suffered rejection on account of Jewish-Christian hostility.

Beyond shedding light on the experiences of inquisitors and converts in the medieval Crown of Aragon, Pere's case raises questions about Jewish attitudes toward apostates and apostasy prior to 1391. Indeed, the charges that Pere leveled against Janto and Jamila Almuli and Jucef de Quatorze are perhaps the most baffling aspect of Pere's case. Did the Almulis and Jucef de Quatorze actually counsel repentant apostates to renounce Christianity and burn at the stake? If so, was their aim truly to save apostates' souls? We shall never know, not least of all because our sources are so problematic. The defendants in the trials of Pere, the Almulis, and Jucef de Quatorze endured prison and torture. The witnesses feared for their lives, and the inquisitors had vested ideological, professional, and pecuniary interests in discovering guilt. Condemning culprits not only enabled inquisitors to punish presumed wrongdoers and thus safeguard Christendom, but it also benefited them personally. The more people inquisitors condemned, the more successful inquisitors appeared and the more revenue they brought in. Further complicating the task of using these records to reconstruct Jewish history, inquisitorial scribes and notaries altered confessions and testimonies through their translations, interpretations, and emendations. On the sole basis of inquisitorial records, therefore, we can draw few definitive conclusions about the Almulis and Jucef de Quatorze.[11]

Upon examining these documents in conjunction with other sources, however, several things become clear. If there existed a religious sensibility among some Jews in Calatayud in the 1330s and 1340s that favored martyrdom by fire as a salvific act for apostates, it was not representative of Jewish attitudes elsewhere in the Crown of Aragon. No evidence suggests that fourteenth-century Jews in other Iberian localities encouraged converts to martyr themselves. However, Jewish horror at apostasy was widespread, and some Jews across the Crown of Aragon and beyond shared a desire to re-Judaize apostates. Moreover, both horror at apostasy and efforts to re-Judaize apostates were inextricably linked to Jewish disdain for the Christian faith and resentment of Christian abuses of Jews.

Pere's case is a powerful lens, then, through which to begin to examine the intersecting worlds of Jews, converts, and inquisitors in the medieval Crown of Aragon. As such, it invites us to look more closely at the nature and consequences of Jewish conversion, and the state of Jewish-Christian relations, in northeastern Iberia during the century prior to 1391.

Jews and Christians in the Medieval Crown of Aragon

Living in self-governing communities known as *aljamas*, Jews constituted between 2 and 6 percent of the population of the Crown of Aragon, and perhaps more than 10 percent of the population of large cities. There may have been up to twenty-five thousand Jews in Catalonia, twenty thousand in Aragon, and ten thousand in Valencia.[12] Considered royal property, Jews enjoyed a degree of protection and certain privileges, but they also endured fiscal exploitation. In addition, the Jews of the Crown maintained close ties to Jews in southern France, whence this study also draws material.[13]

The Christian conquest of Muslim territories created unique conditions for the Jews of Spain from the late twelfth century onward. Jews assisted Christian kings as financial advisors, translators, doctors, and diplomats, and they helped to administer and colonize new domains. Through the early years of the fourteenth century, when the Crown of Aragon reached the peak of its expansion, Jews in the Crown of Aragon are said even to have enjoyed a social, economic, and cultural "golden age."[14] During this period, but also during most of the subsequent decades leading up to 1391, Jews and Christians often interacted productively in the Crown of Aragon. Economic collaboration and interdependence fostered interreligious stability. Christians and Jews embarked on joint business ventures. Butchers of the two faiths bought animals together and provided them with shared pasturage. Jewish doctors treated Christian patients. Jews frequented Christian courts and notaries, and Jews employed Christians in their homes. Records from Vic in the 1330s, for instance, mention a Christian woman who "was in the habit of nursing the children of Jews."[15] In the Crown of Aragon, Jews and Christians also socialized together. Christians in early fourteenth-century Barcelona attended Jewish weddings, circumcisions, and funerals, for example. In 1336, the provost of the monastery of Sant Cugat del Vallès was found gambling with Jews in the *call*, or Jewish quarter, of Barcelona. In 1341, a presbyter in Vilafranca del Penedès joined local Jews for the holiday of Purim and later stumbled out of the *call* drunk, and in the 1370s, it was discovered that the bailiff of Girona was selling licenses to Christians who wanted to gamble in the *call* on Christian holy days.[16] There is even evidence of love affairs between Christians and Jews. In the 1260s, for instance, a Jewish woman named Goig de Palafols and her Christian lover, Guillemó, who were "burning in their love for each other," openly cohabited, with the permission of King Jaume I. In Morvedre in 1325, a Jewish woman named Jorayffa not only fornicated with Christian men but also arranged for encounters between other Christians and Jews.[17]

Collaboration and camaraderie between Christians and Jews were not inconsistent with deep tensions, however, and, throughout the period in question, the peace was tenuous. In the Crown of Aragon, as elsewhere in medieval Christendom, Christian antagonism toward Jews was rooted in the annals of Christian sacred history. Holy Week liturgies and graphic passion plays reminded Christians yearly that Jews were the stubborn rejecters and killers of Christ, and many Christians believed that Jews were inherently malevolent and still conspiring for evil purposes. Jews were the church's antagonists par excellence, and their malice was said to know no bounds. By contrast, the tensions that existed between Christians and the Muslim population of the Crown of Aragon—which was small in Catalonia but large in Aragon and Valencia—were rooted in contemporary political realities. Christians worried, for example, that Muslims might rebel, conspire with Muslims abroad, or abduct Christians and sell them into slavery.[18]

Anxious to keep Jews' destructive potential in check, and eager that the socioreligious order should reflect the Christian claim that Christianity had superseded Judaism, medieval Christians felt strongly that Jews should always be subordinate to them. Instances in which Jews acquired leverage over Christians thus gave rise to outrage. At the Fourth Lateran Council (1215), for instance, the Jewish practice of usury was described as a form of Jewish "oppression" of Christians and as an effort "to exhaust Christians' financial strength," and, in late thirteenth-century Valencia, Christians called for the ouster of Jewish bailiffs, indignant that Jews had been raised above their proper, inferior station.[19] In 1375, Pope Gregory XI condoned sentiments such as these in a letter to King Henry II of Castile. "Jews hate Christians," he wrote, "as those who by divine mercy were received from the detestable hardheartedness of the same Jews into their place as sons of adoption. Therefore . . . the sacred canons forbid Christian freemen to remain subject to the governorship of Jewish slaves and to be cruelly burdened by them."[20]

In the Crown of Aragon, Christians regularly expressed their antagonism toward Jews. Every year during Holy Week, for example, they stoned the walls of Jewish quarters wherein "the sons of the crucifiers" lived.[21] Christians also spread noxious rumors about Jews. In 1321, in the Valencian town of Sogorb, for instance, Christians alleged that a Jew named Mossé had shaped *matzah* in the form of the crucified Christ and burned it in the oven. In addition, Christians accused Jews of poisoning wells and engaging in host desecration and the ritual murder of Christian children.[22] Charges such as these escalated tensions further. In 1327, in Valencia, incensed by accusations of Jewish host desecration, Christians hurled stones at Jewish burial parties and corpses, desecrated the Jewish cemetery, and dumped filth in Jewish graves.[23] On rare occasions, Christian anti-Jewish hostility led to bloodshed. In 1320, in the Aragonese village of Montclús, the French Pastoureaux massacred 337 Jews. In 1348, following the outbreak of the Black Death, which some Christians blamed upon Jews' sins, Christians slaughtered Jews in Barcelona, Cervera, Lleida, Tàrrega, and perhaps also Girona. In Tàrrega alone, Christians killed 300 Jews.[24]

These abuses had a deep impact on the Jews of the Crown of Aragon. Because Jews depended on Christians for survival, they could not respond in kind. Jews, however, found other ways to express their anger at Christians. They deprecated Christians and Christianity in their daily prayers, for example, and they told anti-Christian folktales, such as the *Toledot Yeshu* (*The Life Story of Jesus*), which depicted Christ as a charlatan and Mary as an adulteress.[25] Jewish scholars composed anti-Christian polemics, such as the *Kelimat ha-goyim* (*The Shame of the Gentiles*) of Profiat Duran, the *Bitul ikarei ha-Notsrim* (*The Refutation of the Christian Principles*) of Hasdai Crescas, the *Even bohan* (*Touchstone*) of Shem Tov ben Isaac ibn Shaprut, and the *Keshet*

u-magen (*Shield and Sword*) of Shimon ben Tsemah Duran. The Jewish political and spiritual leader of Barcelona at the turn of the fourteenth century, Rabbi
Solomon ben Avraham ibn Aderet (c. 1233–1310, known by the rabbinic acronym "Rashba"), also penned polemical responses to Christian arguments.[26] In
addition, Jews engaged in informal theological disputations with Christians.
Indeed, Shem Tov ben Isaac ibn Shaprut explained that he hoped that his
Even bohan would serve as a "shield" to Jews by furnishing them with retorts
to Christian arguments.[27] On rare occasions, Jews, too, turned to violence.
In 1308 in Morvedre, after Christians broke into Jewish homes and damaged
property during Holy Week, Jews stoned a church and shouted insults against
Christians and their faith. In 1320 in Montclús, in response to the slaugh-
ter of Jews by the Pastoureaux, Jews rioted, destroyed property, and insulted
Christians.[28]

Christians clearly were aware of Jewish antagonism toward them, and
they even knew of expressions of Jewish antipathy that were intended primarily for internal Jewish consumption. Bernard Gui, the inquisitor of Toulouse from 1307 to 1323, devoted half of the section on "the Jewish perfidy"
in his guide for inquisitors, the *Practica inquisitionis heretice pravitatis* (*Conduct of the Inquisition into Heretical Depravity*), to a discussion of passages
in Jewish prayers—including the Birkhot ha-shahar, the Amidah, and the
Aleinu—that he deemed offensive to Christians.[29] The Catalan Dominican
theologian Ramon Martí recorded a version of the *Toledot Yeshu* in Latin in
his compendium of anti-Muslim and anti-Jewish polemic, the *Pugio fidei adversus mauros et iudaeos* (*Dagger of Faith against Muslims and Jews*, 1278). And
the prolific Catalan Franciscan, Francesc Eiximenis (c. 1340–1409), devoted
nine chapters of his *Primer del Crestià* (*First Book of the Christian*), which he
wrote in Catalan for a lay audience, to defending Christianity against the
attacks of "a great Jewish rabbi" who had impugned Christian dogma and
practice and slandered Christ. It has even been suggested that Eiximenis composed his final work, the *Vita Christi* (*Life of Christ*), specifically in order to
combat the claims of the *Toledot Yeshu*, which he referred to as the "book of
the devil."[30]

The experiences of Jewish converts, and Jewish and Christian attitudes toward converts, as revealed by Pere's case and other little-known sources, allow
us to probe the nature of Jewish-Christian tensions in the medieval Crown
of Aragon during the century prior to 1391 in new ways. As we shall see, they
point especially to features of mutual hostility that spanned this period, char-

acterizing "golden" and darker times alike. They also reveal commonalities in the experiences of Jewish converts, and in Jewish and Christian attitudes toward converts, across medieval Western Christendom.

Book Outline

This study unfolds in three parts, each bookended by short sections that focus on Pere's case. Part I, "Before the Tribunal," explores the inquisitorial prosecution of Jews and converts as an arena of Jewish-Christian conflict in the medieval Crown of Aragon. Chapter 1 examines the inquisitorial prosecution of Jews as a means of defending Christians and Christianity from perceived Jewish attacks. It argues that inquisitors' commitment to protecting converts from corruption by Jews demonstrates the symbolic importance of converts to the church. Chapter 2 analyzes the trials of Janto and Jamila Almuli and Jucef de Quatorze. It details how inquisitors tackled the challenges involved in prosecuting Jews and how Jewish inquisitorial defendants responded to the pressures of inquisitorial scrutiny.

Part II, "At the Font of New Life," examines the lives of Jewish converts who lived in the Crown of Aragon before 1391. Chapter 3 explores converts' backgrounds, their reasons for converting, and the circumstances of their baptisms, and it argues that these factors contributed to Christian skepticism about the sincerity of Jewish conversions. It also considers how Christian authorities responded to the tension between the realities of Jewish conversion and Christian ideals. Chapter 4 turns to converts' experiences following baptism. It suggests that poverty and Christian rejection led many converts to remain bound up in Jewish affairs and caused some to seek to return to Judaism.

Part III, "By the Fire," explores Jewish attitudes toward apostates and apostasy in the medieval Crown of Aragon. Chapter 5 examines Jewish antagonism toward apostates. It argues that a sense of betrayal, anti-Christian sentiments, and the dangers that apostates posed to Jews all fueled this hostility. It shows also that Jews harmed apostates by disinheriting and taunting them and even denouncing them to Christian authorities. Chapter 6 focuses on Jewish efforts to bring apostates back to Judaism. It argues that these constituted bold expressions of Jewish contempt for Christianity and defiance toward Christians.

The Conclusion considers ways in which the implications of this study transcend the history of Jewish conversion and Jewish-Christian relations in the medieval Crown of Aragon, extending to majority-minority relations in Christian Spain more generally, Jewish conversion throughout medieval Western Europe, Jewish and Christian attitudes toward converts in fifteenth-century Spain, and the activities of the Spanish Inquisition.

PART I

Before the Tribunal

Four Arrests

Fra Sancho de Torralba, an inquisitorial commissary in Aragon and the prior of the Dominican monastery of Calatayud, was reputedly zealous in faith and eager to glorify Jesus Christ.[1] On Friday, January 5, 1341, when he learned that the representative of the *justicia* of Calatayud had condemned a Jewish convert to the stake, and that a group of Jews was rumored to have persuaded this convert to court this fate, he rushed to the scene with his partner in matters pertaining to "heretical depravity," Bernardo Duque, the commissary of the bishop of Tarazona. The convert, whose name was Pere, was already starting to burn when the two men arrived. Determined to get to the bottom of the affair, fra Sancho and Bernardo Duque had Pere unbound and turned over to them. They deposited him briefly in the prison of the *justicia*, and then fra Sancho summoned Pere for interrogation.[2]

In the chapterhouse of the aptly named monastery of Sant Pere Mártir, fra Sancho de Torralba opened a formal investigation. Before a handful of clerics and laymen, fra Sancho first asked Pere whether he wished to swear to tell the "pure and undiluted truth" as a Christian or as a Jew.[3] This question was essential, not only because Pere's religious allegiances were unclear, but also because it was crucial to the integrity of the proceedings that Pere take the oath that was most likely to compel him to tell the truth. Pere was not at liberty to respond as he pleased, however, for to request to swear as a Jew would have been to signal impenitence.[4] Even though Pere had been willing to burn to death as a Jewish martyr only hours earlier, therefore, Pere assured the inquisitor that he was a "true and good Christian." As a result, he took his oath in the name of Jesus Christ, with his hand on a crucifix and the Gospels.[5]

Pere then delivered his first confession, in which he recounted the events that had brought him to the stake. He told the tribunal that he had been baptized in Catalonia three weeks earlier and that he had planned to return to his hometown of Calatayud and live there as a Christian. Toward the end of his journey home, however, as he was leaving the village of La Almunia de

Doña Godina (located some thirty-five kilometers northeast of Calatayud), he had been intercepted by a Jewish woman named Jamila Almuli. Jamila invited him into her home, where she lived with her husband, the prominent Janto Almuli, and there Janto and Jamila lamented Pere's apostasy and persuaded Pere to renounce the Christian faith. In addition, they told Pere that, if he proclaimed his return to Judaism before the *justicia* of Calatayud, he would incur the death penalty and become a Jewish martyr. An apostate named Abadia had done so in 1334, the Almulis explained, and Abadia's soul was now "safe with God." Instead of portraying himself as having heroically resisted the Almulis' entreaties, as a "true and good Christian" might have, Pere testified that after taking leave of the Almulis he "immediately tore down the road" to Calatayud and did as the Almulis had advised.[6]

Pere's first confession must have alarmed fra Sancho de Torralba, for it suggested not only that Jews had led a convert to renounce Christianity—a crime for which inquisitors in the medieval Crown of Aragon regularly prosecuted Jews—but also that they had done so in an extraordinary manner. Instead of keeping Pere's return to Judaism secret, the Almulis had convinced Pere to broadcast his repentance, first before the *justicia* of Calatayud, and then at the stake before an even larger Christian audience. Moreover, the Almulis had managed to manipulate the *justicia* of Calatayud into helping to carry out their plan. These acts trumpeted Jewish defiance.

Fra Sancho de Torralba lost no time in continuing his investigation. He went straight to the Almulis' home in La Almunia de Doña Godina. He dragged Janto, who was ill, out of bed, and he brought Janto and Jamila back to Calatayud. Then, on January 8 and 12, respectively, he began to interrogate the husband and wife. Unfortunately, the Almulis' testimonies from this stage of the proceedings have not survived.

We do not know where Pere was taken after he first testified because portions of the records of his trial have been lost. It is likely, however, that he was imprisoned once again, in accordance with standard inquisitorial procedure. If he was, then five months of incarceration seem to have loosened his tongue further. When, on May 28, 1341, Pere came before the tribunal for a second time, he announced that he wished "to add some things that he [initially] had omitted on account of forgetfulness."[7]

In his second confession, Pere recast himself as the innocent victim of a Jewish conspiracy that extended far beyond the Almulis. He explained that efforts to re-Judaize him began over dinner on the night of Thursday, January 4, in La Almunia de Doña Godina, at the home of a Jewish cobbler named Salomon Navarro and his wife, Miriam. When Pere told the Navarros that he had converted to Christianity, they led him to the Almulis' home. There, another influential member of the local Jewish community, Jucef de Quatorze—whom the inquisitor fra Bernat de Puigcercós would call "one of the preeminent Jews of Calatayud"—joined the group. Pere portrayed Jucef de Quatorze as the ringleader, and he testified that Jucef de Quatorze told him that he, along with Janto and several additional Jews, had re-Judaized Abadia in 1334.[8] In addition, Pere now maintained that he resisted the pressure to return to Judaism and burn at the stake. "Lord Jucef," he had cried, "I beg you not to lead me to err so greatly and abandon the Christian law, for I accepted it with devotion and without any force or violence. Do not put me in peril of death!" But Pere said that these protestations had no effect. The Jews did not relent until he agreed to follow their instructions.[9]

Pere's second confession led fra Sancho de Torralba to a particularly prized suspect. As it emerged later in the proceedings, fra Sancho was convinced that Jucef de Quatorze had a history with the inquisition. According to fra Sancho, in 1326, the inquisitor fra Guillem Costa had arrested Jucef, together with other Jews from Calatayud, including two of Jucef's relatives, on charges of circumcising Christians and re-Judaizing converts. On that occasion, Jucef reportedly had abjured "giving support, or in any way cooperating in helping anyone . . . who was baptized go over, or return, to the Jewish perfidy."[10] According to Pere's second confession, however, after this alleged abjuration, Jucef had brought two more Christians—first Abadia, then Pere—over to Judaism. Jucef was, then, a repeat offender, a particularly incorrigible and dangerous culprit who merited death at the stake. On the basis of Pere's second confession, the tribunal immediately concluded that Jucef de Quatorze was guilty as charged. "From the aforesaid things it is clearly apparent," wrote the notary Guillem de Roca, "that Jucef de Quatorze committed grave offenses against the [Catholic] faith that are utterly to be detested by the faithful."[11]

With these arrests and interrogations, fra Sancho de Torralba set in motion a momentous series of confrontations between Jews, converts, and inquisitors. In the two chapters that follow, we shall begin to unravel the implications of Pere's story. After situating the trials of Janto and Jamila Almuli and Jucef de Quatorze in the broader context of the work of medieval inquisitors, we shall consider what these proceedings reveal about inquisitorial approaches to the prosecution of Jews and analyze the ways in which Jewish defendants responded to inquisitorial scrutiny.

Chapter 1

Defending the Faith: Medieval Inquisitors and the Prosecution of Jews and Converts

> Perfidious Jews try, whenever and wherever they can, secretly to
> pervert Christians and bring them to the Jewish perfidy, especially
> those [Christians] who previously were Jews but converted and
> received baptism and the faith of Christ.
> —Bernard Gui, c. 1323[1]

Pope Gregory IX surely never dreamed, when he appointed the first inquisitors in 1231, that medieval inquisitions would become a nexus of conflict between Christians and Jews. As the head of an increasingly self-conscious and assertive church, Gregory's immediate aim was the eradication of Christian heresy. The pope assigned members of the newly founded Franciscan and Dominican orders to this task and, in conjunction with local bishops, these friars set about using Roman inquisitorial procedure to lead "the writhing serpent" of heresy out from "the bosom of the sinner."[2]

Whether by converting hearts or destroying bodies, inquisitors were determined to stamp out heresy. To this end, they initiated proceedings at will. In order to encourage witnesses to speak freely, inquisitors withheld from the accused the names of those who testified against them, as well as the specific crimes with which they were charged. They resorted to coercive measures, such as imprisonment and torture, when confession, "the queen of proofs," was not forthcoming, and they assigned penances—such as arduous pilgrimages and the wearing of symbols representing particular crimes—to facilitate and publicize heretics' return to the church and the saving power of her sacraments. When, however, a heretic was found to be impenitent or a repeat offender, he or she was understood deliberately to have rejected God's favor and the opportunity for atonement that inquisitors sought to mediate. In such cases, inquisitors, who as clerics were not permitted to shed blood, turned individuals over to secular officials to burn at the stake. Inquisitors' jurisdiction reached even into the grave. When inquisitors determined that a heretic had died impenitent, they exhumed and burned his or her corpse.[3]

The origins of inquisitorial activity in the Crown of Aragon can be traced to the late twelfth and early thirteenth centuries, when kings Alfons I, Pere I, and Jaume I launched campaigns against Christian heretics who had fled to the Crown of Aragon to escape persecution in Provence and Languedoc during the Albigensian Crusade (c. 1208–29). Ramon de Penyafort, who served as confessor to King Jaume I, chaplain to Pope Alexander IV, and Dominican master general from 1238 to 1240, was instrumental in putting Dominican inquisitors to work in the Crown by 1237. Penyafort is credited with compiling an inquisitorial manual in 1241 or 1242 and, in 1242, he and the reforming archbishop Pere de Albalate helped to produce guidelines for inquisitorial protocol at the provincial council at Tarragona.[4]

By the time of Pere's case in 1341, inquisitors in the Crown of Aragon possessed a wide range of experience. They had investigated Cathars, Waldenses, Templars, Beguins, and Spiritual Franciscans, as well as the works of the philosopher and alchemist Arnau de Vilanova. In addition, they had come to form part of an intricate network of operations. An inquisitor based in Barcelona appointed local commissaries to conduct investigations. Proceedings required the presence of additional men of good standing, as well as the help of notaries and scribes and the advice of lawyers and theologians. Royal officials helped inquisitors detain, torture, and execute alleged heretics and, beginning in the reign of Jaume II, kings agreed to pay inquisitors an annual salary of one hundred lliures.[5] Bishops, who shared with inquisitors the duty of ridding Christendom of heresy, also collaborated with inquisitors. Thus, in Pere's case, for example, fra Sancho de Torralba worked closely with Bernardo Duque, and fra Bernat de Puigcercós requested the permission of the bishop of Tarazona, Bertran de Cormidela, to have the defendants tortured and to sentence them.

In the pages that follow, we shall explore a remarkable feature of inquisitorial activity in the medieval Crown of Aragon, namely, the prosecution of Jewish converts, whose numbers were few, and professing Jews who, as non-Christians, did not fall squarely within inquisitors' jurisdiction. After examining the extent and impact of this work and considering some of the theoretical and practical challenges it involved, I shall argue that inquisitors prosecuted Jews primarily in order to punish them for perceived attacks against Christians and the Christian faith, which often involved re-Judaizing converts. I shall suggest that inquisitors' focus on safeguarding Jewish converts attests to the importance of Jewish conversions to the medieval church as a means of demonstrating Christianity's superiority to Judaism and weakening the Jewish enemy.

Prosecution and Its Consequences

Bernard Gui, the inquisitor of Toulouse from 1307 to 1323, devoted an entire chapter of his influential guide for inquisitors, the *Practica inquisitionis heretice pravitatis*, to "the Jewish perfidy," and he listed "Jewish converts to Christianity who had returned to their old religion" alongside Cathars, Waldenses, Pseudo-Apostles, Beguins, and sorcerers as one of the six types of heretics that inquisitors were likely to encounter. In so doing, Gui addressed an arena of inquisitorial activity that was, by his day, well established. Dominicans, who manned most medieval inquisitorial tribunals, became involved in Jewish affairs as early as 1233, when Jews from Montpellier who wanted to ban Maimonides' *Guide for the Perplexed* and the *Book of Knowledge* of his *Mishneh Torah* may have turned over copies of these works to friars who consigned them to the flames. Some scholars have suggested that the Paris Disputation of 1240, which was sparked by a Jewish apostate's claim that the Talmud blasphemed God, the Christian faith, and Christians, constitutes an early example of inquisitorial dealings with Jews.[6]

Inquisitors were not interested merely in Jewish texts, however, and, in southwestern Europe, they investigated dozens of Jewish individuals, communities, and converts to Christianity. In the Crown of Aragon, where inquisitors appear to have been far less active than in southern France and northern Italy, surviving evidence indicates that inquisitors received at least seventy denunciations of Jews between 1265 and 1391 and that they prosecuted Jews on at least thirty occasions. In fact, inquisitors in the medieval Crown prosecuted Jews more frequently than they prosecuted converts, who are known to have been denounced only about fifteen times. High-ranking Dominicans oversaw most of these cases. For example, fra Bernat de Puigcercós, who prosecuted Jews and converts on at least six occasions, served as the Aragonese provincial prior and as the prior of the Dominican monastery of Barcelona and, in 1330,

Pope John XXII appointed him inquisitor of all the territories of the Crown of Aragon.[7] Fra Joan Llotger, who was involved in at least five investigations of Jews and converts, convinced King Jaume II to act against the Templars in 1307 and condemned the works of Arnau de Vilanova on Spiritual Franciscanism in 1316.[8] Fra Nicolau Rossell, who oversaw three cases involving Jews and converts, was made a cardinal in 1356.[9]

Inquisitorial prosecution constituted one of the principal threats to the prosperity and security of Jews in the Crown of Aragon, for inquisitors imposed devastating penalties. During the first quarter of the fourteenth century, for example, inquisitors exiled ten Jews from Tarragona and imposed an exorbitant fine of 35,000 Barcelona sous on the entire community. Although King Jaume II later reduced the fine of the ten exiled Jews to 23,000 Barcelona sous, the fine of the rest of the *aljama* of Tarragona to 20,000 Barcelona sous, the fine of the neighboring *aljama* of Valls to 5,000 Barcelona sous, and the fine of three Jews from Tarragona who converted on this occasion to 11,000 Barcelona sous, these sums were still ruinous. King Jaume II decried "the want and very great poverty with which . . . the[se] Jews [were] manifoldly oppressed." In Mallorca around the same time, inquisitorial proceedings resulted in the imposition of a fine of 150,000 florins and appear also to have led to the seizure of a synagogue that was subsequently turned into a chapel.[10] As a result of the inquisitorial prosecution of the *aljama* of Calatayud by fra Guillem Costa during the 1320s, Jews were imprisoned, books were confiscated, and two houses of study narrowly escaped destruction. In addition, fines were imposed that hurt the *aljama*'s economy so badly that Jaume II exempted the Jews of Calatayud from major taxes for four years.[11] In the 1350s, the inquisitorial prosecution of the Jewish *aljamas* of Taus and Exea likewise led to the imprisonment of Jews, the imposition of fines, and the confiscation of property.[12] Overwhelmed by these developments, in 1354, when representatives of Jewish communities from Catalonia and Valencia gathered to discuss their problems, they agreed that inquisitorial prosecution was a grave threat and agreed to ask King Pere III to petition Pope Innocent VI to limit inquisitors' powers.[13]

Improbable Inquisitorial Defendants

The prosecution of Jews by medieval inquisitors was incongruous, for inquisitors' primary goal was to root out Christian heresy. In 1199, in the bull *Vergentis in senium*, Pope Innocent III defined Christian heresy as a form of divine treason, a "wandering away in the faith of the Lord."[14] So conceived, Christian heresy was a crime that Jews could not commit. Since Jews were not "in the faith of the Lord," it was impossible for them to stray from it. Moreover, since the medieval church taught that Jews were deprived of God's grace, Jews could not possibly benefit from the opportunities for reconciliation that *inquisitio heretice pravitatis* promised Christians. Indeed, short of converting to Christianity, Jews were incapable of repenting in the Christian sense of returning to Christ.

The prosecution of Jews also presented procedural challenges. For example, many standard inquisitorial penances—such as wearing large, yellow crosses to signal one's status as a repentant sinner—plainly were inappropriate for Jews.[15] During the trials of the Almulis and Jucef de Quatorze, fra Bernat de Puigcercós pondered this difficulty, musing in a draft of the final sentence that, unlike Christian clerics, Jews could not "be suspended, excommunicated, or deposed, for such punishments were not fitting for Jews."[16]

In addition to theoretical and practical obstacles, the inquisitorial prosecution of medieval Jews faced opposition by the kings of the Crown of Aragon. Kings considered Jews their personal property, and they insisted that Jews were theirs alone to judge. Thus, for example, in 1284, upon learning that inquisitors were proceeding against Jews from Barcelona who allegedly had welcomed *relapsi* into their homes, King Pere II declared that he, and not inquisitors, should be responsible for investigating the matter. Likewise, in 1292, Jaume II ordered a halt to proceedings initiated by inquisitors against Jews in Girona and Besalú. In 1356, Pere III decreed that a Jew named David of Besalú, who had been charged with blasphemy, should be released from inquisitorial prosecution. In 1379, upon hearing that a Jew named Isaach Vidal Ravalla of Peratallada had been mistreated by inquisitors, Pere declared that he would not tolerate that Jews, "his treasure," be unjustly oppressed, and he asserted that the right to punish Jews belonged to the king and to no one else. In 1380, the Infant Joan sought to arrange a meeting of representatives of Jewish *aljamas*, as well as a meeting of learned Christians in order to draft legislation that would protect Jews from the abuses of inquisitors. In 1384, when a Jew from Valencia named Salomon Nasci was tried, along with Christians, on charges of devil worship, Joan protested, in a letter to the bishop of Valencia, that "that which pertains to the church should remain with the church, and that which regards the rights and jurisdiction of the lord king should remain his." In 1387, as king, Joan petitioned Pope Clement VII to recognize his exclusive jurisdiction in cases involving Muslims and Jews.[17]

Neither theoretical objections, procedural complications, nor royal protests stymied inquisitors. The theologian and inquisitor general, Nicolau Eimeric, vigorously tackled the theoretical objections to the inquisitorial prosecution of Jews in his treatise, *Super iurisdictione inquisitorum contra infideles fidem catholicam agitantes* (*On the Jurisdiction of Inquisitors over Infidels Who Agitate against the Catholic Faith*, c. 1370). Drawing on the doctrine of the plenitude of papal power, Eimeric argued that if the pope had jurisdiction over infidels, then inquisitors, as the pope's delegates, did, too. In addition, citing missives that popes had sent to inquisitors in the Crown of Aragon, Eimeric argued that inquisitors of the Crown of Aragon had a special mandate to proceed against Jews and Muslims. Finally, building on a line of reasoning that had begun to gain popularity in the eleventh century, Eimeric maintained that Jews could, in fact, properly be considered heretics, for example, when their views departed from those that Jews and Christians were supposed to share—such as the belief that God created heaven and earth, for instance—or when they engaged in behavior, such as demon worship, that was anathema to Judaism and Christianity.[18]

Inquisitors circumvented the procedural challenges involved in prosecuting Jews by making slight adjustments. For example, Jewish defendants took their oaths on the Ten Commandments, instead of on the Gospels. Thus, Janto and Jamila swore to tell the truth "on the Ten Commandments that God gave Moses at Mount Sinai, while physically touching them."[19] Also, skirting the difficulty that Jews could not properly repent in the Christian sense of returning to Christ, fra Bernat de Puigcercós had Janto Almuli abjure his alleged crimes "as if he were penitent." Similarly, he explained to Jamila Almuli that her abjuration was "in the place of" the one that, "in the case of a Christian," would have the force to render her a repeat offender.[20] This careful language signals that fra Bernat de Puigcercós was aware of the fundamental shift in the nature of *inquisitio* that the prosecution of Jews involved. As we shall see, when it came to investigating Jews, rhetoric about repentance was actually a façade for an operation whose primary aim was to punish.

Finally, demonstrating the limits of royal power, inquisitors disregarded kings' repeated commands to desist from prosecuting Jews.[21] Inquisitors could afford to do so because kings were chronically remiss in paying inquisitors' salaries. The registers of King Pere III reveal, for example, that between 1356 and 1384, the inquisitor fra Jaume Domènech was not paid even once. Year after year, officials recorded the growing debt owed to him, and Domènech eventually died without being paid.[22] In his inquisitorial manual, the *Directorium inquisitorum* (*Guide to Inquisitors*, c. 1376), Nicolau Eimeric lamented that because temporal princes did not support "so wholesome and so necessary an institution" as the papal inquisition, the institution was left to support itself.[23] Indeed, we have evidence that, as early as the 1340s, inquisitors were using the earnings of their tribunals to fund their activities. Thus, for example, in Janto and Jamila's final sentence, fra Bernat de Puigcercós declared that he would use the defendants' confiscated assets to build an inquisitorial prison in Calatayud.[24] In 1354, Pere III granted the inquisitor fra Nicolau Rossell permission to take his salary from the earnings of his tribunal, and in 1366, he granted the same permission to Nicolau Eimeric. When the Jews of Montblanc were prosecuted between 1389 and 1391, in addition to having their property confiscated and paying fines, they were required to cover inquisitors' expenses.[25]

Blasphemy

As learned churchmen bent on destroying error, inquisitors considered Judaism false and reprehensible. Fra Bernat de Puigcercós called it "the wicked way of damnation."[26] Yet, as fra Bernat pointed out in a draft of the final sentence for the Almulis and Jucef de Quatorze, inquisitors did not proceed against Jews "on account of the errors in which they persevered." After all, he continued, Jews were "tolerated by the Church and allowed to persevere and die in their error." Similarly, toward the end of the thirteenth century, the inquisitor of Pamiers, Arnaud Déjean, reassured Jews that the Catholic Church supported their presence and tolerated their rites.[27] However, insofar as Jews were deemed "enemies of the Christian faith"—as the notary Guillem de Roca stated during the trial of Jucef de Quatorze—who tried to lead Christians into error, inquisitors did consider Jews proper targets for inquisitorial investigation.[28] Thus, it was in the name of defending the Christian faith and protecting Christians from Jewish machinations that inquisitors prosecuted Jews, focusing especially on the offenses of blasphemy, Judaizing cradle Christians, and bringing converts back to Judaism.[29]

Dominicans expressed outrage over allegedly blasphemous Jewish writings throughout the period in question. Following the Barcelona Disputation of 1263—at which the Jewish convert Pablo Christiani confronted the towering Jewish scholar Nahmanides—Christiani's mentor, Ramon de Penyafort, decried the words "disparaging [the] Lord and all the Catholic faith" that Nahmanides had uttered and that he subsequently committed to writing (presumably in his still extant *Vikuah,* or *Debate*). Penyafort spearheaded efforts to censor Jewish writings, and he was supported in this endeavor by Pope Clement IV (the former archbishop of Narbonne, Guy Foulques), who decreed that the author of a certain "book of lies" about a disputation with Pablo Christiani should be punished for his impudence—"preferably by death or mutilation."[30]

During the first quarter of the fourteenth century, one century after Dominicans first burned Jewish books in Montpellier, inquisitors just north of the Crown did so again. In 1319, Bernard Gui ordered the public burning of the Talmud. In 1321, in response to Pope John XXII's bull, *Dudum felicis recordationis*, which required that Franciscan and Dominican friars examine Jewish books and destroy those containing offensive passages, the inquisitor and bishop of Pamiers, Jacques Fournier (later Pope Benedict XII), likewise called for the burning of volumes of the Talmud.[31]

Inquisitors were concerned also about blasphemy in Maimonides' *Mishneh Torah.* Bernard Gui decried the work's "deceits and falsehoods" and "many errors and blasphemies against the faith of Christ" in his *Practica inquisitionis.*[32] In 1346, the bishop of Girona, Arnau de Montrodon, sent a letter to the inquisitor fra Guillem Costa, informing him that he had confiscated books belonging to Jews, "the iniquitous enemies of the name of our savior, Jesus Christ," on account of the words they contained "against the Lord . . . [and the] holy Catholic faith," and he enclosed a passage from a book he called *De regulis.*[33] In 1389, the Dominican inquisitorial commissary fra Guillem de Tous of the monastery of Tarragona initiated proceedings against Jews from the town of Montblanc on the grounds that they possessed copies of the blasphemous *Talmud of Rabbi Moses of Egypt.* It is possible that Arnau de Montrodon and fra Guillem de Tous were particularly offended by a passage from the *Shofetim* section of the *Mishneh Torah* that stated that Jesus and Mohammad merely prepared the way for the Messiah. Pablo Christiani helped to bring this passage to the attention of Christian authorities during the Barcelona Disputation. Thereafter, King Jaume I ordered the confiscation and burning of all copies of the section *Shofetim* of the *Mishneh Torah,* and this section was regularly excised by Christian censors.[34]

When inquisitors in the Crown of Aragon prosecuted Jews for blasphemy, however, it was most often on account of public verbal attacks on Christianity—"heretical words" spoken aloud that, as the bishop of Girona Jaume de Trilla put it in 1373, might easily "infect the Lord's sheep."[35] In his draft of the final sentence for the Almulis and Jucef de Quatorze, fra Bernat de

Puigcercós stressed the particularly reprehensible nature of public blasphemy. He explained that the Almulis and Jucef de Quatorze were blameworthy not only because they "led certain Christians, who were previously Jews, to return to the Jewish perfidy *in secret*," but also because they "led them *publicly* to profess said perfidy, *publicly* to deny the faith of Christ, and *publicly* and with abominable words to blaspheme Christ and his mother and the law of Christ" (emphasis mine).[36] Brazen Jewish outbursts could sow doubt in the hearts of far more Christians than could Hebrew words tucked away in books.

Sharing this concern, in 1302, the Dominican inquisitor fra Joan Llotger and the bishop-elect of Barcelona, Ponç de Gualba, investigated three prominent Jewish merchants from Barcelona—Bonsenyor and Cento de Forn and Mosse Toros—for allegedly "having spoken certain contumelious words and la[in] violent hands on the image of the glorious Virgin and sp[at] in her face" while traveling in Mamluk Alexandria.[37] About a decade later, King Pere III and an inquisitor condemned a Jew from Perpignan named David of Besalú for uttering words against the Christian faith. During the third quarter of the fourteenth century, proceedings were opened against a Jew from Pals who was accused of saying "many heretical things against the power of God and the chastity and virginity of blessed Mary." Around the same time, a Jew from the town of Peratallada named Isaach Vidal Ravalla was accused of declaring publicly, in the town square, before the *justicia* Bernat de Belloc, "How can you have so much to say about that woman [that is, the Virgin Mary] who gave herself to a man like a whore?" In 1390, a Jew from Zaragoza named Avraham Obex was denounced to fra Martín Gruñuel, the representative of fra Eximen Navassa, for having offended the Catholic faith "in the presence of some Christians."[38]

Judaizing Cradle Christians

In addition to prosecuting Jews on charges of written and spoken blasphemy, inquisitors in the late thirteenth and early fourteenth centuries also prosecuted Jews on charges of encouraging Christians to Judaize. In his *Directorium inquisitorum*, Nicolau Eimeric defined Judaizing broadly as anything from observing Jewish rites and holidays and "doing the other things that Jews habitually do together," to officially converting to Judaism.[39] Indicating the gravity of the offense, Bernard Gui referred to it in the opening lines of the chapter on "the Jewish perfidy" in his *Practica inquisitionis*, declaring: "perfidious Jews try, whenever and wherever they can, secretly to pervert Christians and bring them to the Jewish perfidy." Even the Catalan Carmelite priest Felip Ribot, who was a staunch critic of the inquisitorial prosecution of infidels under most circumstances, conceded that inquisitors could "punish" Jews who "led Christians into their execrable rite."[40]

From the church's perspective, the evils involved in Judaizing could not be overstated. Judaizing led not only to the loss of Christian souls, but specifically to the particularly appalling loss of Christian souls to the faith of the reject- ers and alleged killers of Christ. As early as the fifth century, the Theodosian Code remarked that it was "graver than death and crueler than massacre when someone abjure[d] the Christian faith and bec[ame] polluted with the Jewish credulity." Similarly, during the third quarter of the fourteenth century, Clem- ent IV remarked in his bull, *Turbato corde*: ". . . many reprobate Christians, denying the truth of the Catholic faith, have transferred themselves damnably to the Jewish rite, which appears the more condemnable, since thereby the most holy name of Christ is blasphemed more recklessly by hostility in the family."[41] Christian horror at apostasy to Judaism was so great that Judaizing was deemed the work of the devil. Thus, in 1316, Bishop Ponç de Gualba of Barcelona described a Christian woman named Johanna from the town of Stella in Navarre—whom a Jew from Barcelona named Jucef Levi (alias Jucef Galiana) and two Jewish women from Castile, Huruceta and Vilida, had alleg- edly converted to Judaism—as having gone over to Judaism "at the instigation of the devil."[42]

Accusations that Jews had Judaized cradle Christians were relatively rare. Yet a few cases have come to light, in addition to that of Johanna. According to the fifteenth-century chronicler Guillaume Bardin, for example, in 1278 inquisitors exhumed and burned the cadaver of a cradle Christian who had gone over to Judaism, died as a Jew, and been buried in a Jewish cemetery near Toulouse.[43] During the summer of 1311 or 1312, the inquisitor fra Joan Llotger, together with Archbishop Guillem de Rocabertí of Tarragona, investigated charges that several Jewish *aljamas* in Catalonia had assisted two German Christians who had converted to Judaism and been circumcised in Toledo.[44] In 1352 and 1353, the inquisitor and Dominican provincial fra Nicolau Rossell prosecuted members of the Aragonese *aljamas* of Taus and Exea, including Avraham and Isaach Coro, who were found guilty of the circumcision of a Christian whom they had brought over to Judaism "by means of cunning practices."[45]

In two more instances, it is possible that boys or men who were said to have been circumcised by Jews had Jewish mothers, or mothers who had converted from Judaism to Christianity. Thus, these individuals may have been considered Jewish by Jews, who followed the law of matrilineal descent, and Christian by Christians, who believed that the offspring of mixed unions should adhere to Christianity.[46] Indeed, in contrast to Johanna, who was described as "the daughter of a Christian woman and a Christian man," these individuals were each described as the son of one Christian parent. One, a boy or man whom Jews from Calatayud were accused of circumcising in the 1320s, was referred to as "the son of a knight" who was "Christian in nature." The other, a boy or man whom Jews from Tàrrega were accused of circumcising in 1329, was referred to as "the son of a Christian."[47]

Re-Judaizing Converts

Far more frequently than inquisitors investigated the Judaizing of cradle Christians, they investigated the re-Judaizing of converts. Inquisitors' concern about converts returning to Judaism was no doubt heightened by the entry into the Crown of Aragon of hundreds of Jews who had been expelled from France during the last decade of the thirteenth century and the first quarter of the fourteenth. A first wave of refugees arrived in 1293 and a much larger influx in 1306. Some of these refugees had been baptized north of the Pyrenees, and they sought to return to Judaism in Iberia.[48] A number of inquisitorial investigations of the period clearly involved suspected French *relapsi*. For example, when, in the 1320s, fra Guillem Costa prosecuted members of the *aljama* of Calatayud, it was not only on charges of circumcising two Christians, but also for reportedly helping a baptized Jewish woman from France (*Gallicam*) return to Judaism. In 1342, during his trial, Jucef de Quatorze specifically referred to these proceedings as "the inquisition against the French."[49]

Later in the fourteenth century, additional French converts crossed the Pyrenees into the Crown of Aragon, drawing further inquisitorial attention. Thus, between January and May 1360, the Franciscan inquisitor Bernat Dezpuig investigated several Jews from Borriana who were alleged to have aided relapsed Provençal converts, and, during the 1370s, a number of converts who had been baptized *in Provincia* (an expression that Jean Régné suggested may refer to Languedoc) were denounced to the vicar general of the inquisitor general of the Crown for living as Jews. One was a man living in Besalú, whom a Jew named Aaron had allegedly helped and hidden. Another, named

Jucef Mosse, was turned over to the inquisitor of Rosselló. A third, who was captured and tried in Castelló d'Empúries, repented of Judaizing and publicly abjured his error. A fourth, who lived in Solsona and was known as lo Salser, asked that it be made known at his death that he had died as a Jew. (A note was made in the inquisitorial register to investigate the Jews who might have encouraged lo Salser to say this.) Yet another, a woman living in Girona who had married a Jew named Salomon, was denounced by a Jew named Aaron Jucef, who claimed that she had tried to bribe him to hide her return to Judaism. Another woman who lived in Banyoles was said to have fled when she learned that Aaron Jucef had denounced her.[50]

Inquisitorial concerns about the re-Judaization of converts predated the French expulsions by several decades, however. In 1265, in Catalonia, for example, the Dominican inquisitor fra Pere Cadireta (whom Christians murdered in 1277) prosecuted a Jewish convert named Berenguer Durand for Judaizing and confiscated his possessions.[51] As early as 1267, Pope Clement IV officially authorized inquisitors to proceed both against Jewish converts who returned to Judaism and also against the Jews who helped them. In the bull *Turbato corde*, Clement wrote to inquisitors, present and future, as follows: "With a troubled heart we relate what we have heard: A number of *bad Christians* have abandoned the true Christian faith and wickedly transferred themselves to the rites of the Jews. . . . Against Christians whom you find guilty of the above you shall proceed as against heretics. Upon Jews whom you may find guilty of having induced Christians of either sex to join their execrable rites, or whom you may find doing so in the future, you shall impose fitting punishment" (emphasis mine).[52]

When Pope Gregory X reissued this bull in 1274, he specified that these "bad Christians" included Jewish converts to Christianity. "With a troubled heart we relate what we have heard," the new version began, "not only are *certain converts from the error of Jewish blindness to the light of the Christian faith known to have reverted to their prior perfidy*, but even very many [cradle] Christians, denying the truth of the Catholic faith, damnably went over to the Jewish rite" (emphasis mine).[53] At the end of the thirteenth century, in the bull *Contra Cristianos*, Pope Boniface VIII reiterated that Christians who converted and converts who returned to Judaism were to be treated like heretics and that inquisitors were to treat those who helped cradle Christians and converts go over to Judaism like "abettors, shelterers, and protectors of heretics."[54] In the mid-fourteenth century, Pope Innocent VI commissioned a Franciscan inquisitor in Provence, fra Bernard Dupuy, to take action against

Jewish converts who were said to have reverted to Judaism, and in 1360, in the Catalan town of Peralada, Dupuy's representative, Arnau de Carmensó, a lector at the monastery of Valencia, read the pope's missive aloud.[55]

Inquisitors in southwestern Europe prosecuted a number of *relapsi* during the century that followed the promulgation of *Turbato corde*. In 1278, Pope Nicholas III directed that a group of French Jews who had been forcibly baptized, returned to Judaism, were arrested by inquisitors, and refused to repent after more than a year in prison be burned at the stake. In 1312, Bernard Gui posthumously tried a Jewish convert named Joan (formerly Josse) who had returned to Judaism and died as a Jew, and he had his remains exhumed and burned. In 1319, Gui detained a convert from the town of Sérignac whose name was also Joan, who was baptized in Bretz and, three years later, returned to Judaism in Lleida. In 1338, the inquisitor of Provence, Jean de Badis/Badas, sought to arrest an Iberian convert named Alfonso Díaz, who was thought to be living with Jews in the county of Dauphiné or Savoie.[56] In 1341, in Calatayud, fra Sancho de Torralba initiated proceedings against our protagonist, Pere, who had publicly renounced Christianity. About 1373, an inquisitor and the bishop of Girona, Jaume de Trilla, arrested a convert named Jaume de Faro (formerly a Jewish doctor) on charges of blasphemy and Judaizing.[57]

In addition to prosecuting *relapsi*, medieval inquisitors prosecuted the Jews who allegedly had encouraged *relapsi* to return to Judaism. In fact, inquisitors prosecuted the latter far more often than the former. Some inquisitors were apparently so quick to accuse Jews of seeking to re-Judaize converts that, in 1281, Pope Martin IV had to remind inquisitors that Jews should not be accused of encouraging converts to return to Judaism if all that was known was that the Jews and converts had been engaged in conversation.[58] Practical considerations may have driven inquisitors to focus on Jews. As we have seen, inquisitors often used the earnings of their tribunals to fund their activities. As, on average, converts were very poor compared to Jews, from a financial perspective, inquisitors would have preferred to prosecute Jews. Inquisitors may also, however, have considered Jews to be more culpable than the converts whom they allegedly re-Judaized. Fra Bernat de Puigcercós, for example, noted in his draft of the final sentence for the Almulis and Jucef de Quatorze that Janto, Jamila, and Jucef "were more guilty than he who was burned [that is, Pere], for they were the entire reason for which the burned one erred, and the reason for which he persevered in error to the point of death." Janto, Jamila, and Jucef were, according to fra Bernat, "makers, abettors, and defenders of heretics" who, according to canon law, "deserved to be punished more than heretics."[59] In his *Practica inquisitionis*, Bernard Gui affirmed the importance of prosecuting abettors of heresy. "The end of the office of inquisition is the destruction of heresy," Gui wrote, "which cannot be destroyed unless heretics are destroyed, who also cannot be destroyed unless their receivers, favorers, and defenders are destroyed."[60]

Surviving evidence indicates that inquisitors prosecuted Jews suspected of bringing converts back to Judaism on many occasions beyond those involving *relapsi* from France. In 1284, for example, an inquisitorial tribunal in Brignoles investigated charges that a Jew from Manosque named Avraham de Grassa had facilitated the re-Judaization of the baptized daughter, Agnes (formerly Belia), of his wife, Rosa. In the early 1290s, in Apulia, the inquisitor fra Bartolomeo de Aquila fined a Jew from Naples for bringing a convert back to Judaism.[61] There were similar proceedings in the Crown of Aragon, as well. In 1284, for instance, Dominican friars investigated the Jewish *aljama* of Barcelona for sheltering regretful converts. In 1313, the archbishop of Tarragona, Guillem de Rocabertí, and the inquisitor Joan Llotger prosecuted the Jewish *aljama* of Montblanc for helping a convert named Joan Ferrand return to Judaism. In 1315, the bishop of Barcelona, Ponç de Gualba, investigated charges that a Jew from Barcelona named Chaim Quiç had convinced a convert named Bonafos to return to Judaism. In 1323, the archbishop of Tarragona, Ximeno Martínez de Luna i Aragó, prosecuted a Jew from Valls named Isaach Necim for having sheltered a convert who had returned to Judaism.[62]

Like Judaizing cradle Christians, abetting the return to Judaism of converts was considered the work of the devil.[63] Both crimes led to the loss of Christian souls and specifically to their loss to the church's age-old antagonists. In fact, technically, re-Judaizing converts was simply a particular instance of Judaizing Christians. Thus, in his *Practica inquisitionis*, Bernard Gui specified: "perfidious Jews try, whenever and wherever they can, secretly to pervert Christians and bring them to the Jewish perfidy, *especially those [Christians] who previously were Jews but converted and received baptism and the faith of Christ*" (emphasis mine).[64] On account of the special significance of Jewish converts to Christian authorities, however, the implications of re-Judaizing converts were not identical to those of Judaizing cradle Christians. In some ways, they were even more grave.

The medieval church prized conversions to Christianity. Spreading the Good News was a fundamental Christian objective. It saved souls, enlarged the body of Christ, and advanced the coming of God's kingdom. Moreover, conversions were evidence of the strength and vitality of the Christian faith. A surge in conversionary fervor swept thirteenth-century Western Europe, and the conversion of infidels was a particularly pressing concern in the Crown of Aragon, where Muslim and Jewish populations had swelled as a result of the Christian conquest of Muslim territories. Indeed, several natives of Catalonia—including Ramon Llull, Arnau de Vilanova, Ramon de Penyafort, and Ramon Martí—spearheaded efforts to convert infidels by means of preaching, and Christians of all ranks in the Crown showed support for conversion, for example, by serving as godparents to neophytes.[65]

It appears, however, that Jewish conversions to Christianity were a special *desideratum*. Although the kings of the Crown of Aragon issued legislation meant to encourage the conversion of both Jews and Muslims, and although Muslim conversions—often driven by the promise of liberation from slavery—probably outnumbered Jewish conversions, the kings of the Crown served as godparents to Jewish converts far more frequently than to Muslim converts.[66] Although thirteenth-century Dominicans in the Crown of Aragon studied Hebrew and Arabic—perhaps for missionary purposes—there is no indication that friars preached to Muslims, whereas there is abundant evidence that they preached to Jews.[67] And, although backsliding occurred among Muslim converts as among Jewish converts, there is barely a trace of inquisitorial concern regarding Muslim converts.[68]

The importance of Jewish conversions surely was heightened by the fact that these were relatively hard to come by. The higher social and economic status of many Jews certainly made Jewish conversions more attractive, too, as wealthy and educated individuals were perceived as less likely to convert for the sake of material gain. Christian theology, however, which posited a unique relationship between Judaism and Christianity, also informed a predilection for Jewish conversions. From a theological perspective, Jewish conversions enjoyed special status, on the one hand, on account of the merits of Jews' forefathers. Indeed, Christian theologians deemed it especially appropriate that, as the original "chosen people" and the progenitors of the prophets and Christ, Jews should recognize Christian truth and join the "new Israel." Thus, in 1236, Pope Gregory IX opened a missive regarding two Jewish converts as follows: "Although we open the heart of fatherly piety to all who come to the Christian faith, we embrace more dearly those converted from Judaism. We hope that, since sometimes a naturally wild olive tree grafted onto a good olive tree bears agreeable fruits, contrary to its nature, all the more so will branches broken from a sacred root, which are better grafted onto their olive tree, in accordance with their nature."[69]

On the other hand, Jewish conversions were of particular significance on account of the imputed sins of Jews' ancestors. The status of Jews as the archvillains in Christian sacred history elevated the importance of Jewish conversions in at least two ways. First, insofar as Jews were believed to be trying insidiously to corrupt Christians and undermine Christianity, conversions reduced these threats by turning Jews into Christians. Arnau de Vilanova argued along these lines in his *Informació espiritual* (1309), suggesting that Jews ought to convert in order "to avoid the corruption of Christians."[70] Similarly, Ramon Martí argued in his *Pugio fidei* that it was more important to convert Jews than Muslims because there was "no enemy more capable of inflicting injury than a familiar one, and there [wa]s no enemy of the Christian faith more familiar and more unavoidable than the Jew."[71]

Second, every conversion of a Jew to Christianity confirmed the triumph of *Ecclesia* over *Synagoga* that the church had long touted. Christians understood Christianity's rapid spread and its political and military might as evidence of God's favor and Christianity's supersession of Judaism. They viewed Jews' abject fate as a people—that is, the destruction of the Temple and Jerusalem, Jewish exile, and Jews' prescribed subordinate status in foreign lands—as evidence of God's rejection of the Jews and Judaism's defeat. Nevertheless, Christians were disconcerted by Judaism's tenacity and by the prosperity of many Jews, and they feared that Jews were capable of grievously injuring Christians and Christianity. Jewish conversions to Christianity, therefore, were welcome reminders of Christianity's preeminence, as well as milestones on the road to Christianity's final victory over Judaism. Indeed, according to Christians from Saint Paul to Ramon Martí and Francesc Eiximenis, the eventual conversion of all Jews would herald Christ's return in glory. For Christians, then, converting Jews was the ultimate way to destroy Jews and triumph over them.

In sum, inquisitors' special focus on prosecuting backsliding converts and the Jews suspected of encouraging them to return to Judaism was about more than trying to stop the loss of Christian souls to maleficent Jews. It was also about participating in the Christian missionary impulse, seeking to bring to fruition the special destiny of the Jewish people as understood by Christian theologians, trying to eliminate malignant members of society, and preserving the victory of Christianity over Judaism that transpired, in theory at least, in the soul of every Jewish convert.

Inquisitorial prosecution—whether for blasphemy, Judaizing cradle Christians, or re-Judaizing converts—looked very different from a Jewish perspective, of course. To Jews, it constituted a particularly devastating form of Christian attack. As such, the inquisitorial prosecution of Jews perpetuated the cycle in which Christian persecution deepened Jewish bitterness, which, in turn, reinforced Christian fear of Jews.

Chapter 2

From Resistance to Surrender: Jewish Responses to Inquisitorial Prosecution

> With all due respect to the lord inquisitor, he should not have
> proceeded as he did.
> —Jucef de Quatorze, 1342[1]

The Jews whom Pere blamed for his misadventures were terrified when they learned that they were suspected of "crimes of heretical depravity." Jucef de Quatorze fled to Valencia, where he was arrested and put on trial by the inquisitorial commissary fra Berenguer Saiol. Salomon and Miriam Navarro prepared to flee to Castile, where medieval inquisitions never took root. Before they could leave, however, fra Sancho de Torralba sent the *justicia* of the neighboring town of Ricla, Gosalbo de Grades, to arrest Salomon and escort him to Calatayud for interrogation.[2]

As Jews who sought to evade inquisitors' grasp physically, Jucef de Quatorze and the Navarros were not alone. In 1303, for example, a Jew from Valls named Isaach Necim abandoned his property and escaped after he was charged with sheltering a convert who had returned to Judaism. In 1323, King Jaume II lamented that "many of the most terrified [Jews of Lleida] had fled" on account of inquisitorial prosecution. In 1364, a Franciscan inquisitor in Arles named Hugo de Cardillon complained to Pope Urban V that he was unable to prosecute certain Jews who had re-Judaized converts because they had taken refuge abroad. A register kept by the vicar general of the inquisitor general of the Crown in the 1370s records that when a baptized Jewish woman who had returned to Judaism was denounced, she escaped "on account of fear of the inquisitors."[3]

Other Jews in and around the medieval Crown of Aragon took a preemptive approach to inquisitorial prosecution. In late thirteenth-century Languedoc, for example, Jews requested reassurance from the newly appointed inquisitor of Pamiers, Arnaud Déjean, who promised that he "ha[d] no intention of imposing upon [them] any serious or unusual innovations." Jews also petitioned popes for protection from inquisitors, with some success. For example, concerned that Jews might be the victims of false accusations, Pope Martin IV specified that the accuser of a Jew was to post a bond, and if the case against the accused could not be proven, the accuser was to receive the penalty that would have befallen the accused. Moreover, on the grounds that Jews—even the wealthy among them—were *impotentes*, that is, people who lacked the power to harm their accusers, popes repeatedly decreed that inquisitors should reveal to Jewish defendants the names of their accusers.[4]

As nearly complete transcripts of inquisitorial proceedings against Jews from the medieval Crown of Aragon, the records of the trials of Janto and Jamila Almuli and Jucef de Quatorze afford a unique opportunity to examine in detail a spectrum of Jewish responses to inquisitorial prosecution. These responses included appealing for help to Jewish communal leaders and the king, cooperating with inquisitors in the hope of receiving mercy, attempting to invalidate the prosecution's witnesses, denouncing inquisitors for procedural irregularities, taking advantage of inquisitors' attention to harm personal enemies, and breaking down under the stress of torture and prolonged imprisonment. In the pages that follow, we shall see how, by actively trying to shape their fates by drawing on a wide range of resources, the Almulis, the Navarros, and Jucef de Quatorze became key actors in an inquisitorial investigation.

Negotiations and Appeals: October 1341–January 1342

After proceedings were initiated against Janto and Jamila Almuli in Calatayud in January 1341, King Pere III transferred the trials to the tribunal of fra Bernat de Puigcercós in Barcelona, on account of the seriousness of the charges. On Wednesday, October 24, 1341, at the Dominican monastery of Santa Caterina, fra Bernat de Puigcercós picked up where fra Sancho de Torralba had left off. He began by interrogating Janto and Jamila Almuli separately, in the presence of the notary Guillem de Roca and the Dominicans fra Bertran d'Abella and fra Simó Serdina.[5]

At first, Janto and Jamila professed total ignorance. Both maintained that they had never met Pere, who was from Calatayud, about thirty-five kilometers northeast of La Almunia de Doña Godina. Jamila added that she would not even recognize Pere if she were to see him, and she declared that it would have been impossible for Janto to have convinced Pere to return to Judaism, as Janto was bedridden at the time of his alleged encounter with Pere. Janto and Jamila also each testified that Janto had not spoken with Abadia—the convert whom Janto Almuli, Jucef de Quatorze, and other Jews allegedly convinced to return to Judaism and die at the stake in 1334—after his baptism.[6]

Testimony that the Almulis' son, Jucef Almuli, gave at his parents' trials suggests, however, that Janto and Jamila were not telling the truth. For example, on Thursday, October 25, 1341, Jucef Almuli testified that, when he went to live in the Morata de Jalón (because he was suspected of having killed a fellow Jew during a fight in Zaragoza), on at least one occasion he dispatched Pere to deliver a message to his parents. In addition, when fra Bernat questioned Jucef Almuli about his parents' relationship with Pere—whether it was true that Pere's mother had once lived near his parents, for instance, and how frequently Pere had dined with them—Jucef Almuli did not dismiss these questions out of hand. Instead, perhaps dubiously, he claimed that "he did not remember."[7]

Testimony that Salomon Navarro gave on November 29, 1341 also suggests that Pere had been acquainted with the Almulis prior to their alleged encounter in January. Salomon, who lived near the Almulis in La Almunia de Doña Godina, told the tribunal that on the night of Thursday, January 4, 1341, when he learned that Pere had converted to Christianity, he sent his wife, Miriam, to tell the Almulis that "Alatzar" was in their home and that he was now a Christian.[8] Salomon would not have been likely to refer to Pere simply by his Jewish first name unless the Almulis knew him.

By denying any relationship to Pere, Janto and Jamila Almuli may have been stalling for time, for, from his cell in the prison tower of Castellnou, Janto was trying to use his connections to escape from his predicament. One such connection was Samuel Benvenist, a prominent member of the Jewish community of Barcelona who was, among other things, the founder of a local synagogue.[9] Janto must have thought that Samuel's wealth and influence would command the respect of fra Bernat de Puigcercós. Janto sent his son,

Jucef Almuli, to invite Samuel to his cell and, when Samuel arrived, Janto begged him to intercede on his behalf before the inquisitor.[10]

According to Janto Almuli and Samuel Benvenist, who also testified before fra Bernat de Puigcercós, Samuel initially refused to help Janto. Both men maintained that Samuel told Janto that "no one could help him more than he could help himself, by telling the truth," for, in inquisitorial investigations, "he who confessed the full truth received greater mercy than he who denied it."[11] It is possible that, by "the truth," Samuel meant "that which fra Bernat wanted to hear." That is, Samuel may have wanted Janto to plead guilty—even if he was innocent—in the hope that he would receive a lighter penalty.

In spite of Samuel's understandable reluctance to involve himself in Janto's troubles with the inquisition, Samuel eventually appeared with Jucef Almuli before fra Bernat de Puigcercós. Janto had asked Samuel and Jucef to tell the inquisitor that he "would confess the truth that he had initially denied if the inquisitor would have mercy on him." Fra Bernat was not interested in this offer, however. Indeed, in keeping with the best inquisitorial practice as described in Bernard Gui's *Practica inquisitionis*, the inquisitor was determined to reject all appeals for special treatment. He curtly told Samuel and Jucef to inform Janto that he would proceed justly. He would consult royal advisers, scholars, and religious men in determining Janto's final sentence and, if he condemned Janto to death, he would ask the king to have mercy on him, "as [wa]s the custom when heretics [we]re relinquished to the secular arm." Surely Janto was not reassured by the inquisitor's response. It was standard practice for inquisitors to turn heretics over to secular officials with a plea for mercy. This plea, however, was a mere formality.[12]

Samuel Benvenist was not Janto's only hope. Indeed, Janto had a second plan under way. He had begun negotiations with the royal bailiff and treasurer of Queen María, Pere Justas, in order to obtain a royal remission for his alleged crimes. Janto had reason to believe that King Pere III might come to his rescue, for he had made significant contributions to the royal fisc. Indeed, in return for Janto's service to the Crown, Pere III had reduced his taxes in 1323.[13] Moreover, Janto probably knew of several instances in which the previous king, Jaume II, had been persuaded to exempt wealthy Jews from Calatayud from punishments and fines. In 1319, for example, Jaume II granted Jucef de Quatorze a royal remission for having wounded another Jew, in exchange for two thousand Jaca sous. In 1321, Jaume II granted Mosse Abenforna a royal remission for having wounded a relative of Jucef de Quatorze named Isaach, in exchange for three hundred Barcelona sous. Moreover, in 1326, Jaume II revoked various inquisitorial fines and confiscations that had been imposed on Sulema and Ora de Quatorze, in exchange for ten thousand Jaca *sous*. Also in 1326, Jaume II was asked by the Infanta María to remit Isaach Abenalafu's portion of a community-wide inquisitorial fine on the grounds that Isaach was too valuable a source of royal income.[14]

Janto did not place all his faith in the king, however. He was also considering confessing to the crimes of which he was accused. Janto's ability to confess, however, was constrained. As Janto told Samuel Benvenist and Jucef Almuli, and as they, in turn, told fra Bernat, Janto had assured Pere Justas that "the things that Pere the neophyte had said against him" were "completely false," and that "he knew nothing about them." As a result, Pere Justas "believed that Janto was innocent and blameless," and he had "worked very hard to help Janto." Indeed, Pere Justas had told the king and the archbishop of Zaragoza that Janto was completely innocent. Moreover, Pere Justas had "pledged his fealty to the lord king concerning this, promising him under the fealty by which he was held by the lord king that said Janto was innocent and blameless." If Janto now confessed to the charges against him, as Samuel Benvenist urged, this would render Pere Justas "contemptible to the king," and Janto would lose all chances of obtaining a royal remission. In fact, on October 24, 1341, Janto confided in Samuel Benvenist and his son Jucef that, if he were to confess "the truth," "the lord king would kill him and seize all of his belongings."[15]

Janto's dilemma was cruel. If he remained silent and the king failed to come to his aid, fra Bernat de Puigcercós would deem him impenitent and turn him over to the secular arm for execution. If Janto confessed, however, he might avoid an inquisitorial death sentence, but surely he would receive some other harsh punishment and, in addition, he would incur royal wrath and harm Pere Justas. Faced with these alternatives, Janto initially contemplated confessing. Indeed, he had Samuel Benvenist and Jucef Almuli ask fra Bernat whether the proceedings could be suspended for twelve days in order to give him a chance to ask Pere Justas for forgiveness. Fra Bernat refused, declaring that "he did not need to grant any favors in this affair." Moreover, the inquisitor added that he was pressed for time as he feared that Janto might soon die on account of his illness, and he wanted the case to conclude "in favor of the faith and in exaltation of the name of Christ." Janto decided, then, that it would be better to "keep the truth quiet."[16]

Janto's appeal to the king nearly bore fruit. On January 16, 1342, less than three months after Janto and Jamila first professed their innocence before fra

Bernat de Puigcercós, Pere III agreed to grant Janto's request for a royal remission. The account books of the royal treasury record a payment of five thousand Barcelona sous out of a promised ten thousand made by the Almulis in exchange for a royal remission given on account of their having been charged with being responsible for the renunciation of Christianity and return to Judaism of "some Christians who previously were Jews."[17] Janto and Jamila should, at this point, have been on their way to freedom. Demonstrating the limits of royal power, however, the Almulis' trials proceeded unhindered. Janto's efforts to use his powerful connections to extricate himself from the proceedings had come to naught.

Strategic Cooperation: November–December 1341

Meanwhile, in Calatayud, fra Sancho de Torralba continued to assist in the investigation, and he interrogated Solomon and Miriam Navarro. The Navarros lacked the Almulis' wealth and connections, and they approached their predicament very differently from the Almulis. In fact, they showered the tribunal with information about the re-Judaizations of Pere and Abadia with no apparent worry regarding self-incrimination.

At the residence of the *justicia* of La Almunia de Doña Godina on December 7, 1341, Miriam declared, for instance—in accordance with Pere's second confession—that she and her husband had brought Pere to the Almulis' home on the night of Thursday, January 4 and been present throughout the meeting during which Pere was persuaded to return to Judaism and burn at the stake. At the Dominican monastery of Sant Pere Mártir on November 28, 1341, Salomon said that he had attended Abadia's re-Judaization in 1334. Miriam and Salomon also implicated additional Jews in the case. Salmon testified that his daughters were present when Pere arrived at his home for dinner on January 4, and Miriam mentioned that the Almulis' daughter-in-law, Velida (Jucef Almuli's wife), was at the Almulis' home that evening.[18]

The testimonies of Salomon and Miriam Navarro were rich in detail. Miriam related, for instance, that when Pere arrived at their home on January 4, they were eating a meal of marinated greens (*caules*), bread, and wine, and that the Jews celebrated Pere's renunciation of the Catholic faith at the Almulis' home by drinking wine.[19] Miriam also displayed a keen awareness of Pere's emotional state. Pere began to tremble, she said, when Janto urged him to renounce Christianity and, on account of Pere's trepidation, the Jews had to assure Pere that the "temporal punishment" of burning at the stake would "pass quickly." They also had to repeat that by dying at the stake "he would acquire eternal life and be a martyr before God." In addition, Miriam noted that "the men as much as the women Judaized [*judayçaverunt*] Pere . . . leading him to renounce the Catholic faith."[20]

Salomon Navarro gave a similarly vivid portrayal of events. He testified, for example—as did Pere and Jamila—that Janto was reclining by the fire when he entered his kitchen on the night of January 4. In addition, Salomon described Abadia's re-Judaization. He told the tribunal that it took place in a Jewish communal gathering space above the butcher shop in the Jewish quarter of Calatayud. During the proceedings, Abadia was surrounded by "very important and pious" Jews from Calatayud, including Aaron Abenafia, Samuel Alpestan, Mosse Amnalguer, Rabbi Mahir Amnalguer the elder, Rabbi Mahir's son Rabbi Salomon, David Avenrodrig, Salomon Avensaprut Ezquierdo, Isaach Habealuz, Avraham Mocatil, Avraham Pasagon's son Jucef, Salomon Passariel, Jucef de Quatorze, Jucef de Quatorze's son Jaco, Sabbat del Sach, Isaach Sadoch, and Sadoch Ullaçeni. Salomon also told the tribunal that, directly following Abadia's re-Judaization, he witnessed Jucef de Quatorze announce to his wife, Jamila: "Know that we Judaized [*judayçavimus*] Abadia, and we instructed him to ask the *justicia* of Calatayud to have him burned immediately." Moreover, straining credulity, Salomon claimed that later that day, as he went about the Jewish quarter of Calatayud, he came upon Avraham Mocatil and Salomon Passariel, two of the Jews who had been involved in re-Judaizing Abadia, and he overheard Avraham say to Salomon: "Abadia's case has been taken care of," to which Salomon Passariel responded: "It has, indeed."[21]

The testimonies of Salomon and Miriam Navarro largely concurred with one another and with Pere's two confessions. All of these narratives agreed that Janto and Jamila Almuli had convinced Pere to renounce Christianity and return to Judaism and that the only way to save his soul was to die at the stake as a Jewish martyr. One glaring inconsistency, however, suggests that at least one person may have been wrongly accused of involvement in Pere's re-Judaization. Miriam Navarro portrayed Jucef de Quatorze as a central player in Pere's re-Judaization, as did Pere in his second confession. But Salomon Navarro initially omitted any mention of Jucef and instead portrayed Janto Almuli as the lone ringleader, as did Pere in his first confession. Indeed, Salomon first mentioned Jucef de Quatorze one week after he first testified, when fra Sancho de Torralba asked whether he wished to add anything to his previous testimony.[22] Jucef de Quatorze may have been present at Pere's alleged re-Judaization, and Pere and Salomon Navarro may have been trying to protect him. Alternatively, Jucef may not have been involved, and Salomon and Pere may have been pressured to testify against him.

In spite of the contradictions in the record, fra Sancho de Torralba concluded that Jucef de Quatorze was principally responsible for Pere's re-Judaization. Toward the end of December 1341, he sent fra Bernat de Puigcercós a report in which he stated as follows: "As you will clearly see from the proceedings I am sending you, the neophyte Pere and two other witnesses [that is, the Navarros] who were present in the home of Janto Almuli and saw all the things that were done regarding said neophyte . . . all agree on time, day, hour, place, and method, and they do not disagree about anything. . . . You should know that Jucef de Quatorze was the one who did the most and led the neophyte Pere to renounce the [Catholic] faith." Upon receiving this letter, fra Bernat de Puigcercós sent for Jucef, who was still being held in Valencia by fra Berenguer Saiol.[23]

The Navarros' effusiveness before fra Sancho de Torralba's tribunal may have been motivated by a desire for mercy. Indeed, the Navarros may have believed that, as Samuel Benvenist warned Janto Almuli, in investigations conducted by inquisitors of heretical depravity, "he who confessed the full truth received greater mercy than he who denied it." According to Bernard Gui, individuals who voluntarily came forth, confessed, and betrayed their associates deserved to be pardoned. The Navarros did not voluntarily come forth; they first tried to flee to Castile. But they certainly confessed to crimes and denounced other Jews. Therefore, although they both professed complicity in Pere's re-Judaization, and although Salomon also professed complicity in Abadia's, neither Salomon nor Miriam were formally charged by fra Sancho. In fact, when Miriam Navarro was called to testify on December 7, 1341, one week after Salomon gave his testimony, she was described as "having been set free." After she testified, she and Salomon disappeared from the records of the proceedings.[24]

The Invalidation of the Prosecution's Witnesses: February 1342

As neither Samuel Benvenist nor King Pere III had proved able to extricate Janto Almuli from the proceedings, Janto was forced to confront the inquisition on his own terms. Still unwilling to confess to the crimes of which he was accused, Janto tried to subvert the proceedings against him by taking advantage of one of the few procedural protections available to inquisitorial defendants, namely, the right to invalidate the prosecution's witnesses. Inquisitorial procedure required that tribunals disqualify the testimony of mortal enemies of the accused. A shrewd defendant therefore would try to guess the identities of his or her accusers and seek to invalidate their testimony by naming them as mortal enemies.

On Wednesday, February 20, 1342, the scribe and notary Guillem de Roca visited Janto in the residence of the provost of Tarragona in Barcelona, where Janto was being held "without shackles or handcuffs," and asked him to list his mortal enemies. Janto said he had many enemies because people were jealous of him, but he maintained that, on account of his illness, he could not remember exactly who they were, and he asked for time to think. Guillem visited Janto twice the following day—first at the hour of terce, then at compline—and Janto still would not speak. Finally, on Monday, February 26, Janto was ready.

Janto cast his net widely, claiming, for instance, that he had "many" enemies in the town of Ricla and that, moreover, "all" the Jews of Calatayud were his enemies because they had once sold some property that belonged to him, and Janto had denounced them to the king.[25] Janto's enemies in Ricla included a Jew named Juste d'Almudever and the four sons of a Jew named Bita Suri, who blamed Janto's son, Jucef Almuli, for the murder of a Jew from Calatayud. Janto also maintained that a Jew named Mosse el Roig from La Almunia de Doña Godina was his enemy, and that "many" other Jews from La Almunia had quarreled with him when he insisted that the king had exempted him from having to contribute with them to the castellan of Amposta. Janto also named several Christians as enemies. He mentioned the son of a certain Juan Justo, whom fra Sancho de Torralba had assigned to guard Janto's home after Janto was arrested, and who had taken advantage of his assignment to help himself to Janto's possessions. Janto also named a Christian cleric who owed him money, as well as a certain Miguel Peires from La Almunia de Doña Godina, who had seized a vineyard that Janto had bought from Miguel's father, Esteban.[26]

Nearly all the enemies whom Janto named bore no obvious relation to the case against him. Janto did, however, list three relevant individuals. One was Salomon Navarro, who, as we have seen, had placed Janto at the scene of Pere's re-Judaization. Janto told Guillem de Roca that Salomon Navarro, whom he explained was known also as "Salamò Moreno," was his enemy because Janto's nephew, Safidia, had once punched Salomon Navarro in the face during an argument over taxes. In addition, Janto named Rabbi Isaach Beallul of Calatayud, whom both Salomon Navarro and, later, Jucef de Quatorze claimed had been present at Abadia's re-Judaization. Janto explained that Rabbi Isaach Beallul was his enemy because Janto's brother, Jafuda, had once wounded Rabbi Isaach's son, Abrafim, in the hand. Finally, Janto named Rabbi Salomon Amnalguer, a scribe and tax collector from Calatayud and the son of Rabbi Mahir Amnalguer. Salomon Navarro had testified that Rabbi Salomon was present at Abadia's re-Judaization, and Miriam Navarro had recounted how, on the night of January 4, Jucef de Quatorze told Pere that he and Janto had urged Abadia to renounce the Catholic faith "in the presence of Rabbi Salomon, son of Rabbi Mahir, Salomon Passariel, Rabbi Mahir, and many others." Janto told Guillem de Roca that Rabbi Salomon was his enemy because Janto's nephew had been hurt in a fight that had erupted when Rabbi Salomon Amnalguer threw the belongings of a Jew named Bonanat out of his house for not paying his taxes. In retaliation, Janto continued, Janto and some friends had had Rabbi Salomon captured in Ricla.[27]

In light of how many enemies Janto named, it is noteworthy that he did not mention most of the Jews whom Salomon Navarro and, later, Jucef de Quatorze said were present at Abadia's re-Judaization. Indeed, had Janto been present at Abadia's alleged re-Judaization—or even known about it— one would think that he would have named everyone associated with the proceedings in an attempt to disqualify damaging testimony.

During this time, it appears that Janto was in close communication with Jamila, who was also being held, "without shackles or handcuffs," in the residence of the provost of Tarragona in Barcelona. Indeed, husband and wife seem to have coordinated their answers to the questions of Guillem de Roca. On Wednesday, February 20, Jamila, like Janto, told Guillem that she and Janto had many enemies because people were jealous of them, but that she needed time to deliberate before naming specific individuals. On Thursday, she, too, claimed that she still could not remember the names of her enemies. Finally, on Monday, she had an answer: she declared that her enemies were the same as her husband's.[28]

The Almulis' attempt to disqualify the witnesses for the prosecution was unavailing. In spite of the assertions of Janto and Jamila, fra Bernat de Puigcercós did not discard Salomon Navarro's incriminating testimony. It is possible that Janto failed to convince the tribunal that Salomon Navarro was truly his *mortal* enemy. No note to this effect appears in the records, however. In his determination to convict Janto, the inquisitor may have decided to ignore the Almulis' claims.

Direct Confrontation: March–April 1342

In the meantime, Jucef de Quatorze arrived from Valencia. On Thursday, February 28, 1342, after he swore "on the Ten Commandments that the Lord God gave Moses on Mount Sinai, while physically touching the book of the Ten Commandments, that he would tell the complete and pure truth about all the things regarding which the lord inquisitor would ask him and about any other acts that he had committed to the detriment of Christians and the Christian faith," Jucef answered questions about the enemies he apparently had listed already before fra Berenguer Saiol in Valencia.[29]

Like Janto Almuli, Jucef de Quatorze tried to undermine the proceedings by invalidating potential witnesses for the prosecution. The first mortal enemy he named was the bailiff of Calatayud, Fernando Exemenis. Jucef had once denounced Fernando before the king, accusing Fernando of doing a poor job as bailiff and endangering the Jewish *aljama* of Calatayud. Jucef also listed as mortal enemies the bailiff's scribe, Juan de Jaca, and the bailiff's attendant, Pedro Exemenis de Sayés. Then, Jucef listed as his mortal enemy a Jewish merchant from France named Cuxo, whom he claimed had gathered French *relapsi* in his home at the time of the inquisitorial investigations of the *aljama* of Calatayud in the 1320s. Jucef explained, perhaps in an effort to distance himself from such deeds in the eyes of the tribunal, that he was "very angry" at Cuxo because Cuxo's actions had caused many men of Jucef's lineage to lose all their possessions as a result of inquisitorial prosecution. Jucef next listed a tailor from La Almunia de Doña Godina named Bonanat and his two sons, relatives of Janto Almuli. These men, Jucef explained, blamed him for fra Sancho de Torralba's arrest of Janto Almuli and swore that Jucef "would lose his life and all of his belongings."[30]

Finally, Jucef listed Salomon and Miriam Navarro, his only mortal enemies with any apparent relation to the charges against him. Jucef de Quatorze was sure that "Navarello" had denounced him. In fact, he told fra Bernat de Puigcercós that he knew that fra Sancho de Torralba had captured Salomon Navarro and that the inquisitor had asked Salomon if he knew whether anything "against the Christian faith" had been done in the Jewish quarter of Calatayud. Moreover, even though inquisitorial proceedings were supposed to unfold in strict secrecy, Jucef de Quatorze also reported that the *justicia* of Ricla, Gosalbo de Grades, had informed him that he was considered guilty in the case. To Jucef's mind, this confirmed that Salomon Navarro had accused him. (Suggesting further leaks, three months later, Jucef told the tribunal that the jurist Juan de Yrastra also told him about developments in the proceedings.)[31] With vitriol, Jucef told fra Bernat de Puigcercós that Salomon Navarro was nothing but "a cobbler, a pauper, a gambler, and a cheater, who g[ot] drunk and [into] such a state that he would say [anything] against all truth." Moreover, Jucef continued, Salomon was "very angry" because Salomon suspected that his wife, Miriam, had had an affair with Jucef. Jucef explained that he had not, in fact, had an affair with Miriam, but that his son, Jaco de Quatorze, might have. Determined to prove that Salomon was truly his *mortal* enemy, Jucef de Quatorze "said several times that Navarello would behave and act in such a way that Jucef would lose his life and all that he owned."[32]

Jucef de Quatorze's claims about Salomon Navarro's hatred for him may well have been true. Yet, as we saw above, Salomon Navarro did not implicate Jucef de Quatorze in the re-Judaizations of Pere or Abadia the first time he testified before the tribunal. He implicated Jucef only when he was prodded for more information one week later. Salomon, then, does not appear actually to have been intent on harming Jucef.

Like the list of enemies that Janto Almuli formulated, that of Jucef de Quatorze is remarkable in its omission of the Jews whom Salomon Navarro named—and whom Jucef himself later would name—as present at Abadia's alleged re-Judaization. If Jucef de Quatorze had indeed been present at, or known of, such an event, one would expect that he would have tried to establish that everyone there was his mortal enemy.

On March 5, 1342, before learning of fra Bernat de Puigcercós' response to his list of enemies, in one of the most striking moments of his trial, Jucef de Quatorze inveighed against the proceedings against him in the presence of fra Bernat, fra Bertran d'Abella, Guillem de Roca, and Samuel Benvenist (whom fra Bernat had apparently summoned).[33] Jucef declared that, "with all due respect to the lord inquisitor," prior to interrogating him about his enemies and the causes of these enmities, he should have made known to him the entire proceedings, shared with him the questions that had been put to witnesses, and provided him with a lawyer. Jucef also complained that, because he was being held captive, he was not able to procure witnesses who might vouch for the enmities he had alleged. He asked to be released on bail so that he might go to Calatayud to round up these witnesses.[34]

Jucef's outburst gave voice to widespread Jewish sentiments. In 1354, Jewish delegates from *aljamas* in Catalonia and Valencia would seek a papal bull ordering inquisitors to grant Jewish suspects the right of counsel and furnish them with a statement of the charges against them. In 1360, Pope Innocent VI approved a similar petition from Jews in Arles, Marseilles, and elsewhere in Provence and Forcalquier.[35] Moreover, as recently as 1325, King Jaume II had reminded fra Sancho de Torralba that papal bulls required inquisitors to reveal to Jewish defendants the names of accusers and witnesses.[36] In spite of these considerations, fra Bernat de Puigcercós quashed Jucef's objections. Determined, in the spirit of Bernard Gui, not to let any "impediments aris[e] from judicial rules or the wrangling of advocates" and to "shorten the proceedings as much as possible by depriving the accused of the ordinary facilities of defense," the inquisitor explained that the issues Jucef had raised were irrelevant.[37] In the business of inquisition, "only the truth was sought, without the order of law and the din of formal legal proceedings." Indeed, precisely because he sought "only the truth," fra Bernat continued, he would not provide Jucef de Quatorze with an attorney, for no one knew the truth better than Jucef himself. The inquisitor also refused to release Jucef de Quatorze on bail on the grounds that this simply was not permitted in capital cases.[38]

Jucef de Quatorze still did not give up. Two weeks later, on March 19, he told Guillem de Roca that he wanted the inquisitor to show him the questions that would be posed to the individuals called upon to testify about his enemies. He also requested that the inquisitor allow his personal agent to go to Calatayud to find appropriate witnesses, claiming that his agent would know better than himself who might seek to harm him, as Jucef had been away from Calatayud for about a year. Jucef was so certain of his entitlement to these measures that he demanded that "the aforesaid things be inserted and added in the [written records of the] present proceedings."[39]

This time, fra Bernat de Puigcercós made some minor concessions. Although he did not permit Jucef to send his agent to Calatayud, on the grounds that no one could know Jucef's enemies better than Jucef himself, he agreed to show Jucef the questions that would be posed to witnesses. In addition, he allowed Jucef to propose some individuals who might serve as witnesses to support his claims about his mortal enemies.[40] These procedural victories were of little consequence, however. Of the eighteen Jewish and Christian witnesses whom Jucef de Quatorze proposed, fra Sancho de Torralba summoned eleven Jews to testify, "individually and in secret," in the Dominican monastery of Calatayud, before himself, fra Gillermo de Rigulis, fra Mateo Maça, and the notary Gil Sánchez de Sanchaznar. According to fra Sancho, all eleven claimed that they did not know that Jucef de Quatorze had any enemies.[41]

Given the conflict-ridden nature of Jewish communities in the medieval Crown, Jucef de Quatorze's strong character, and the rivalries and spats in which he and his family were involved, it is implausible that Jucef had no enemies. We know from royal correspondence, for example, that around 1319, Jucef wounded Mosse Amnalguer, the son of the scribe and tax collector Rabbi Salomon Amnalguer of Calatayud, and dragged him by the hair. In addition, a member of the Teruel branch of the Quatorze family named Samuel son of Sanson was imprisoned during the first decade of the fourteenth century for gouging out the eye of a Jew named Mosse, who was the son of Jacob Avenfelaça.[42] Perhaps the witnesses whom Jucef de Quatorze proposed were intimidated, or fra Sancho de Torralba falsified his report. We know for certain only that, on April 19, 1342, fra Bernat de Puigcercós received fra Sancho's confirmation that these witnesses had denied that Jucef de Quatorze had any enemies.[43] As a result, Salomon Navarro's testimony was used also against Jucef de Quatorze.

Capitulation and Manipulation: March 1342

By March, Janto Almuli had languished in prison for more than six months. Neither the pleas of Samuel Benvenist nor the royal remission had had any effect on the progress of the proceedings, and Janto's attempt to invalidate the prosecution's witnesses had failed, as well. Janto capitulated. On March 5, 1342, at the Dominican monastery of Barcelona, in the presence of Guillem de Roca, fra Bernat de Puigcercós, fra Bertran d'Abella, and fra Pere Carner, Janto answered in the affirmative to the following questions, posed by fra Bernat:

1. Whether he led the neophyte Pere, who previously had been called Alatzar as a Jew, to renounce the faith of Christ and return to the perfidy of the Jews.
2. Whether he said to Pere: "Oh wretched man, how could you err so greatly as to renounce the law of Moses, the law of the one and true God, and accept the Christian law, which is empty and dead and in which no one can be saved."
3. Whether he also said to Pere: "I advise you to renounce and dismiss said emptiness or empty law and take back the law of Moses."

4. Whether he told Pere that Abadia had renounced and dismissed the Christian law in accordance with the advice of Janto and some other Jews.

5. Whether he told Pere that Janto and some other Jews had made Abadia renounce the Christian faith in Calatayud.

6. Whether he told Pere that, following his advice, Abadia had had himself burned in Calatayud, "in contempt of the Christian faith."

7. Whether he told Pere that Pere would have to do the same thing if he wanted "to be saved."

8. Whether, at first, Pere hesitated and said he wanted to think about this.

9. Whether, at that point, Janto repeated the aforesaid words, pressuring Pere most strongly to renounce the Christian faith.

10. Whether his wife, Jamila, and his daughter-in-law, Velida, were present.

11. Whether these two women joined Janto in pressuring Pere, telling him that he would be saved if he did as he was told.

12. Whether, on account of this pressure, Pere agreed to renounce the faith of Christ.

13. Whether, in the presence of Janto, Jamila, and Velida, Pere renounced the faith of Christ.

14. Whether Janto then told Pere to go to the home of the *justicia* of Calatayud and ask the *justicia* to burn him, or have him burned, on account of having committed so great a crime as "having renounced the law of the one God and accepted the empty and dead law of the Christians and been baptized."

15. Whether Janto told Pere that, if, on account of these words, the *justicia* did not wish to have him burned, Pere should threaten to have a notarized statement made against the *justicia*.

16. Whether Janto told Pere that, before being given over to the fire, he should ask that the fingers with which he had made the sign of the cross be amputated, the skin of his forehead that chrism had touched be ripped off, and the skin of his knees that he had bent before the crucifix be flayed.[44]

Janto also told the inquisitor that, during the course of his encounter with Pere, he had indeed sent for Jucef de Quatorze, and he explained that Jucef had arrived and approved of his words and pronounced even stronger ones, leading Pere to renounce the faith of Christ.[45]

Janto's confession was extracted by means of detailed leading questions. Yet Janto responded evasively or negatively to several additional questions of this kind, suggesting that his admissions may have had some probative significance. Janto claimed, for example, that because he had been very sick he could not remember whether he told Pere that, if the *justicia* did not want to have him burned, he should tell the *justicia* and those around him that "Christ, whom Christians worship, is not God, nor was he [ever] God, or else he would not have died; instead, he was an accursed bastard and the son of the greatest whore." He claimed also that he could not remember whether he told Pere that, once he had spoken these words, the *justicia* would proceed against him without any delay. And he insisted that on account of his illness he could not remember exactly what Jucef de Quatorze said to Pere.[46] Janto also testified that he had not seen Miriam Navarro leading Pere to his house and that he did not know whether Miriam or Salomon had led Pere there, or whether Pere had come on his own. In addition, Janto said that, although he had encouraged Abadia to renounce the Christian faith and burn at the stake, he had not been present at the gathering in Calatayud at which Abadia formally agreed to follow this course.[47]

At the end of the session, Janto made a denunciation of his own, which clarified the role he now claimed to have played in Abadia's re-Judaization. He declared that Rabbi Salomon Amnalguer—whom Salomon Navarro said was present at Abadia's re-Judaization, and whom Janto Almuli named as a personal enemy, perhaps to disqualify any testimony he might give—was primarily responsible for pressuring Abadia to renounce Christianity and burn at the stake. He explained that Rabbi Salomon had instructed Abadia to ask that the skin of his forehead that chrism had touched be flayed, the skin of his knees that had bent before the crucifix be torn off, and the fingers with which he had made the sign of the cross be amputated, and that Rabbi Salomon had urged Abadia to ask to be burned at the stake and thus "die in the law in which he had been born." Janto added that Rabbi Salomon had brought Abadia to him—presumably in the privacy of his home in La Almunia of Doña Godina—and asked Janto to second his advice. Janto confessed that he had done so, telling Abadia that this was the only way to save his soul.[48]

The tribunal of fra Bernat de Puigcercós carefully noted Janto's denunciation of Rabbi Salomon Amnalguer. The scribe who made the final copy of the trial records marked the folio containing Janto's incriminating statements with a large cross to facilitate future reference. He also included a mention of the accusation in the opening paragraph of the manuscript.

On the same day, before the same tribunal, Jamila Almuli also capitulated and responded in the affirmative to detailed leading questions regarding Pere's case. She admitted, for example, that Miriam Navarro had indeed come to her home and informed her and Janto that "Alatzar, who had been a Jew, was at Salomon's house, and he had been made Christian," and she asserted that Janto had instructed Miriam to bring Pere to him. Jamila also affirmed that, upon seeing Pere, Janto had exclaimed, "Wretched man! How could you have renounced the holy and good law of the one true God and embraced a law that is empty, false, and dead?" Like her husband, Jamila maintained that, when Pere initially demurred upon receiving Janto's instructions, she had pressed Pere to follow Janto's advice, and she agreed that Jucef de Quatorze had arrived during the course of the evening and echoed Janto's words.

There were three points, however, that Jamila did not confirm. First, possibly in an attempt to protect her daughter-in-law, she claimed that Velida had been away at the mill on the evening of January 4. Second, she insisted that she did not remember many of the words that had been spoken that evening, as she had been coming and going from the room where Janto was bedridden. Third, she said she knew nothing about Abadia.[49]

Confession under Torture: April–July 1342

On April 15, 1342, fra Bernat de Puigcercós declared that, based on the information he had received, "it was clear that Jucef de Quatorze was guilty" of the crimes with which he was charged.[50] Trying to elicit a confession, fra Bernat summoned Jucef and questioned him about Abadia's case, asking:

1. Whether Jucef ever knew a Jew named Abadia.
2. Whether he knew that Abadia had been baptized, when or where he had been baptized, what his Christian name was, or who was present when he was "made Christian."
3. Whether he knew that Abadia later returned to "the perfidy of the Jews," or where, when, or in whose presence this occurred.
4. Whether he knew that, after Abadia returned to the "perfidy of the Jews," he came to Calatayud and there, before the *justicia*, he publicly denied the faith of Christ and said that "no one can be saved in the faith of Jesus Christ and the Christians because the law of the Christians is an empty and false one in which no one can be saved,

because Jesus Christ, whom Christians worship, was not God nor the son of God, but, rather, an accursed bastard and the son of the greatest whore, and he deceived the world; and, therefore, the law of the Christians is false and empty and no one can be saved through it."

5. Whether he knew that Abadia then said that because he had embraced the law of the Christians, which was empty and false, and because he had been baptized, he deserved to be burned and that he asked the *justicia* to be burned.

6. Whether he knew that Abadia publicly renounced Christianity and was burned by the *justicia*.

7. Whether he knew that Abadia did all of this according to the instructions of some Jews, and whether he knew who these Jews were, or when and where they did this.

8. Whether Jucef was present at this event and one of the principal participants.

9. Whether he knew that Abadia sought advice from some Jews from Calatayud regarding the renunciation of Christianity. Whether those Jews had told Abadia that "there was no way he would be able to be saved unless he said and did all of the above . . . but if he did and said those things and was burned, he would be a martyr before God." Whether he knew who was present and where and when this occurred.

10. Whether he knew that, at this meeting, Jews told Abadia that he would not be able to be saved unless he asked the *justicia* to amputate the fingers with which he had made the sign of the cross and to tear off the skin of his forehead on which chrism had been placed when he was baptized and the skin of his knees that he bent before the crucifix, "showing honor for the crucifix."

11. Whether Jucef was present at this meeting and one of the principal participants.[51]

Jucef de Quatorze responded negatively to all of these questions. He told the tribunal that he used to know Abadia and had seen him frequently coming and going from Calatayud, and that he had heard that Abadia had been baptized, but he did not know when or where he had been baptized, what his new name was, or who had been present at his baptism. Jucef also said that he had heard that Abadia had returned to Judaism and that it was for this reason that he had gone to Calatayud and been burned. Jucef insisted, however, that he did not know when this had happened or who had been present, and that he knew nothing about Abadia's having acted upon the advice of Jews.[52]

Fra Bernat de Puigcercós next asked similar questions regarding Pere's case, and again Jucef denied all involvement. He said that he had never met a Jew called Alatzar, nor had he known that a Jew by this name had been baptized, taking the name Pere. He added that he was never in La Almunia de Doña Godina or in any place where he interacted with or counseled this man.[53]

A month and a half later, on May 27, 1342, fra Bernat de Puigcercós interrogated Jucef further, asking:

1. Whether he knew by what means Janto and Jamila Almuli had led Pere to renounce the Christian faith, return to "the execrable rite and perfidy of the Jews," and court death at the stake.
2. Whether he knew if Salomon Navarro and his wife, Miriam, had participated in these "crimes" and what exactly they had done.
3. Whether he knew if Janto and Jamila Almuli had led Abadia to renounce the Christian faith.
4. Whether he knew if Jews had counseled Abadia in a room above the butcher shop of Calatayud.
5. Whether he knew if Salomon Passariel, Avraham Mocatil, Samuel Alpestan, Salomon Avensaprut Ezquierdo, and others had been present at Abadia's re-Judaization. If he knew of other Jews who had been present, who were they?[54]

Jucef de Quatorze still maintained his innocence. He said he never saw Janto and his wife commit the crimes with which they were charged, he knew nothing about the Navarros' participation in Pere's case, he knew nothing about the Almulis' involvement in Abadia's case, and he knew nothing about Abadia's re-Judaization.[55]

On June 8, 1342, fra Bernat de Puigcercós lost patience and sent Jucef to the torture chamber in the palace of the bishop of Barcelona. There, Jucef was prepared for a form of torture known as *garrucha* or *strappado*, in which the prisoner's wrists were tied from behind, the prisoner was then hung by his wrists from the ceiling with weights hanging from his feet, and he was then allowed suddenly to drop—stretching and sometimes dislocating his arms and legs, and sometimes leading to long-term nerve, tendon, and ligament damage.[56]

Jucef's arms had been twisted and tied behind his back, but his body had not yet been raised off the ground, when he began to speak. Responding to the questions of fra Bernat de Puigcercós, in the presence of Guillem de Roca, fra Bertran d'Abella, and the jurist Pere Cendra, Jucef listed fifteen Jews who allegedly had been present at Abadia's re-Judaization. Nine of these—Jucef de Quatorze himself, Aaron Abenafia, Samuel Alpestan, Mosse Amnalguer, Salomon Avensaprut Ezquierdo, Isaach Habealuz, Avraham Mocatil, Salomon Passariel, and Isaach Sadoch—had been listed also by Salomon Navarro.[57] When fra Bernat asked Jucef how he knew that these Jews had been present, Jucef responded that he had attended Abadia's re-Judaization. He added, echoing one of the charges that fra Bernat had read to him a week earlier, that this re-Judaization had taken place on a morning seven years ago, in a room above a butcher shop in Calatayud. Jucef also said that he had been present at Pere's re-Judaization.[58]

After Jucef de Quatorze made these statements, his arms were untied, and fra Bernat de Puigcercós had his confession read to him for confirmation. Later that day, Jucef was taken to the Dominican monastery of Santa Caterina where, at vespers, he was brought before fra Bernat, and again he confirmed what he had said.[59]

Even after these confessions, Jucef remained defiant. On June 12, 1342, for example, when fra Bernat asked whether he wished to renounce the protestations he had made against the trial procedure on March 5 and 19, Jucef responded that he needed time to think. Only when the inquisitor persisted did Jucef agree to retract his objections, saying that "he did not wish to argue or litigate with the lord inquisitor." For the rest of that day, however, and on June 14 and 17, as well, every time fra Bernat asked Jucef a question about Pere or Abadia, Jucef claimed that "he could not remember."[60]

On June 19, Jucef de Quatorze made a denunciation of his own, much as Janto Almuli had done when he denounced Rabbi Salomon Amnalguer. Jucef told the tribunal that at the end of Abadia's re-Judaization a Jew named Jafuda del Calvo had spoken harsh words against the Christian law and against Christ and the Virgin. Jucef added that the other Jews who were present had not approved of these words, and some had even reprimanded Jafuda. It is not clear what Jucef de Quatorze hoped to gain from this denunciation. Jucef had not listed Jafuda as an enemy, and neither he nor Salomon Navarro had claimed that Jafuda was present at Abadia's re-Judaization. Moreover, Jafuda del Calvo had recently died.[61] The tribunal showed little interest in this denunciation, and the scribe who made the final copy of the proceedings did not mark for easy reference the folio on which it appears.

The proceedings were drawing to a close, and fra Bernat de Puigcercós wrote to the bishop of Tarazona, Bertran de Cormidela, requesting permission to sentence the accused. On June 21, a defeated Jucef de Quatorze begged fra Bernat for mercy. One week later, Jucef de Quatorze and Janto and Jamila Almuli promised fra Bernat that they would abjure their alleged crimes and solemnly swear never again, by word, deed, or any other means, to lead any Christian over to Judaism or to be present at, or give council or aid in, related affairs.[62]

Becoming a Relapsed Heretic: July 1342

Before fra Bernat de Puigcercós could sentence Jucef de Quatorze to the stake as a repeat offender, he needed to certify that Jucef had once before abjured leading Christians over to Judaism. On fra Bernat's behalf, fra Sancho de Torralba asked Bernardo Duque and Juan Gómez de Zamán—commissaries of the bishop of Tarazona—to assist in this endeavor. These three men inspected all the trial records they could find in Calatayud. They did come across some abjurations made during the inquisitorial prosecution of the *aljama* in the 1320s, including those of Jucef de Quatorze's relatives, Sulema and Ora, which they enclosed for fra Bernat to review. In a letter that fra Bernat received on July 27, 1342, however, Bernardo Duque and Juan Gómez de Zamán explained that they had been unable to find any proof of a prior abjuration by Jucef de Quatorze. They lamented that the late inquisitorial notary, García Martín, had left his records "badly organized and scattered on separate sheets [*dispersos per cedulas*] and not inserted into trial dossiers [*et non in processibus insertas*]." Nevertheless, the two commissaries assured fra Bernat de Puigcercós that they had no doubt that Jucef de Quatorze had participated in a community-wide abjuration in 1326. If such a general abjuration had not taken place, they explained, the *aljama*'s school and synagogue, which had been slated to be destroyed, would not have been spared. Indeed, the commissaries "firmly believed in their souls" that they could confirm that Jucef de Quatorze had previously abjured.[63]

In 1310, in Toulouse, when proof of the prior abjuration of a suspected relapsed heretic could not be found among the papers of the Holy Office, the inquisitor ruled that the defendant would have to be prosecuted as though for a first offense.[64] Fra Bernat de Puigcercós, however, accepted the commissaries' dubious assurance.

When fra Bernat de Puigcercós asked Jucef de Quatorze about his previous abjuration, Jucef de Quatorze answered that he had no recollection of it, and that he remembered only that he had been interrogated under oath during the inquisitorial investigations of the 1320s. Fra Bernat de Puigcercós insisted that it was not possible that Jucef de Quatorze could have forgotten this abjuration for, during that time, many Jews from Calatayud had been condemned to prison. Jucef responded that he did recall that many Jews had been gathered in the cloister of the Dominican monastery of Sant Pere Màrtir, but he did not remember what had been said or read.[65]

Exasperated, fra Bernat de Puigcercós sent Jucef de Quatorze back to the torture chamber. There, "before he even laid eyes upon the instruments of torture," Jucef declared that the things said in the letter of Bernardo Duque and Juan Gómez de Zamán were true. Later, "having been stripped of his *gramasia* by the guards so that they might torture him, yet not stripped of his *supertunicali* nor having been tied down," Jucef confessed that, in 1326, he and other Jews had sworn on the Ten Commandments never again to do anything against the Christian faith and never in any way to help any Christian men or women return or go over to the "Jewish perfidy." Jucef also named thirteen Jews who had allegedly abjured along with him in 1326. After this, he was taken to the monastery of Santa Caterina where, in the presence of fra Bernat de Puigcercós, fra Bertran d'Abella, fra Bernat Simó, and Guillem de Roca, he confirmed this confession. Jucef de Quatorze was now, officially, a relapsed heretic.[66]

The attempts of the Almulis, the Navarros, and Jucef de Quatorze to escape from the inquisition illustrate a range of ways in which Jews responded to inquisitorial prosecution. The Almulis and Jucef de Quatorze put up resistance to no avail. But the Navarros, who threw themselves on the mercy of fra Sancho de Torralba, were rewarded with liberation. There was one particularly powerful recourse, however, that none of these Jews appear to have contemplated. As we shall see in Chapter 3, during the fourteenth century, inquisitors in the Crown of Aragon reduced the penalties of Jewish defendants who converted to Christianity. By converting, the Almulis and Jucef de Quatorze presumably would have demonstrated that they genuinely regretted their alleged crimes and that, moreover, their repentance was authentic in the sense that it involved turning toward Christ. Indeed, in a draft of the final sentence for the Almulis and Jucef de Quatorze, fra Bernat implied that the only way a Jew could truly repent for crimes against Christians and the Christian faith was by converting to Christianity. "I will consider [a Jew] impenitent," he wrote, "as long as he remains a Jew."[67]

In addition, however, by converting to Christianity, the Almulis and Jucef de Quatorze would have given fra Bernat de Puigcercós the satisfaction of conquering Jewish souls, thereby scoring victories for the church and rendering Christendom more secure. The Almulis and Jucef de Quatorze stopped short of giving the inquisitor this pleasure. They may have confessed to crimes they did not commit, and they certainly denounced fellow Jews, but they would not join the ranks of the Christian foe.

Four Condemnations

In a draft of his final sentence, fra Bernat de Puigcercós recommended sending Jucef de Quatorze and the Almulis to the stake on the grounds that, as Jews, all three individuals were impenitent, in spite of their promises to abjure. Fra Bernat could not fathom that Jews could repent sincerely of having harmed Christians and the Christian faith.[1] Between August 5 and 7, 1342, however, a group of legal and religious experts challenged this proposal. These advisors argued that, although there was no question that Jucef de Quatorze should be relinquished to the secular arm as a relapsed heretic, and although all three Jews certainly should be punished "most severely," the Almulis should not share the same fate as Jucef de Quatorze, for the Almulis were not relapsed heretics.[2]

Between Thursday, August 8 and Saturday, August 10, fra Bernat de Puigcercós convened yet another group of scholars in the episcopal palace of Barcelona.[3] The entire transcript of the trial of Jucef de Quatorze was read aloud, the committee deliberated, and, finally, it agreed to the following. Janto Almuli, "who [had] erred much more than Jamila," would be condemned to perpetual prison in "the worst prison" of Barcelona, the tower of Castellnou, until a new prison, paid for with his confiscated assets, was built in Calatayud. At Castellnou, Janto was to have nothing but bread and water, "so that his life might be more death than life, and death a solace and pleasure greater than life." Jamila would also be imprisoned in Castellnou. Jucef de Quatorze, however, would be relinquished to the secular arm for execution.[4]

The next day—Sunday, August 11—at the cemetery of the church of Santa María del Mar in Barcelona, the alleged crimes of the Almulis and Jucef de Quatorze were broadcast before a "great multitude of people of both sexes" summoned by the town crier, as well as before notables such as the archbishop of Aix-en-Provence, Armand de Narcés, the vicar of Barcelona, Arnau d'Erill, the bishop of Barcelona, Ferrer d'Abella, the five *consellers* (counselors) of Barcelona, canons of the city, and other prominent clerics and legal experts.

Guillem de Roca read the final sentence aloud—in Catalan, for all to understand—railing against the Almulis and Jucef de Quatorze for having "erred
and sinned cruelly and gravely against the holy mother Church, against the
holy Catholic faith, and against the holy law of Christians."[5] Meanwhile, the
Almulis and Jucef de Quatorze probably stood in shackles on a high platform
and were paraded forth, each in turn, as their offenses and penalties were
enumerated.

We do not know for certain what became of Pere, Janto and Jamila Almuli, and Jucef de Quatorze. We know only that, during Pere's trial, most of
whose transcript has not survived, Pere repented of his actions, begged to be
reconciled to the Christian law, and abjured and renounced all heresy. As a
result, the death sentence that the *justicia* of Calatayud had imposed on him
was lifted, and he was condemned instead to prison for life.[6] Janto and Jamila
may have died in the tower of Castellnou. And, barring some development of
which we have no record, on Monday, August 12, 1342, Jucef de Quatorze was
tied living to a high post—with a chain around his neck and ropes under his
arms, around his waist and groin, above and below his knees, and around his
ankles—and consumed by the flames that he and the Almulis allegedly had
recommended to Pere and Abadia.[7]

PART II

At the Font of New Life

Alatzar and Abadia, Baptized

Two Jewish converts to Christianity—Pere and Abadia—were at the heart of the proceedings against Janto and Jamila Almuli and Jucef de Quatorze. Pere first denounced the Almulis and Jucef de Quatorze to the tribunal of fra Sancho de Torralba, and fra Sancho proceeded with the investigation in order to punish the Almulis and Jucef de Quatorze for persuading Pere and Abadia to renounce Christianity and burn at the stake. Nevertheless, the records of the trials of the Almulis and Jucef de Quatorze reveal little about Pere and Abadia. Regarding Pere, they tell us that his Jewish name was Alatzar, he was the son of a Jew from Calatayud named Isaach Camariel, he once worked as a messenger for the Almuli family, and he and his father frequently ate at the home of the cobbler, Salomon Navarro.[1] He was baptized in Catalonia in mid-December 1340 in the village church of Sant Pere de Riudebitlles. The local vicar presided and, according to custom, four godparents were present—a Benedictine monk called Borràs, a layman called Gironella, and two women, Molnera and Bellesa.[2] We learn nothing about what led to Pere's conversion, however, and we do not know how old Pere was at his baptism. Regarding Abadia, the trial records relate only that he had been a Jewish peddler and that he was baptized in La Almunia de Doña Godina following the baptisms of his sister and brother-in-law.[3] We do not know Abadia's Christian name.

We are not entirely at a loss in attempting to reconstruct the world of Pere and Abadia, however, for nearly two hundred other Jewish converts from the medieval Crown of Aragon emerge from royal and episcopal correspondence, inquisitorial records, and rabbinic *responsa* composed between the late thirteenth century and 1391. Surviving evidence about these additional converts is fragmentary. Most converts surface in the documentation only once, and sources usually provide a mere snapshot of a situation, leaving its background and resolution open to conjecture. Furthermore, because not all references to converts have yet been culled from records, because much documentation has been lost, and because many converts probably never figured in written sources, it is difficult to make meaningful generalizations regarding, for instance, the relationship of Jewish conversions to factors such as age, sex, profession, geography, or period.

In spite of these limitations, however, extant sources preserve remarkable vignettes, and they enable us to draw tentative conclusions about some broad features of Jewish conversion in the medieval Crown of Aragon. In the next two chapters, we shall begin to examine the revelations of these sources, focusing first on converts' motivations for converting and the circumstances under which they were baptized, and then on converts' fates after baptism. Throughout, we shall consider the relationship between the church's lofty ideals for Jewish conversion, Christians' negative perceptions of converts, and the grim realities of converts' lives. We shall also observe similarities between the Crown of Aragon and other realms in medieval Western Europe with regard to converts' experiences and Christian attitudes.

Chapter 3

Between Doubt and Desire:
Jewish Conversion, Converts,
and Christian Society

Divine inspiration and my own will [led me to be baptized].
—Pere, 1341[1]

The medieval Crown of Aragon was home to a wide variety of Jewish converts—
men and women, the single and the married, parents and children. Several
converts had been wealthy or learned as Jews, such as the physician Vincenç
Esteve, whose possessions King Jaume II promised to protect from confiscation in 1307; the physician brothers Romeu and Pere de Pal, who converted
during the second quarter of the fourteenth century; the physician Pere de
Gràcia, who converted prior to 1347; the physician Jaume de Faro, who converted during the third quarter of the fourteenth century; and the son of the
queen's treasurer, Juan Sánchez de Calatayud (formerly Isaach Golluf), who
was baptized about 1389.[2] Many others, however, were of humble origins. Abadia, for example, had been a peddler, and Pere, too, appears to have been
poor. Two other converts were tailors before their conversions—one of them
baptized in the church of Sant Jaume in Barcelona in 1308, taking the name
Nicolau de Montsó, the other baptized about 1370, taking the name Jaume
Bisnes.[3] In the pages that follow, we shall examine additional indications that
many converts had been impoverished as Jews.

Although forced baptisms did occur in the Crown of Aragon prior to
1391, many Jewish conversions were not accompanied by violence.[4] In fact,
there is evidence that some Jews carefully planned their baptisms. These

individuals were baptized far from home, either alone or with close relatives, and in the presence of up to four, sometimes wealthy, godparents. As Christian authorities in the medieval Crown widely encouraged Jewish conversion, one might expect that these ostensibly voluntary converts would have met a warm welcome. Indeed, by contrast to converts whose baptisms had been coerced and whose devotion would have been suspect automatically, these converts potentially were enthusiastic about joining the Christian fold. Christians, however, recoiled from them and, in many ways, continued to view them as Jews.

In this chapter, we shall seek to understand this reaction. Following an overview of expressions of Christian conversionary enthusiasm in the Crown of Aragon that render the rejection of converts all the more intriguing, I will argue that Christian prejudice against converts was shaped both by Christian concerns about the immutability of Jewishness and also by Christian awareness of the circumstances that led many Jews to baptism. Although many Jews turned to baptism by choice, these converts were far from the pure and pious souls of Christians' dreams. Indeed, many had sought through conversion, first and foremost, to escape from personal difficulties. In closing, we shall explore how some Christian authorities tried to mitigate the dissonance between their desire for, and the troubling realities of, Jewish conversion.

Christian Conversionary Enthusiasm

In 1353, in a begging license issued to a convert named Daniel Verger, the bishop of Girona, Berenguer de Cruïlles, proclaimed that Jewish conversion involved "abandoning the treachery of Jewish blindness," "putting the errors of darkness to flight," and "converting to Christ himself, God, the true light." Some thirty years later, in a begging license issued to a convert named Joan Gervasi, the bishop of Girona, Berenguer d'Anglesola, expressed the hope that Jewish conversions would lead to the salvation of the entire people of Israel and to the vigorous spread and growth of the Christian religion before all the "enemies of the orthodox faith."[5] As these declarations suggest, Jewish conversion was an unimpeachable cause. Indeed, as we discussed in Chapter 1, promoting conversion to Christianity was consistent with the missionary impulse fundamental to Christianity, as well as with the pious priorities of Christian leaders throughout medieval Western Europe, including prominent thirteenth-century Catalan intellectuals, such as Ramon de Penyafort, Ramon

Martí, Ramon Llull, and Arnau de Vilanova. Moreover, Jewish conversions held special significance insofar as Jews were considered the malevolent rejecters and killers of Christ. Conversions represented the elimination of dangerous enemies and the ongoing triumph of the "new Israel."[6]

Eager to participate in bringing Jews to Christ, Christians of all ranks in the thirteenth- and fourteenth-century Crown of Aragon demonstrated support for Jewish conversion. Like the kings of England, France, and Castile, the kings of the Crown of Aragon issued legislation aimed at improving converts' lives.[7] At the Council of Lleida on March 12, 1243, for example, King Jaume I declared that no Jew or Muslim who sought to become a Christian should encounter impediments of any kind. To this end, he ordered that converts be allowed to retain their belongings, which Christians normally confiscated, and receive their inheritances, which relatives often withheld. The king also warned that anyone who ridiculed converts would be fined. In addition, in an effort to recruit more converts, Jaume I commanded officials to compel Jews and Muslims to attend conversionary sermons. Jaume II reissued portions of this legislation in 1296, 1300, and 1311.[8]

Kings also provided incentives for conversion by pardoning Jews who had been convicted of crimes but subsequently opted for baptism. Thus, about 1325, after a Jew who had killed another Jew converted to Christianity, taking the name Ramon Fuster, Jaume II exonerated Ramon, "in honor of God and the Catholic faith." Similarly, in 1347, Pere III decreed that if a Jew who was condemned to hang or undergo some other form of corporal punishment (with the exception of stoning) expressed the desire to be baptized, he was to be released for this purpose, and his corporal punishment was to be cancelled. Likewise, about 1381, King Pere pardoned a Jew who had been assigned the penalty of lashes, after he converted to Christianity together with his wife and five children, taking the name Jaume Romeu.[9] As it was not unusual for kings to pardon Jews in exchange for money, it is probable that Jews of humble means, who could not afford to pay the king, were most likely to convert under these circumstances.[10]

Even a mere promise to convert could result in a pardon. In 1385, when a Jewish father and son from Barcelona named Isaach and Vidal Xam, who were imprisoned for assaulting their relative Jaya, wrote to King Pere promising to convert, the king "granted them a remission from lawsuits and gave guarantees over their property." One year later, a convert named Pere Despla—who may have been the former Isaach or Vidal Xam and was in prison on account of debts he owed Jaya—promised the king that his wife and children would convert if the king were to release him from prison. The king granted Pere six months to travel to Mallorca to convert his family.[11]

Kings also offered baptism to Jews who had been convicted of crimes as a means of enabling these individuals to die a quicker and less painful death. Some Christian authorities sought to demonstrate Jewish inferiority by hanging Jewish criminals by their feet, instead of by their necks, or by suspending on either side of them a ferocious dog.[12] In fact, in 1315, the Jews of Mallorca begged Jaume II to outlaw these customs, explaining that it took a man who was hung by his feet up to three days to die. This petition does not seem to have been granted, although in 1347 Pere III did make an effort to shorten the suffering of Jews who had been condemned to hang upside down, by decreeing that a stone should be tied to the neck of such a condemned Jew in order to accelerate his death.[13] By choosing baptism, Jews who had been condemned to hang could at least curtail their agony. Thus, in 1303, two Mallorcan Jews who were accused of having forged money were "dragged through the city, ridiculed, baptized on their way to the gallows, and then hung," presumably as Christians, that is, by their necks.[14]

Inquisitors and bishops in the Crown of Aragon also provided an incentive for Jewish conversion. They had mercy on Jewish defendants who converted to Christianity. In 1312, for instance, the inquisitor fra Joan Llotger and the archbishop of Tarragona, Guillem de Rocabertí, reduced the fines of three members of the *aljama* of Tarragona who converted to Christianity.[15] Similarly, in or before 1375, after a Jew from Peratallada named Jacob Isaach was baptized, taking the name Pere de Saumana, the bishop of Girona, Bertran de Montrodon, ordered that his debts, possessions, and two daughters be returned to him. These girls, whose religious status is not known, had been placed in the care of a Christian woman, Elvira, the wife of Gilabert of Cruïlles, who initially refused to relinquish them.[16]

During the second half of the thirteenth century and the early fourteenth century, it was also the case that Franciscan and Dominican friars sporadically preached to Jews. It seems that most of these sermons were bitter rants that functioned primarily as verbal attacks against Jews and Judaism and as theological demonstrations geared toward Christian onlookers. Indeed, there is no evidence that mendicant sermons were successful as a proselytizing measure. Yet, these campaigns were billed as missionary efforts and, as such, they fit into the matrix of a society that was bent on encouraging Jewish conversion.[17]

Finally, Christians lay and religious, rich and poor, demonstrated support for Jewish conversion by serving as godparents to converts. Like the kings of

France and England, the kings of the Crown of Aragon sponsored individual conversions.[18] Pere III served as a godfather, for instance, to a woman named Caterina, who was the daughter of a convert named Andreu Contijoc.[19] In addition, records of the king's almsgiving mention "a Jewess whom the king had baptized,"[20] as well as an adolescent named Joan who was baptized in Alcira when the king visited.[21] Christian men and women of high social rank followed kings' example. For instance, one of Pere's two godfathers, the Benedictine monk Borràs Tacó, was the procurator of the prior of a monastery near Sant Pere de Riudebitlles, Antonio da Bagnasco. The godparents of Joan de Ruibech, who was baptized in Barcelona in 1378, included the squire Joan de Ruibech, and the godparents of Andreu d'Abella, who was baptized in Barcelona in 1380, included the squire Ferrer d'Abella and Lady Constancia, the wife of the nobleman Francesc de Perallos. Similarly, just north of the Crown, in mid-thirteenth-century Manosque, the godparents of a convert named Raymbauda (formerly Regina) included Lord Raymbaud d'Esparron and his sister, Lady Artauda.[22] Other godparents, however, were of lower social status. The godparents of Joan de Ruibech also included a tailor named Pere Vebre, for example, and the godparents of a convert named Nicolau de Montsò, who was baptized in Barcelona around the turn of the fourteenth century, included a blacksmith.[23]

Conversion as Escape

Although Christians in the Crown of Aragon demonstrated support for Jewish conversion, as a group they extended a chilly welcome to converts. Indeed, far from embracing converts, Christians marked them as a group apart. As elsewhere in Western Europe, Christians memorialized converts' unique identity by referring to converts in writing as "neophyte," "convert," "having been baptized," "having been made Christian," or "ex-Jew."[24] These terms were used even decades after a conversion had taken place. For example, in his *Directorium inquisitorum*, composed about 1376, Nicolau Eimeric referred to the convert Ramon de Tàrrega as "Ramon the neophyte," even though Ramon had been baptized thirty years earlier and had become a prominent Dominican theologian.[25] Furthermore, the designation "baptized one" was sometimes applied to the children of Muslim converts in the Crown of Aragon, suggesting that converts' special nature could be understood as able to pass from one generation to the next.[26]

As a group apart, Jewish converts were not merely a subcategory of Christians. Instead, it was widely feared that they were not entirely Christian and that, to quote from the Fourth Lateran Council (1215), Jewish converts did "not entirely cast off the old man" but "retain[ed] remnants of the[ir] former rite."[27] In other words, Christians suspected that converts were of an intermediate status and therefore still, to some extent, Jews. Reflecting this sense, some Christians continued to treat converts like Jews. In 1375, for example, shortly after Pere de Saumana was baptized, the bishop of Girona, Bertran de Montrodon, had to remind his officials to treat Pere kindly, "as a Christian, as [wa]s fitting."[28] Moreover, some judicial rules for Jews were applied to converts. In 1381, for example, King Pere III specified that converts needed to bring Jewish—and not Christian—witnesses to support their suits.[29]

Multiple factors informed the Christian conviction that Jewishness inhered in converts. In 1290, in a bull addressed to inquisitors in Aix, Arles, and Embrun, Pope Nicholas IV suggested that converts kept Jewish customs. He claimed that they brought candles to synagogue, held vigils on the Sabbath, and showed devotion for the Torah scroll "as if through a nefarious kind of idolatry, by displaying patent signs of devotion and reverence."[30] Understandings of the process of religious conversion may have informed Christian skepticism, as well. During this period, conversion was regarded as a lifelong journey, a work forever in progress. Baptism was an important step along the way, but it was not expected instantaneously to transform a Jew in all regards.[31]

In addition, there existed a sense that Jewishness entailed membership in a "nation," a *gens*, as Pope Alexander III had put it about 1173. Thus, in 1320, the Infant Alfons described the convert Joan d'Osca as hailing "from the Jewish nation or people" (*a judayca gente vel populo*) and, in a missive from 1383, King Pere III described the convert Leonor Muniz as having converted from the Jewish "stock" (*genus*) to the Christian "faith" (*fides*).[32] The view that Jewishness passed from generation to generation prevailed among Jews, and it had a long history among Christians, as well. In the fifth century, for example, the Gallo-Roman nobleman Sidonius described a particular convert as "a Jew by race [who had] chosen to be accounted an Israelite by faith rather than by blood."[33] Christians must have wondered whether conversion could truly trump ethnicity and whether Jewishness could really be left behind.[34]

Evidence from the medieval Crown of Aragon suggests that, while concerns regarding the indelibility of Jewishness contributed to Christian suspicion of converts, Christian suspicion was shaped also by clear indications that many Jewish converts had turned to baptism not in the course of a spiritual odyssey but in an effort to improve the conditions of their earthly existence. As we have seen, inquisitorial defendants and convicted criminals converted to Christianity to avert or reduce punishments. Other Jews, however, converted to extricate themselves from conflicts with the Jewish community. For example, some prospective converts sought to flee the consequences of Jewish excommunication—also referred to as *herem, alatma,* or, in its less severe form of shorter duration, *nidui.* Jewish excommunication cut the condemned person off from the Jewish community socially, religiously, and financially for violating communal norms. Sometimes it involved expulsion from the Jewish quarter and, on occasion, it even deprived the condemned person of a tombstone.[35] A *responsum* of the Jewish political and spiritual leader of Barcelona, Rabbi Yom Tov ben Avraham Ishbili (1250–1330, known by his rabbinic acronym as "Ritva"), recounts how a Jewish mother named Jamila and her four children—Oro, Tsevah, Nissim, and Yosef—apostatized after they were banned from the town of Daroca for five years, "on account of many major and minor [offenses against] all the people of the town."[36] Similarly, around 1327, after two sons of a Jew named Baruch Mocatil were placed under *herem* for physically attacking Bonsenyor Gracià, the secretary of the *aljama* of Barcelona, one of these men converted to Christianity.[37]

Aware that the excommunicated might apostatize, Jewish authorities sometimes revoked, or decided against issuing, edicts of excommunication. This happened, for example, in the case of a Jewish culprit named Avraham ben Yosef ben Plas, who had snuck into a synagogue in Daroca "one night, when everyone else was sleeping in their beds," and broken the doors of the ark in order to steal the "silver apples that sat on top of the holy Torah scroll." Avraham was going to be banished from Daroca for five years and prohibited from marrying or trading with any Jew from Daroca during that period. In addition, if he were to violate the terms of his excommunication, his head would be shaved, and he would receive lashes. Avraham's mother, Jamila, convinced Ritva to annul the decree, however, on the grounds that, if excommunicated, her son would "be tempted into idol worship," that is, he would convert to Christianity. Ritva explained that he consented to do so in order that this young man might "return in repentance and not go out to a bad culture" (*veshe-lo yetse le-tarbut raah*).[38] Similarly, about 1375, the family of an adulterer named Isaach ibn Açfora persuaded Rabbi Isaac ben Sheshet ("Rivash," then a rabbi in Zaragoza) to assure Isaach that no action would be taken against him. Like Avraham's mother, Isaach's relatives feared that excommunication would lead to apostasy.[39] In Xàtiva about 1383, a Jewish family threatened to apostatize if imprisoned or excommunicated.[40]

Other Jews turned to baptism to escape Jewish prohibitions regarding marriage and adultery. A *responsum* of Ritva tells, for instance, of a Jewish couple that had a child together and then learned that their union was incestuous according to rabbinic law. Desperate to save their child from being an outcast, the couple wanted to know if they could marry, in order to legitimize their child, and then divorce. If they were not allowed to do so, they warned, they would apostatize. In this case, the threat of apostasy did not sway Ritva. Ritva refused to sanction such a marriage, declaring, "We are not beholden to cheaters and evildoers!" and he recommended that the man be whipped for his sin.[41]

This couple actually may have apostatized, for, as Christians, they probably would have been permitted to marry. Indeed, even though canon law normally forbade marriages between persons who were related within seven degrees of kinship by blood, exceptions were made in cases involving converts in order to encourage conversion. In the early fifteenth century, for example, the antipope Benedict XIII allowed two couples of Jewish converts to wed, one in Toledo and one in Tortosa, in spite of the fact that their unions were technically incestuous.[42] Christian authorities also allowed converts to practice other marital customs that were typically forbidden among Christians. In a letter to the bishop of Livonia, for example, Pope Innocent III specified that converts were allowed to continue contracting marriages several generations in advance and to stay in already established levirate marriages "so that something good, planted with a weak root, not be destroyed, but be strengthened and faithfully brought to perfection."[43]

A *responsum* of Ritva's teacher, the Jewish political and spiritual leader of Barcelona, Rabbi Solomon ben Avraham ibn Aderet (c. 1233–1310, "Rashba"), tells of a case in which a married Jewish woman converted to Christianity in order to obtain a bill of divorce and join her Jewish lover. Demonstrating that this woman's conversion was not motivated by a commitment to Christianity, she and her new partner then moved to Toledo, where they lived as Jews and were assumed to be husband and wife.[44] In another instance involving conversion and marriage, about 1378, a Jew from Toledo was baptized in the cathedral of Girona, taking the name Ramon Malars. Directly following his baptism, Ramon married a Jewish convert from Alcalá named Teresa. It is likely either that Teresa was previously married or that some other legal impediment had made it impossible for Ramon and Teresa to marry as Jews.[45] In yet another case, in the 1380s, a Jewish woman left her husband, a tailor named Astruc, converted to Christianity, taking the name Eulalia, and married a Jewish convert named Bernat de Mutros.[46]

Eulalia's case demonstrates that conversions such as these could, in turn, lead to additional baptisms whose ulterior motives were patent, as well as to legal conundra. When Astruc learned of Eulalia's new marriage, he "immediately" turned to the bishop of Barcelona, Ramon d'Escales, "brought himself forth to be converted to the Catholic faith," and requested that, "if legally possible," his marriage to Eulalia should be declared to supersede the marriage between Eulalia and Bernat. We do not know how the bishop ruled. We know only that the bishop began by seeking to prevent further developments. First, he demanded that the vicar of the Church of Santa María de Caldes de Montbui and the priests of the city and diocese of Barcelona under no circumstances proceed with the solemnization of the marriage of "these converts" (presumably Eulalia and Bernat) *in facie ecclesie*, thus making their union sacramentally complete.[47] Then, concerned that there might be adultery, as Eulalia still might be married to Astruc, the bishop added that "the two" converts (*ambo*, again presumably Eulalia and Bernat) were "to cease and desist completely from all cohabitation," until he should determine whether their marriage was valid, enabling them to remain together.[48]

Baptism also served as a response to violence within the Jewish community. As the most common means of resolving disputes in and around the medieval Crown of Aragon, violence was widespread. Indeed, at least sixty murders of Jews by Jews have been documented in the Crown between 1257 and 1327, and Jews also were accused repeatedly by fellow Jews of rape.[49] In fact, the families of Janto Almuli and Jucef de Quatorze were themselves involved in a number of violent acts. Janto's brother Jafuda was said to have wounded the son of Rabbi Isaach Beallul. His nephew injured a Jew from La Almunia de Doña Godina, and his son, Jucef, was suspected of murder.[50] For his part, Jucef de Quatorze was accused of dragging the son of Rabbi Salomon Amnalguer by the hair, and a member of the Teruel branch of the Quatorze family was imprisoned during the first decade of the fourteenth century for gouging out the eye of a fellow Jew.[51] Some victims of aggression, such as a man named Simon, who was assaulted in 1338 in Manosque, while in synagogue with his brother, ran for the baptismal font.[52]

Within the Jewish community, violence also permeated the private sphere. In or shortly before 1304, in Manosque, a Jewish woman named Marioneta sought to flee from her husband, Samuel Bonastrug, who was in the habit of hitting her so hard "that the whole neighborhood would gather [in horror]." Marioneta begged her brother, Davinet de Portali, to save her from Samuel, and she warned him that if he did not come to her assistance she would "leave in the company of a Christian lady" and, presumably, receive baptism.[53] We do not know what became of Marioneta. In light of the cases of Teresa, Eulalia, and the woman mentioned in the *responsum* of Rashba, however, it is possible that Marioneta's words were not merely an idle threat and that Marioneta actually left the Jewish community. In the environs of Morvedre about 1367, upon the encouragement of a Christian woman named María Sanç, a Jewish woman named Astruga left her husband, Gençon Levi, and converted to Christianity, taking the name Constança.[54]

Finally, some Jews in the Crown of Aragon converted on account of poverty. In spite of the general prosperity of Jewish *aljamas*, socioeconomic disparities among Jews were great, and the number of poor Jews grew during the second half of the fourteenth century, due to the effects of poor harvests, plague, and war.[55] Conversion to Christianity may have been attractive to some Jews in dire financial straits who thought it would eliminate their debts. Conversion did not always work this way, however. About 1327, a Jew from Xàtiva who was heavily indebted to a certain Astruc Aleç was baptized, taking the name Bonanat Ferrari. The Jewish *aljama* of Xàtiva had no intention of letting Bonanat abandon his debts, however, and it confiscated his houses.[56]

We cannot always know what moved Jews to seek baptism. It is likely that some sincere conversions transpired. In addition, the reasons for the conversions of a handful of converts who had been wealthy or learned as Jews—such as Vincenç Esteve, Romeu and Pere de Pal, Pere de Gràcia, Jaume de Faro, and Juan Sánchez de Calatayud—remain unclear.[57] Extant evidence demonstrates, however, that, in the Crown of Aragon prior to 1391, a wide variety of desperate Jews turned to baptism seeking respite from a host of ills.

The pressure that many prospective Jewish converts felt to improve their unpleasant circumstances may—together with clerical eagerness to baptize Jews—explain the haste in which many Jews were baptized. Indeed, in the Crown of Aragon, Jews were baptized throughout the year, instead of on the dates traditionally reserved for adult initiation into the Catholic Church, namely, Easter, Pentecost, and sometimes Christmas. Pere declared on January 5, 1341 that he had begun his six-day journey to Calatayud fifteen days after his baptism, suggesting that he was baptized on Saturday, December 16, 1340. The convert Andreu d'Abella was baptized on the feast of Saint Andrew, which fell on Wednesday, November 30 in 1379. Joan de Sant Servin, formerly the Jewish doctor Donçach Javefull of Perpignan, was baptized in Castelló d'Empúries on Tuesday, October 19, 1372. In 1377 in Besalú, three Jews—David Gerson, Mosse Valensí, and Isaach Biton—were baptized on Palm Sunday (March 22). In 1381, four Jews in Rheims were baptized on the Feast of All Saints (November 1). King Jaume I must have known that baptisms were taking place throughout the year, for in 1252, he decided to level a fine of twelve morabetins on any convert who was not baptized on Easter, Pentecost, or Christmas.[58]

The rush to baptism left little time for instruction in the Catholic faith. Neophytes often were described as requiring catechesis, just as infants need "the milk of sweetness."[59] Some Christians tried to educate new converts. For example, in mid-thirteenth-century Manosque, Lord Raymbaud d'Esparron took his goddaughter, Raymbauda, under his wing. Raymbauda spent two years in his household, where she "received [the sacrament of] Penance and the Eucharist . . . once a year . . . and did what Christians did," praying, fasting, going to church, and hearing Mass. Similarly, in the 1360s in Anduze, the convert preacher Joan Catalan housed and instructed Jewish converts following their baptisms.[60] It seems, however, that most Jewish converts, like Joan (formerly Baruch), who was forcibly baptized by the Pastoureaux in Toulouse in 1320, "did not know what Christians believe[d] or why they believe[d] what they believe[d]."[61]

Prospective converts' desire to break away from their predicaments and start anew also may explain why Jews tended to be baptized far from home. Examples of "destination baptisms" abound. Joan de Sant Servin of Perpignan was baptized in or before 1372 in Castelló d'Empúries, for instance, and the three Jews who were baptized in 1377 in Besalú—taking the names Marc Moner, Joan Turon, and Joan Estrader—hailed, respectively, from Solsona, Palencia, and a town in Castile that is abbreviated in the record as "Venech."[62] Throughout the fourteenth century, prospective Jewish converts headed to the bustling hubs of Barcelona and Girona, perhaps in search of economic opportunity. Two Jews from Zaragoza were baptized in Barcelona about 1350, for example, the first taking the name Joan Serra and the second, the name Francesc de Papiolo. In 1359, a Jew from Monteposullo was baptized in Girona, taking the name Tomás. In 1378, a Jew from Castile named Jacob de Lorancha was baptized in the cathedral of Girona, taking the name Pere Castell. In 1379, a convert from Castelló d'Empúries was baptized in the cathedral of Girona, with his wife Brunisendis and his son Ramon Ros, taking the name Pere Alfons de Luna. In 1380, a convert from Teruel was baptized in the cathedral of Barcelona by the canon and hebdomadary Berenguer de Matamala, taking the name Andreu d'Abella.[63] Some Jews were baptized especially far from home. Some time prior to 1371, for example, a Jew from Puigcerdà was baptized in Ille-sur-Têt, France, taking the name Pierre de Gérone. In 1378, two of his children were baptized in Ille-sur-Têt, as well. About 1378, a Jew from Cologne made his way to Barcelona, where he was baptized at the church of Santa María del Mar, taking the name Joan de Ruibech.[64]

Jews' familiarity with Christian culture surely enabled prospective converts to envision and perhaps even idealize conversion to Christianity. Prospective converts would have been aware that the church wanted Jews to convert and that clerics would welcome prospective converts. Moreover, as Jews and Christians depended on one another for professional services and also socialized together, prospective converts may have seen themselves fitting easily into Christian society. Many even would have had Christian acquaintances, if not friends, whom they might have hoped would ease their transition. At the same time, however, because Jews and Christians were theologically at odds and fundamentally suspicious of one another, conversion to Christianity sent a message of radical rejection to converts' Jewish antagonists. And because Jews and Christians were juridically autonomous, and political power resided with Christians, conversion promised to enable converts to evade the grasp of their Jewish enemies, while providing some with new opportunities for retaliation against Jews. In short, conversion to Christianity could seem an attractive and effective way to address a range of troubles.

As the other religious minority in the Crown of Aragon, Muslims also were aware that the church desired their conversion. Therefore, they, too, used baptism to try to find sanctuary from personal difficulties. Some converted to become free from debts. Muslim slaves converted in the hope of being liberated, and in 1274, a Muslim man converted, presumably to evade punishment, after he was accused of stealing horses from his Christian neighbors. The laws known as the *Furs* of Valencia (1261) included specific provisions relating to Muslims who turned to baptism in order to avoid penalties.[65]

The conditions that made conversion to Christianity appealing to Jews and Muslims in dire straits in the Crown of Aragon existed also in other lands dominated by the Catholic Church. As the following examples illustrate, in northern Europe, too, Jews turned to baptism as a means of escape. They converted to evade punishment, for instance, as when in London in 1253, a Jew named Hake (Isaac), son of Mosse, converted to avert execution.[66] They converted in response to Jewish excommunication, as in the case of Nicolas Donin (who served as the Christian disputant at the Paris Disputation of

1240), who chose baptism after he was banned by the Jewish community in La Rochelle about 1225, apparently for having rejected rabbinic Judaism.[67] Jews also converted, or threatened to convert, to escape unhappy marriages. Thus, according to a *responsum* of Rabbi Meir of Rothenburg, a Jewish woman named Leah "rebelled against her husband," and when she was warned that she might lose her *ketubah* and dowry and be forced to wait many years for a divorce, she threatened, among other things, to apostatize.[68] In addition, in medieval England (and southern Italy), Jews converted on account of abject poverty.[69]

These commonalities are striking in light of a scholarly tradition of treating the history of the Jews of Spain as fundamentally distinct from that of the Jews of northern Europe. In fact, the Jews of these two realms have been contrasted specifically with regard to their attitudes toward conversion. In particular, the Jews of medieval German lands have been described as more likely to choose martyrdom over forced baptism than those of Spain.[70] Recent research has complicated this dichotomy, showing not only that Jewish responses to the prospect of forced baptism could be similar in Spain and northern Europe, but also that the two realms had much in common when it came to voluntary conversions.[71] Our observations about the motivations of Jewish converts in the Crown of Aragon strengthen the argument that Jewish conversion had significant common features across medieval Western Europe. Evidence that we shall examine in Chapter 4 about converts' fates after baptism shall strengthen this argument further.

Between Rhetoric and Reality

Christians in the Crown of Aragon surely were aware of the pattern of Jews converting to escape personal problems. It would have been obvious, for example, that the conversions of convicted criminals, inquisitorial defendants, the excommunicated, the lovelorn, the abused, and the poor were primarily a means to an end other than becoming part of the body of Christ. Aside from concerns about the extent to which some converts might continue to observe Jewish customs, about the incremental nature of religious conversion, and about the immutability of Jewishness, therefore, Christians had ample evidence that many Jewish conversions were insincere. Converts' unsavory former identities certainly disconcerted Christians further. Convicted criminals, inquisitorial defendants, individuals who had violated Jewish communal norms, adulterers, victims of violence, and the poor did not make for attractive additions to the Christian flock. Moreover, insofar as convicted criminals, inquisitorial defendants, and individuals who had violated Jewish communal norms were deemed proven menaces to society, their conversions introduced dangers beyond those that might have been associated simply with converts' Jewish origins. These converts not only embodied Christians' fears about Jews, but they also threatened to be vectors of additional ills.

In certain other times and places, Christian authorities made efforts to prevent fraudulent conversions. For example, during the fourth and fifth centuries, the emperors Arcadius and Honorius decreed that Jews who sought to evade punishment or payment of debts through baptism were to be admitted to the church only after they had been found innocent or paid their debts. Honorius even allowed Jewish converts to return to Judaism if their baptisms obviously had been driven by ulterior motives.[72] In a similar effort to forestall insincere conversions, it was decreed at the Council of Agde in 506 that prospective Jewish converts should spend eight months as catechumens so that it might be determined whether they entered in "pure faith" and "merit[ed] the grace of baptism."[73] Closer to our period, in northern Europe, communal charters that were issued by Emperor Henry IV to the Jews of Worms in 1090, and confirmed by Frederick Barbarossa to the Jews of the empire in 1157, specified that prospective Jewish converts were to be held for three days "so that it be clearly known if indeed they repudiate[d] their law because of the Christian faith or[, instead,] by virtue of some injury they ha[d] suffered."[74] At the metropolitan council of 1246 at Tarragona, in response to the complaints of feudal lords whose Muslim slaves were converting to Christianity, it was determined that pastors should wait "a few days" before baptizing Muslims, in order to determine whether these prospective converts "walk[ed] in darkness or light."[75]

During the thirteenth and fourteenth centuries, however, other responses to the disquieting realities of Jewish conversion predominated. One such response involved the ritual purification of Jewish converts through acts that symbolized the casting away of converts' former selves and the creation of a fresh start. Both in northern Europe and Iberia, the practice of divesting converts of their possessions (which persisted in spite of royal prohibitions) appears to have functioned as a form of cleansing. Clearly, this practice served several purposes. It enriched the recipients of converts' belongings and, when the goods in question devolved to royal officials, it symbolically indemnified the king for the loss of a serf.[76] In addition, when converts' belongings were said to have been acquired through the "ill-gotten gains of usury," and they were returned to the owner or converted to pious purposes, the practice fulfilled the instructions of Thomas Aquinas regarding the profits of usury.[77]

This practice also served, however, as a rite of purification. First, a letter that Pope Urban V composed in 1363 documented the existence of—and disavowed—the belief that the practice distanced converts from their Jewish pasts by taking away their material connections to that past. Urban described how a group of clerics and laymen had seized the possessions of a convert in the diocese of Constance under the disingenuous pretext that it was "not permitted to the faithful to retain goods that were gained during a wicked time without the ruin of salvation." The pope lamented that these Christian thugs actually had been "cloaking a desire for booty with the appearance of Christian purity, and longing for their own profit."[78] Second, the repudiation of worldly possessions supposedly enabled converts to break free from the vice of avarice and walk, instead, in the ways of Christ. Thus, in 1350, the bishop of Girona described a convert named Guillem de Llinyola as having chosen "to be poor, active with the zeal of the orthodox faith, rather than a Jew, abounding in the riches of this world." His words echoed those of Pope Innocent III, who, in 1199, in a letter to the abbot of the monastery of Saint Mary de Pratt in Leicester, described how a convert had abandoned his property in order to "follow Christ, rather than wallow in the mire of wealth."[79]

Finally, the act of giving up one's belongings physically may have represented the repudiation of Judaism. The main privileges of German Jewry since the days of Henry IV put the two acts on a par, stating: "just as [converts] have relinquished the law of their forefathers, so did they abandon also their possessions." Echoing this statement and several declarations that were issued thereafter, in 1364, Pope Urban V similarly mentioned converts' "riches" and their "Jewish error" in the same breath. He described a group of converts in southern France as "completely having given up the Jewish error of blindness and all their riches and goods." Episcopal missives from the fourteenth-century Crown of Aragon sometimes employed the same verb—"to reject" (*dimittere*)—in relation to converts' material possessions and Judaism.[80]

At least twenty begging licenses that the bishops of Girona issued to converts during the fourteenth century linked converts' relinquishment of their belongings and their repudiation of Judaism even more closely. These documents referred to both acts simultaneously when they noted that particular converts brought with them into Christianity "nothing but their bare bodies" or "nothing but their pure hearts."[81] Christians' ultimate hope, of course, was that converts would carry neither tangible nor intangible traces of their former lives. In illustration of this aspiration, some Jews not only relinquished their belongings, but they also were baptized naked.[82]

Baptism itself was the ultimate rite of purification. Sacramentally, it removed the stain of sin, and some documents thus referred to it as a "washing" (*lavacrum*).[83] In the font, Jewish converts were said to be "renewed," "regenerated," and "reborn in the holy mother church." They emerged like "newborn" or "tiny" infants.[84] According to records from the papal almonry at Avignon that were issued in 1325, Jewish converts were given new clothes: a linen shirt (*camisia*), pants, stockings, shoes, a hood, and a belt.[85] In addition, converts were assigned a new name, often that of one of their godparents. Thus, for example, the godson of the squire Joan de Ruibech was named Joan de Ruibech, and the goddaughter of Lord Raymbaud was named Raymbauda.[86] Composed in twelfth-century Germany, the alleged autobiography of the convert Herman of Cologne (formerly Judah ben David ha-Levi) combined these elements in fluid prose. The author described how, at baptism, Herman's flesh "took on the purity of an infant. The Church, a virgin mother, gave birth to [him] in a new infancy. Through the washing of regeneration, [he] was stripped of the skin of the old existence . . . [and,] just has [he] changed the order of [his] former ways in this washing, so also did [he] change the name that belonged to [him]."[87]

Another response to the troubling tension between Christian aspirations and the realities of Jewish conversion involved the composition of idealized portrayals of individual conversions. In begging and preaching licenses, for example, kings and bishops stressed the depth of Jewish conversions, describing converts as having converted "thoroughly" or "with their whole heart and soul."[88] Clerics touted the piety of even the most obviously fraudulent conversions. For example, when writing about Pere de Saumana, who converted in order to recover his confiscated children and property, the bishop of Girona, Bertran de Montrodon, declared that Pere had converted "devoutly and humbly."[89] In addition, bishops trumpeted the spiritual significance of converts' relinquishment of their property, even though most converts seem to have had no choice in the matter, asserting that converts gave up their possessions "freely and spontaneously," "inspired by the grace of the Holy Spirit," "for the love of Christ," and "in order to gain celestial glory."[90]

Clerics in and around the Crown of Aragon also participated in the Christian tradition of legitimizing conversions by portraying them as miracles. This was the case when, for example, about 1371, the bishop of Elne, Pere de Planella, wrote to the bishop of Barcelona, Berenguer d'Erill, about the conversion of a Jewish woman named Blanca. Drawing on a trope present in the writings of the French Dominican Vincent de Beauvais (d. c. 1264) and the thirteenth-century Castilian *Cantigas de Santa María*, Pere de Planella described how, after struggling to give birth to a child for nine days and nights, Blanca "recognized her creator," "venerated his mother, the Virgin Mary," and pledged that, if her agony eased, she and her infant would "convert and be reborn." As soon as she made this promise, Blanca reportedly was liberated from pain, and she gave birth to a boy. The child, however, was as "black as coal." Yet the instant the boy was baptized and anointed with the sign of the cross, "all of his blackness was turned, through the power of the Holy Spirit, into whiteness." Upon witnessing "so great a miracle," Blanca, her husband, and their four other children converted, and eighty additional Jews "flew over" to the Catholic faith. Vividly illustrating the cleansing, transformative power of baptism, this story was meant to show that the conversions of Blanca, her family, and the Jewish onlookers were authentic. Blanca's conversion and that of her infant had been confirmed by divine signs, and the conversions of the other Jews were born of awe at the saving power of Christ.[91]

In a letter composed in 1381 to Bishop Bertran de Montrodon of Girona, the canon of Girona, Miquel de Sant Joan, described another miraculous conversion. In this case, four Jews in Rheims were said to have received a vision of a beautiful boy during Mass, when the host was elevated following the words of consecration. Moved to convert, these Jews had clamored "Baptism! Baptism!" and promptly been welcomed into the Christian faith. One took the name Tonsanus. Miquel de Sant Joan established the spiritual pedigree of these converts by showing that they had been deemed worthy of receiving a divine vision.[92]

Accounts of miraculous Jewish conversions dated back to late antiquity, and they emerged in medieval northern Europe, as well. The twelfth-century French Benedictine monk, Guibert de Nogent, wrote, for instance, of a miracle that occurred upon the baptism of a Jewish child from Rouen, who was seized during the First Crusade. "After the holy words had been said and the sacrament performed," Guibert recounted, "when they came to the part where a candle is lighted and the melted wax is dropped on the water, a drop of it was seen to fall separately all by itself, taking the shape of a tiny cross on the water so exactly in its minute substance that no human hand could have made a similar one so small." This sign was understood not only as confirming a religious transformation but also as predicting this child's future career as a monk. Another northern European account of a miraculous Jewish conversion detailed how the family of a Jew who allegedly attacked a consecrated host in Paris at Easter in 1290 (stabbing it with knives and tossing it in boiling water) converted upon seeing the wafer become an image of the crucified Christ.[93]

Stories like these, in which the church scored an incontrovertible victory over Judaism, were intended to circulate widely. Thus, Miquel de Sant Joan told Bertran de Montrodon that either the Jewish converts from Rheims themselves were to spread word of the miracle he had described, or Bertran should do so.[94] Repeated over and over, such tales might have alleviated Christian unease regarding individual Jewish converts, and they also perpetuated hopes about the positive potential of Jewish conversion in general. The very need for such narratives, however, underscores the irony that, although many converts turned to baptism primarily to distance themselves from Jews—indeed, precisely *because* this, and not faith in Christ, was the main motivation of many converts—in the eyes of Christians, converts remained more Jewish than Christian. Rites of purification and miracle stories were a weak balm for this predicament.

In the Crown of Aragon and beyond, pious Christians desired Jewish conversions, yet the realities of Jewish conversion fell short of Christian ideals. Many Jews who sought baptism were marginalized individuals who hoped, first and foremost, to extricate themselves from personal difficulties. They were baptized in haste and possessed only superficial knowledge of Christianity. In an effort to ameliorate the state of Jewish conversion, some Christians instructed new converts in Catholic doctrine and practice. In an attempt to ease converts' way among Christian skeptics, Christian authorities stressed the regenerative power of rites of Christian initiation, and they portrayed individual conversions as divinely sanctioned. In spite of these efforts, however, Christians suspected that converts were still in some ways Jewish. This suspicion, in turn, surely deepened the Christian fears about Judaism's tenacity that contributed to making Jewish conversion a great *desideratum* in the first place.

Chapter 4

Homeward Bound:
The Fates of Jewish Converts

> If you accept baptism, you will be called a dog, a son of a dog, both by Christians and also by Jews. You will live in poverty, and he who today will not give you a coin will not give you another in an entire year. And so you will suffer great privation and, out of despair, you may soon beg to die.
>
> —Inghetto Contardo, 1286[1]

In the environs of the medieval Crown of Aragon, a handful of Jewish converts fared well after baptism, including several individuals who had been wealthy or learned as Jews. At least two converts rose in the ranks of the Dominican order. Pablo Christiani served as the Christian disputant at the Barcelona Disputation of 1263, and Ramon of Tàrrega, who converted in 1346 or 1347 at the age of eleven, became a theologian.[2] Others received royal privileges. For example, the physician Vincenç Esteve and the son of the queen's treasurer, Juan Sánchez de Calatayud, were exempted, by Jaume II and Joan I, respectively, from having to renounce their material possessions.[3] In addition, several converts were granted lucrative employment—often pertaining to Jewish affairs—by members of the royal family. In 1305, for instance, the convert Bertran of Jorba was granted a monopoly over the sale of meat to the Jews of Montblanc by Queen Blanca. This probably meant that Bertran received the earnings from the sale of meat to Jews and that he appointed the local *shohet*, or ritual slaughterer. In 1307, a convert named Joan Ferrand was appointed bailiff of Jews and Muslims in Teruel by Jaume II. The convert Romeu de Pal of Tàrrega served as a royal surgeon. In 1331, he was granted a monopoly over the sale of meat to the Jews of Cervera by King Alfons III and, in 1343, he accompanied Pere III on his campaign in Mallorca and received four hundred Barcelona sous as compensation. In 1388, the convert Jaume Romeu was granted a franchise to operate the *tafureria*, or gambling house, of the Jewish *aljama* of Valencia by King Pere III.[4]

Given Christians' deep suspicion of Jewish converts, however, it is not surprising that, unlike the exceptional converts listed above, many converts did not fare well. In fact, even some of those who received royal assistance encountered obstacles to prosperity as Christians. Only one year after Bertran de Jorba was granted a monopoly over the sale of meat to the Jews of Montblanc, for example, Jewish and Christian protests led Queen Blanca to remove Bertran from this post, and King Jaume II informed Rashba that the Jewish *aljama* of Montblanc would have to pay Bertran one thousand Barcelona sous in order to settle the affair. Christians, who had supplied local Jews with meat until the appointment of Bertran, must have resented the fact that a convert had taken part of their business, and Jews presumably recoiled from the idea that an apostate should profit from their patronage. In Mallorca in 1308, Jews also objected to buying meat from apostates, and the concession to Romeu de Pal of the meat stand of the Jews of Cervera in 1331 generated further controversy.[5]

In addition, Ramon of Tàrrega, the Jew turned Dominican theologian, was eventually arrested by inquisitors for heretical theological opinions, and he died in prison in 1371. The records of Ramon's inquisitorial trial are no longer extant, and we do not know whether Ramon's identity as a Jewish convert was a focus of his trial. However, even though Ramon's objectionable teachings lacked any obvious relation to Judaism, the sixteenth-century commentator on the *Directorium inquisitorum* of Nicolau Eimeric, Francisco Peña, remarked that Ramon's fate demonstrated that "even though [Ramon] had changed his religion, he had not changed his habits."[6]

In this chapter, we shall examine the difficult circumstances that the majority of Jewish converts faced following their baptisms. In so doing, we shall see that, as a result of poverty, Christian rejection, and personal grievances against Jews, many converts continued to interact with Jews, often in antagonistic ways. In some cases, however, poverty and Christian rejection led disaffected converts to seek to return to Judaism.

Converts as Wandering Beggars

Unlike Vincenç Esteve and Juan Sánchez de Calatayud, most converts in the Crown of Aragon gave up their possessions upon converting to Christianity. As we discussed in Chapter 3, this act was imbued with symbolic meaning about the renunciation of Judaism. It also, however, had grave practical consequences. Having, "according to custom," "thoroughly relinquished all of [their] temporal goods," "given up the resources that [they] had possessed as Jew[s]," abandoned "all of their belongings," and renounced "all of the things in the world that they had previously owned," many converts were destitute.[7] Jewish relatives often aggravated converts' poverty by withholding their inheritances.[8] Moreover, some converts lacked skills with which they might earn a living as Christians. A convert from Toledo named Juan Fernández who made his way to Catalonia, for instance, lamented that "he did not know how to practice any trade with his hands with which he might support his family because he was of the lineage of Sadoch," that is, a priest. Juan was probably a Talmud scholar who thought that Christians would best understand his predicament if he likened himself to a Christian cleric.[9]

Penniless, shunned by Christians, and ostracized by Jews, many converts became beggars. As such, they wandered the Crown of Aragon and beyond in search of Christian charity. In fact, travel was a hallmark of the existence of Jewish convert beggars across Western Europe, such that converts bridged regions not only by being baptized far from home, but also through their wayfaring after baptism.[10] During the fourteenth century, convert beggars passed through the Crown of Aragon from as far afield as Lisbon, Toledo, Avignon, Toulouse, Paris, Saint Denis, and Rheims.[11] Constantly on the move, the convert Joan de Ruibech, originally from Cologne, found himself in Barcelona on March 17, 1378 and in Girona on April 3, 1378.[12] A letter of Pope Urban V indicates that some converts maintained this way of life for over a decade. A certain Petrus from the diocese of Constance, who "had abounded in temporal goods" prior to his baptism, begged "door to door" with his wife and children for sixteen years.[13]

On occasion, convert beggars traveled in groups. Thus, when bishops in fourteenth-century Barcelona and Girona—like some of their counterparts in northern Europe—issued begging licenses authorizing Jewish converts to beg throughout their dioceses, they issued several that were to be shared by groups of converts.[14] For example, in 1350, the bishop of Girona, Berenguer de Cruïlles, issued a single license to the converts Joan Serra, Pere de Terre, Bernat de Palaciolo, and Ramon Esquert. In 1371, the bishop of Barcelona,

Berenguer d'Erill, issued a single license to Blanca, her family, and the eighty Jews who allegedly converted upon witnessing her survival of childbirth and the transformation of her infant. In 1377, the bishop of Girona, Bertran de Montrodon, issued a single license to three converts: Marc Moner (formerly David Gerson), Joan Turon (formerly Mosse Valensí), and Joan Estrader (formerly Isaach Biton). The license issued to Blanca and her entourage reveals that Christians sometimes collected alms on behalf of Jewish convert beggars. In this license, Berenguer d'Erill instructed the rectors, vicars, and presbyters of the diocese of Barcelona each to choose one or two parishioners to collect alms for Blanca's group. Possibly, Berenguer thought that Christians would be more likely to give to fellow cradle Christians who represented converts than to converts themselves.[15]

These begging licenses—which were supposed to be visible at all times and may have been worn around the neck—stressed converts' extreme poverty.[16] In the license issued to Guillem de Llinyola in 1350, for example, Bishop Berenguer de Cruïlles of Girona declared that Guillem would not be able to sustain "his destitute and miserable life unless he were to be aided mercifully by [Christian] alms." Similarly, in the license issued to Daniel de Verger in 1353, Berenguer cited Daniel's "lack of basic necessities."[17] In the license that Bishop Jaume de Trilla of Girona issued to Jaume de Faro in 1372, Jaume de Trilla explained that Jaume's baptized daughter, Margarita, needed money for a dowry. He reminded Christians that it was a pious act to help girls marry, and he urged them to collect alms for Margarita.[18] Christian aid to Jewish converts, however, did not come easily. Bishops not only advised clergy to "admonish and exhort" their congregants to help converts, but they also promised a partial indulgence to all those "who [we]re truly penitent and ha[d] made confessions and sh[ould] extend their helpful hands to the said individuals who ha[d] been reborn [in Christ]."[19]

Various Christian institutions sought to help poor Jewish converts. In December 1361, for example, the general council of the town of Manresa gave the convert Nicolau de Gràcia thirty Barcelona sous.[20] In addition, the kings of the Crown of Aragon, like the bishops of Barcelona and Girona, issued begging licenses to Jewish converts. In 1378, for example, King Pere III gave a license to a convert named Caterma, whose husband was being held captive in North Africa, so that she would have the right to beg to support herself and her children. The following year, he granted a license to the convert Leonor Muniz, whom he described as "afflicted by old age and poverty," authorizing her to beg anywhere within his dominion.[21]

The kings of the Crown—like those of France and England—also financially supported some converts.[22] In 1303, for example, Jaume II donated sixty-three Barcelona sous to a convert named Bonanat for clothes,[23] and in 1378, 1382, and 1383, Pere III granted aid to several others. In 1378, for instance, he gave five Barcelona sous, six diners to a convert by the name of Joan Ramon, and in 1382 he gave fifty-five Barcelona sous to clothe an unnamed woman convert, five florins to an unnamed male convert, eleven Barcelona sous to another, eleven Barcelona sous to a group of converts from Castile, and eleven Barcelona sous to a convert by the name of Jaume Romeu "for the sustainment of his life."[24]

On occasion, King Pere III took an ongoing interest in a particular convert. In 1378, for example, he gave 50 Barcelona sous to his goddaughter Caterina, the daughter of the deceased apostate Andreu Contijoc, "to help her marriage." Four years later, it seems that Caterina was still in need. The king sent her 73 Barcelona sous and 3 florins "to help with her journey to Barcelona," and promised 4 diners daily for the rest of her life. Shortly thereafter, when Caterina was ill, the king sent her 11 Barcelona sous and, the following year, the king sent her a total of 150 Barcelona sous.[25] Similarly, between 1382 and 1384, the king repeatedly gave money to the young convert Joan, who was baptized when the king passed through the town of Alcira and was in the care of an official of the *escrivà de raciò* named Joan Loral.[26]

In his *Llibre de contemplació en Déu* (*The Book of Contemplation on God*, 1271–74), Ramon Llull lamented that "many [more] Jews would convert if they had a way to live [as Christians]."[27] In effect, the poverty of many converts must have served as a deterrent to Jewish conversion. In addition, it made converts a drain on Christian resources, which were increasingly scarce as the fourteenth century progressed, and war, plague, and famine afflicted the Crown of Aragon.

Converts as Informers

In an ordinance issued in 1354, Catalan and Aragonese Jewish leaders noted that some apostates turned against their former brethren, "bending their bow, making ready their arrow," to shoot by their deadly defamation whomever they pleased.[28] In effect, converts not infrequently harmed Jews. Poverty may have been a motivating factor, as converts often extorted money from Jews. Shem Tov ben Isaac ibn Shaprut explained in the introduction to the *Even bohan*, however, that a desire "to please Christians" also drove this behavior.[29] By positioning themselves against Jews, converts aligned themselves with Christians insofar as they shared with them a common enemy.

Converts often harassed Jews under the guise of seeking to protect Christians and Christianity from Jewish villainy. A query sent to Rashba tells, for example, of converts who persuaded local Christian authorities to forbid the Christian consumption of kosher meat and of wine and bread prepared by Jews.[30] These converts may have argued, as was noted in an ordinance promulgated in 1290 regarding the town of Huesca, that it was outrageous that Christians should regularly consume kosher meat and wine, whereas Jews never touched non-kosher food or drink.[31] Local Jews had to bribe these converts to stop speaking ill of them, and they also bribed Christian priests and judges, who revoked the ban on the Christian consumption of kosher foodstuffs.[32]

Converts repeatedly denounced Jews to bishops and inquisitors for committing offenses against Christians and Christianity. In 1315, for example, the converts Guillem de Belloc and Bonanat Torner captured several Jews from Lleida, including Bonanat's relative, Rovent de Castelldasens, and brought them before the bishop of Barcelona, Ponç de Gualba, on charges of blasphemy. Perhaps moved by pressure from the influential Jewish scholar and merchant Rabbi Mosse Natan of Tàrrega, however, Ponç de Gualba declared Rovent innocent. Moreover, the bishop asked for the release of another Jew whom Bonanat had captured. Nine days later, he acquitted yet another Jew whom Bonanat had denounced, he declared Bonanat a liar, and he instructed the bishop of Lleida to have no faith in him.[33]

In 1324, an apostate named Ramon (who allegedly had been baptized four times) told the scribe of Calatayud, Judah Hochon, that if he did not pay him ten Jaca lliures, Ramon would report him to the local inquisition. Following the advice of his communal leaders, Judah refused to pay Ramon. In response, Ramon denounced Judah, and Judah was arrested and imprisoned by the prior of the Dominican monastery of Calatayud. Ramon was persistent and so he told Judah's wife that, if she paid him, he would have Judah released from prison. Judah's wife gave Ramon one hundred sous and promised one hundred more. Ramon assured her that Judah would soon be set free, but he did not keep his word. When Judah's wife protested, Ramon demanded the remaining one hundred sous. Here, the documentary trail ends.[34]

A register of denunciations made to the inquisitor general of the Crown of Aragon during the 1370s records another convert's scheme to harm Jews.

This convert, the tailor Jaume Bisnes, denounced a Jew named Lupus Abnacay for host desecration, that is, abusing the consecrated eucharistic wafer that the church taught was Christ himself. This was a particularly potent accusation for, over a millennium after Jews allegedly had killed Christ, Christians feared that Jews remained intent on hurting their savior. Jaume claimed that Lupus had bought two gilt-silver chalices containing consecrated hosts from a chaplain and, more interested in the silver than the hosts, he had tossed the hosts to the ground. Jaume, who claimed to have been present, hastened to add that he and other onlookers had reprimanded Lupus and that Lupus had sworn them all to secrecy.[35]

In 1389, a convert denounced a Jew from Montblanc named Vidal Brunell to the inquisitor fra Guillem de Tous of Tarragona for possessing the allegedly blasphemous *Talmud of Rabbi Moses of Egypt*, probably Maimonides' *Mishneh Torah*. This denunciation unleashed a grueling inquisitorial investigation that resulted in the harsh punishment of the entire Jewish *aljama* of Montblanc.[36] Through denunciations such as these, converts presumably hoped to earn Christian trust and respect. The case of Bonanat Torner indicates, however, that converts did not necessarily succeed in doing so.

Converts with an axe to grind against Jews—such as victims of Jewish violence or individuals who had been excommunicated by a Jewish community—may have turned against Jews not only to collect profit or curry Christian favor, but also to take revenge. In 1327, the secretary of the *aljama* of Barcelona, Bonsenyor Gracià, feared that a particular apostate, who had been excommunicated by the Jewish *aljama* of Barcelona for physically attacking him, might retaliate. As a precaution, Gracià paid King Alfons III to guarantee that this apostate would not harm any local Jews.[37]

As in the Crown of Aragon, converts elsewhere in Western Europe turned against Jews. For example, the thirteenth-century French convert, Nicolas Donin, who had been excommunicated by Jews prior to his baptism, spearheaded Christian efforts to condemn the Talmud and, about 1173, an English convert named Theobald of Canterbury provided key testimony in the first known medieval accusation of ritual murder, which was recorded by the Benedictine monk Thomas of Monmouth. Theobald—whom Thomas of Monmouth described as "a converted enemy" who had "been privy to the secrets of our enemies"—informed Christians that Jews were required to shed human blood in order to "obtain their freedom" and "return to their fatherland." He explained that Jews sacrificed a Christian child every year, "in scorn and contempt of Christ, that so they might avenge their sufferings on him; inasmuch as it was because of Christ's death that they had been shut out from their own country and were in exile as slaves in a foreign land."[38]

Although some converts who harmed Jews were trying to convince skeptical Christians that they had transferred their allegiances to Christian society, it is likely that, by focusing their efforts on their former co-religionists, these converts actually reinforced the Christian conviction that converts remained irrevocably tied to Jews and Judaism.

Converts as Missionary Preachers

Converts in the Crown of Aragon also preached to Jews. Mendicant conversionary sermons were scarce by the second quarter of the fourteenth century, and Jewish converts initially appeared to be promising successors to the friars. Indeed, Christian authorities welcomed these "new soldier[s] for Christ," for it was widely agreed that converts' knowledge of Jewish culture would prove useful in converting Jews. Moreover, the itinerant lifestyle of many converts was well-suited to preaching. Thus, Ramon Llull had advocated convert preaching and, in Castile in 1322, the municipal council of Valladolid specifically recommended that Jewish converts be encouraged to preach to Jews.[39]

Between 1263 and 1389, the kings of the Crown of Aragon issued preaching licenses to at least thirteen Jewish converts, authorizing these converts to proselytize their former co-religionists and instructing royal officials to compel Jews to attend their sermons. In August 1263, shortly after the conclusion of the Barcelona Disputation, King Jaume I commanded Jews to welcome Pablo Christiani as a traveling preacher.[40] In 1333, the Infant Pere granted a preaching license to two brothers from Tudela, Pedro Fernández and Jimeno Pérez, which he renewed in 1338. As king, in 1339, Pere granted a license to Pere de la Mercè of Berga; in 1360 to Nicolau de Gràcia of Íxar; in 1377 to Arnau d'Estadella of Huesca; and in 1379 to a convert from Paris named Guillem, as well as to two converts from Valencia, Jaume Romeu and Guillem Català, who were to preach together.[41] In 1308, Jaume II granted a preaching license to a Muslim convert named Jaume Pere, authorizing him to preach to Muslims and Jews.[42]

Preaching licenses frequently stressed the erudition of Jewish converts. For example, the two preaching licenses granted—in 1320 and 1328, respectively—to the convert Juan of Huesca, who was baptized in or before 1303, described Juan as having long been a Jewish rabbi (*magister*) and as an expert in "divine law." The royal surgeon Romeu de Pal received a preaching license in 1344 and was described as well-versed in Latin, Hebrew, and the Old and New Testaments. Pere de Gràcia, formerly a Jewish doctor, received a preaching license in 1347 and was described as learned in Mosaic law. Juan Fernández de Toledo, who received a preaching license in 1389 and may have been a Talmud scholar, was praised for his vast knowledge.[43] Educated converts may have been more likely than others to be attracted to preaching, yet some of these claims were likely exaggerated. It was in kings' interest to stress the erudition of convert preachers for this bolstered the authority of convert preachers and enhanced the image of Jewish converts generally. Learned converts were a boon to Christendom not only because they were probably of high social status and their conversions presumably constituted a particularly strong blow to the Jewish community, but also because their rejection of Judaism and acknowledgment of Christian truth may have been more likely to result from a genuine appreciation of Christian theology.[44]

Convert preachers were said to act in imitation of the apostles of Christ and to follow in their ways, but few succeeded in gaining converts. One who did was Pere de Gràcia. In the preaching license that Pere III gave him in 1352, the king commented with approbation: "You [have] instructed many Jews in the Catholic faith through salvific speeches and lessons, such that . . . they converted to the said faith, having rejected . . . Jewish errors."[45] An episcopal begging license from 1350 lists four converts—Joan Serra, Pere de Terre of Fraga, Bernat de Palaciolo of Tarazona, and Ramon Esquert of Valadorit—who, thanks to Pere's efforts, were "illuminated by the spirit, fled the shadows of error, abandoned the perfidy of Jewish blindness, and were thoroughly converted to Christ, the true light." A begging license from 1352 lists yet another of Pere's disciples, a convert from Zaragoza named Francesc de Papiolo who was baptized in Barcelona.[46] A convert from Anduze named Joan Catalan also reportedly brought about conversions. According to Pope Urban V, by 1364, Joan had converted some thirty Jews from the dioceses of Cuenca, Valencia, Avignon, Vaucluse, and Sisteron. A begging license issued in 1381 by the bishop of Girona, Bertran de Montrodon, notes that a Jewish convert from Toulouse named Joan Alquer, his wife, María, and "many other former Jews" converted upon hearing the preaching of "Joan"—possibly Joan Catalan.[47]

Most convert preachers, however, were not intent on converting Jews. Instead, like converts who blackmailed and informed on Jews, they appear to have been driven by a desire to please Christians and an urge to harm Jews. A far cry from the peaceful ideal of conversionary enthusiasts such as Ramon

Llull, the sermons of most convert preachers were diatribes that incited Christian onlookers to taunt Jews. In 1297, the Jews of Zaragoza complained that converts who preached beyond the bounds of Jewish quarters led Christian bystanders to attack Jews.[48] In the early 1380s, Shem Tov ben Isaac ibn Shaprut, who had recently moved from Navarre to Tarazona, wrote in his *Even bohan* that apostates who disputed with Jews instilled in them doubts about Judaism in order to humiliate them in front of Christians.[49]

Converts in France and Castile tormented Jews with sermons, as well. In 1368, a French Jew named David Quinon complained that converts tried to force Jews to attend their sermons in church. He explained that this practice endangered Jews and that Christians took advantage of these occasions to ridicule Jews.[50] About 1375, in neighboring Castile, Moisés Cohen of Tordesillas, the author of the polemical treatise *Ezer ha-emunah* (*The Support of Faith*), described a sermon delivered by two convert preachers (Juan of Valladolid and a disciple of Alfonso de Valladolid) in Ávila as follows: "Two perverse and hardened men, who had rejected our holy law and taken on a new religion, and who were furbished with a royal letter of authorization, descended upon our communities and convoked Jews wherever and whenever they wanted to discuss their religion with them. . . . In Ávila, they gathered us first in the large church. They posed questions and made speeches that appeared very knowledgeable but were [in fact] nothing but thorns and refuse. . . . They gathered us four times, in front of the entire community and the entire assembly of Christians and Muslims."[51]

To end the vexation of convert preaching, Jews in the Crown of Aragon informed the king that, as the Jews of Mallorca pointed out in 1383, convert preachers not only caused "great damage to Jews," but they were also an insult to Christendom.[52] Perhaps because kings agreed, but surely in exchange for money, kings set about restricting convert preaching. On June 28, 1309, Jaume II forbade converts from entering Jewish quarters. In November 1328, Alfons III limited convert preaching to synagogues, and he told the bailiffs and vicars of the County of Urgell and the *vizcondado* of Ager that convert preachers were to be accompanied by six or eight upstanding Christian men. Also in 1328, Alfons ordered his officials to stop converts from gathering the Jews of Girona wherever they liked, for the Jews of Girona had complained that this violated the privileges of the *aljama* and that, moreover, it was very dangerous to gather Jews outside the synagogue. On August 27, 1343, Pere III forbade converts from entering synagogues and private homes in Mallorca and excused Jews from attending converts' sermons. In 1376, Pere III decreed that converts were to be allowed to preach in Teruel on only one day every year, in the home of the bailiff, before Jews whom the bailiff would select. Pere also excused the Jews of Mallorca, Barcelona, Lleida, Perpignan, Zaragoza, Calatayud, Huesca, Exea, Barbastre, Alcanyís, Valencia, and Xàtiva from converts' sermons, and he prohibited converts, under penalty of fine, from entering these Jewish quarters. In 1383, Pere again ordered, with regard to all the principal *aljamas* of the realm, that no convert should enter a Jewish quarter and that no Jew should be compelled to listen to the preaching and disputations of converts. In addition, he specified that converts who violated these regulations were to be arrested and publicly whipped. [53]

In directives such as these, kings mentioned that convert preachers often sought to extort money from Jews. In May 1390, Joan I ordered his officials in Rosselló not to tolerate converts' abuses of Jews, including their habit of "extort[ing] monies from Jews" and meeting with Jews "rather for the sake of harassment than in the spirit of converting the same Jews to the orthodox faith." And in September 1390, Joan I directed his officials in Valencia not to force Jews to attend converts' sermons, on the grounds that converts' purpose was to extort money and aggravate Jews, rather than to lead Jews over to the Catholic faith (*qui pocius hoc faciunt pro extorquendis peccuniis et pro gravando aljamam ipsam aut eius singulares quam pro reducendo aliquos judeos ad fidem catholicam*).[54]

Regret and Return

If some converts in the Crown of Aragon—and also in Castile and northern Europe—hoped to eke out a living, gain Christian favor, or take revenge on Jews by denouncing Jews or preaching to them, others gave up. In the words of a repentant apostate from early fourteenth-century Toulon, they "greatly suffered and regretted [their conversions] and therefore wished to return to Judaism."[55] In the face of new hardships, then, conversion—this time back to Judaism—once again presented itself as a means of escape.

In medieval Europe, reversion to Judaism was frequently a consequence of violent forced conversions. For example, following the massacres of the First Crusade, dozens of converts from Regensburg returned to Judaism. Likewise, in 1189, a Jew from York named Benedict, who was baptized after "having been so maltreated and wounded by Christians that his life was despaired of," declared to the king only hours after his baptism that he remained a Jew, and he "relapsed into the Jewish errors." Similarly, in the aftermath of the violence of the Barons' War (1264–67), King Edward I of England inquired into the apostasy to Judaism of fifteen forced converts. And, in southern France in 1320, the convert Joan (formerly Baruch) not only returned to Judaism but also attempted to convince inquisitors that his return was permissible according to canon law, as his baptism had been unlawfully coerced. Like Joan, other victims of the Pastoureaux also sought to return to Judaism, as did Jews from France who converted in the face of edicts of expulsion.[56] Some Jews who were baptized in the absence of violence, however, also returned to Judaism. As we saw in Chapter 3, just like Jews who converted at sword's point, many voluntary converts lacked commitment to the Christian faith. When, then, they found themselves destitute and stranded among hostile Christians, it was only natural that they should contemplate retracing their steps.[57]

Returning to Judaism was fraught with risk. To begin, in southwestern Europe, inquisitors were on patrol. Indeed, inquisitors hounded so-called *relapsi* even beyond the grave. In late thirteenth-century Provence, for example, Pablo Christiani and some Franciscan inquisitors removed the bodies of suspected apostates to Judaism from Jewish cemeteries to burn them at the stake.[58] Moreover, some Jews who opposed the re-Judaization of apostates were also on the lookout, and they readily denounced repentant apostates, and the Jews who helped them, to Christian authorities.[59]

In spite of these dangers, as we shall see in Chapter 6, some converts approached Jewish communal leaders and underwent a formal process of re-Judaization that included acts of penance and rituals of purification. Other converts, however, simply relocated, hoping to hide from Jews as well as from Christians. In so doing, converts added yet another leg to a journey across regions that often had begun with baptism far from home and then continued for the sake of begging and preaching.[60] A *responsum* of Rashba tells, for example, of a Jewish woman who converted to Christianity and then moved with her Jewish lover to Toledo, where the couple was known to "go out [in public] as if they were Jews and husband and wife" (*yotsim be-hezkat yehudim, uve-ish ve-ishto*). Similarly, in 1308, a female convert in Xàtiva lamented that her baptized husband had fled to Toledo to return to Judaism. Benvenist Barzilay, who converted to Christianity about 1312 in Tarragona in order to reduce an inquisitorial penalty, taking the name Pere d'Avinyó, returned to Judaism further away, in Tripoli, where he went with a son named Jucef.[61]

Like the use of baptism as a means of escape—and like converts' poverty, converts' tendency to harm Jews, and converts' preaching—efforts to return to Judaism incognito were not unique to the Crown of Aragon. A *responsum* of the great eleventh-century Ashkenazi scholar of Jewish law, Rashi, tells, for example, of an apostate who was baptized in one place and then returned to Judaism elsewhere. Similarly, in the late thirteenth century, an apostate from southern Italy named Andreas wrote that it was well known that poor apostates went "to places where they [we]re not known and revert[ed there] to their origin."[62] Moreover, in 1360, King Pere III deplored that baptized Jews from papal territories were entering his kingdom to return to Judaism:

> Quite a few Jews who [once] desired to go from the Jewish blindness to the true light of Christ and who received holy chrism and baptism in the water of new life, [now,] like dogs returning to their vomit, denying the name of Christ, the holy faith, and the holy Catholic Church, have deceitfully left the County of Venaissin and other places and lands directly subject to the dominion of the same Pope, and fled to our kingdom of Aragon . . . and, living [here], they Judaize and live according to the perfidious Jewish rite of the Jews, blaspheming against the name of our Lord Jesus Christ and the aforesaid Catholic faith.[63]

Incognito or not, the return of converts to Judaism fulfilled the fears of Christian leaders throughout Western Europe. Popes and bishops had long worried that poverty and Christian rejection would drive converts away. In 1169, for example, Pope Alexander III wrote that converts "despaired easily" and might be compelled to forsake the Christian faith on account of indigence and lack of assistance, thus returning to their former religion, "like a dog to vomit."[64] At the Third Lateran Council (1179), Alexander again warned that converts ought to be better off after their conversions than before, lest poverty drive them to despair and they return to Judaism.[65] Similarly, in 1199, Pope Innocent III wrote in a letter to the bishop of Autun that "the shame of poverty, which [converts] are not accustomed to bear easily, [might] force [converts] to look back to the abandoned Jewish perfidy." In the same year, in a letter to the abbot of a monastery in Leicester, Innocent admonished: "Care must be taken that [converts] should be solicitously provided for, lest, in the midst of other faithful Christians, they become oppressed by lack of food; for, lacking the necessities of life, many of them, after their baptism, are led into great distress, with the result that they are often forced to go backward."[66] Likewise, in 1320, Pope John XXII wrote, in a letter to the officials and counts of the County of Venaissin:

It is both unbecoming and senseless that those who while living as infidels enjoyed abundance should, upon turning believers, be forced to beg. We forbid, therefore, all our rectors and other officials in the County of Venaissin and in the other counties and territories subject to the Apostolic See to cause such converted Jews, or those to be converted in the future, to suffer damage in their property and possessions for whatever cause or allow others to injure them. [Christians] ought rather to show themselves favorably disposed toward them and protect them against insults and molestations, so that they realize that they ha[ve] left bondage for freedom, and w[ill] not be forced ignominiously to beg and to relapse.[67]

Episcopal begging licenses in the Crown of Aragon echoed these concerns, encouraging Christians to give alms generously to converts lest, on account of poverty, converts should be compelled to return, "like dog[s] to vomit," to their "original blindness."[68]

The phenomenon of return to Judaism must have struck Christian observers as further proof that many Jewish conversions were fraudulent.[69] Christians themselves, however, were partly responsible for failed conversions. In 1201, Pope Innocent III had written, with regard to Jewish converts, of aspiring to strengthen, and faithfully bring to perfection, something "planted with a weak root."[70] Instead of cultivating converts, however, most Christians forsook and rejected them, reducing the chances that they might flourish. Thus, Christian expectations of Jewish converts became a self-fulfilling prophecy.

Sources from the Crown of Aragon paint a generally dark portrait of medieval Jewish conversion, an endeavor in which pious Christian ideals clashed with a crass reality. Church authorities hoped that Jewish conversions would boost Christian morale but, instead, conversions were often an affront to Christian pride. Efforts to remedy this state of affairs by ritually cleansing converts and spreading miracle stories had little concrete effect. Rejected by Christians, many converts were relegated to a no-man's land, where hopes of ever truly joining Christian society dimmed, and wounds inflicted by former co-religionists festered.

Evidence from northern Europe and Castile indicates commonalities north and southwest of the Crown of Aragon. Christian leaders from England to Castile waxed eloquent about Jewish conversion, enacted laws meant to encourage it, gave charity to converts, served as godparents to converts, and expressed fears about reversion to Judaism. Across these lands, too, however,

Christian suspicion of converts prevailed. Christians memorialized converts' unique status in writing, and rites of purification and miracle stories developed to counteract concerns about lingering Jewishness. Moreover, in northern Europe as in Spain, Jews converted to flee personal predicaments, some converts became wandering beggars, some sought to harm Jews, some worked as Christian preachers, and some tried to return to Judaism. Deeper exploration of these similarities—and of the movement of converts between northern Europe and Spain—promises to contribute to a richer understanding of medieval Jewish conversion and, by extension, of fundamental continuities in the nature of Jewish-Christian relations across medieval Western Christendom.

Two Converts, Repentant

The records of the trials of Janto and Jamila Almuli and Jucef de Quatorze suggest that Pere and Abadia were among the disillusioned and remorseful converts who sought to return to Judaism. According to Salomon Navarro, Abadia repeatedly visited the Jewish quarter of Calatayud after his baptism, and he conversed there with distinguished members of the *aljama*. Moreover, according to Jucef de Quatorze, Abadia told these Jews that he wanted to return to Judaism, and the Jews "approved of what Abadia said he wanted to do and strengthened him in his intent." Jucef de Quatorze commented also that, although he did not remember who had assembled the Jews who officially re-Judaized Abadia, it seemed reasonable to him that Abadia would have convened them himself.[1] In making these claims, Salomon Navarro and Jucef de Quatorze may simply have been trying to deflect blame for Abadia's return to Judaism away from Jews. However, as some converts did actively seek to return to Judaism, it is possible that Salomon and Jucef were telling the truth.

Evidence about Pere's behavior following his baptism suggests that Pere also may have turned homeward of his own accord. According to Pere's first confession, Pere remained near the village of Sant Pere de Riudebitlles in Catalonia for fifteen days after his baptism. Then he began to travel west. Averaging about fifty kilometers per day in the dead of winter, Pere initially associated with Christians. At the end of the first day, for example, during which he passed through Cervera and arrived at the village of Castellnou de Seana, Pere was welcomed at a Christian inn. On the second day, after passing through Lleida, he stopped to eat "Christian food" at a tavern in Alcarràs. Later, in La Granja d'Escarp, he lodged in a Christian home. In the absence of any indication to the contrary, it is probable that, on the third day, after crossing the border from Catalonia into Aragon and arriving in Bujaraloz, Pere again ate and lodged with Christians.

As we have seen, it was common for Jewish converts to wander from town to town. It is striking, however, that Pere headed directly back to Calatayud.

Pere explained to fra Sancho de Torralba that he had planned to reestablish himself there as a Christian, but this is doubtful. Would Pere truly have chosen to live as a Christian surrounded by the Jews among whom he had previously lived as a Jew? Unlike Pere, a number of converts in the medieval Crown stayed far from home, presumably to distance themselves from problematic pasts and protect themselves from the anger of their former co-religionists.[2]

Pere's journey is all the more intriguing in that, on the fourth night, Pere began to eat and lodge with Jews. According to the *Directorium inquisitorum* of Nicolau Eimeric, these were telltale signs of a "re-Judaizing heretic."[3] Upon being prodded by fra Sancho de Torralba, Pere confessed that, in Pina de Ebro, he stayed with a Jew named Mosse Camariel. Pere told the tribunal that he did so because there was nowhere else to obtain food. It is difficult to believe, however, that not a single Christian would have been willing to assist Pere for one night, especially as Pere may, already at this point, have had some money. Pere never mentioned begging and, toward the end of his journey, a Jewish acquaintance refused to *sell* him bread and wine (and invited him to share his meal as a friend). It seems, instead, that Pere sought out Mosse Camariel for personal reasons. "Camariel" was the last name of Pere's father, and Mosse may have been Pere's relative. Indeed, Pere described the Jew with whom he spent the following night as "a Jew whom he did not know," ostensibly in contrast to Mosse.[4]

Pere was evasive in describing his encounter with Mosse Camariel. For example, he told the tribunal of fra Sancho de Torralba that he did not know whether Mosse knew that he had been baptized "because Mosse did not ask him about these things, and he did not tell him." Perhaps Mosse did not know. This would mean that there was no discernable change in Pere's physical appearance following baptism and that Pere comported himself as a Jew in Mosse's home. (Pere admitted to fra Sancho that he ate Mosse's food. He insisted, however, that he did not "pray as a Jew, according to the Jewish rite.") But perhaps Mosse did know of Pere's baptism and also that Pere was contemplating returning to Judaism.[5]

For the remainder of his journey, Pere continued to eat and lodge with Jews, as though in an underground railroad. On the fifth night, in Alfajarín, Pere stayed with the Jew "whom he did not know," and the following day he traveled with this Jew to Zaragoza, where he ate in the home of his companion's sister.

Finally, on the evening of the sixth and penultimate day of his journey, Pere arrived in the village of La Almunia de Doña Godina, about thirty-five kilometers from Calatayud. There, he headed straight to the home of his old acquaintances, Salomon and Miriam Navarro. The Navarros welcomed Pere and, according to Pere's first confession, Pere immediately told Salomon that he was now a Christian. Unfazed, Salomon responded, "See this food. If you want, eat of it. If not, leave it." Pere answered that he did want to partake of the meal, and so, according to Miriam, "he sat and ate bread and greens (*caules*) with oil, and he drank [the Navarros'] wine with them."[6]

According to Pere's second confession and the testimonies of Salomon and Miriam Navarro, the Navarros then escorted Pere through the cold, dark Jewish quarter and into the home of Janto and Jamila Almuli. There, Janto lay by the fire in the kitchen, waiting to turn Pere into a Jewish martyr.

PART III

By the Fire

The Intervention

The records of the trials of the Almulis and Jucef de Quatorze provide direct insight into inquisitorial thought and practice, and they grant valuable glimpses of the experiences of Jewish apostates. They are clouded as a window on to Jewish life, however, both on account of the vagaries of the process of inquisitorial record production, and also because of the nature of the conditions that they documented. Inquisitorial scribes and notaries paraphrased, summarized, and translated material, thereby obscuring the voices of defendants and witnesses. Moreover, to the extent that we can recover these voices, there remains the challenge of interpreting them. Fearing for their lives and the welfare of loved ones, forced to respond to detailed leading questions, and sometimes suffering from the physical and psychological consequences of imprisonment and torture, defendants and witnesses did not necessarily tell the truth. For all of these reasons, we shall never know for sure how Pere and Abadia came to be condemned to the stake.[1]

In spite of these challenges, the charges that Pere and the Navarros leveled against the Almulis and Jucef de Quatorze are worth pondering. Even if they were entirely false—which would require some other explanation for Abadia's burning and Pere's near death, and mean either that Pere and the Navarros jointly fabricated their denunciations in advance (an unlikely possibility given the great personal harm to Pere that the scheme would have entailed) or that Pere fabricated the denunciations on his own and the Navarros decided after the fact to play along—inevitably these charges bore some relation to lived experience. Indeed, as these accusations were meant to be believed, they are evidence at least of common perceptions. In light of these considerations, let us revisit Pere's and the Navarros' accounts of Pere's re-Judaization.

On either the night of Thursday, January 4, 1341 or the morning of Friday, January 5, some thirty-five kilometers from Calatayud in the village of La Almunia de Doña Godina, Jews allegedly surrounded Pere in the home of Janto and Jamila Almuli and sought to re-Judaize him. How Pere got to the Almulis' home is a matter of debate. According to Pere's first confession, Pere spent Thursday night with the Navarros, and he ran into Jamila Almuli the next morning as he was departing for Calatayud.[2] According to Pere's second confession and the testimonies of Salomon and Miriam Navarro, however, the Navarros escorted Pere to the Almulis' home on Thursday night. Indeed, according to Pere's second confession, upon learning over dinner, "amidst other discussions," that Pere had been baptized, Salomon sent Miriam to tell the Almulis that "Alatzar" had been baptized in Catalonia, and that he was now at their house. As soon as Janto heard this, he told Miriam to fetch Pere and Salomon.[3] This second version of the events suggests that there existed some prior understanding between the Navarros and the Almulis. The Navarros knew to inform the Almulis that an apostate was in town, and the Almulis had a plan for how to proceed.

"Welcome, Alatzar!" Janto cried, calling Pere by his Jewish name, when Pere and the Navarros entered the Almulis' kitchen, which Salomon Navarro later referred to as Janto's "secret palace," intimating both that Janto wielded power and also that his operations were clandestine. Surely, Jews routinely referred to apostates by the Jewish names by which they had always known them. Nevertheless, according to Miriam, Pere bristled at the implication that he was still a Jew. "My name is not Alatzar but Pere," he retorted. According to Pere's second confession, Pere went even further. "My name is not Alatzar," he replied, "my name is Pere, for I have been baptized, and I accepted the Catholic faith . . . and through it I believe I shall be saved."[4]

According to Pere's second confession, at this point in the meeting, Janto Almuli sent Salomon Navarro to fetch Jucef de Quatorze, and then, according to Miriam, Janto asked, "Alatzar, what did you do when you went to Catalonia?" "I settled down and stayed for some time, and I was baptized," Pere responded. Upon hearing this, Janto reacted with horror, and he and Jamila set about making Pere feel shame for having apostatized to Christianity and fear regarding the consequences. According to Pere's first confession, Janto cried, "You are a Christian? Wretched man! Why have you done this?" And according to Pere's second confession, Janto and Jamila went on to "accuse Pere of the most grave and intolerable errors he had committed by becoming a Christian, and they began to lead him, by means of persuasive words, to abandon the Christian law and renounce it as empty, false, and deceptive." According to Pere's first confession, Jamila "advised Pere to believe and agree to" her husband's words, and she repeated some of them "several times." Salomon claimed that Janto, Jamila, and the Almulis' daughter-in-law, Velida, all pressured Pere to renounce the Christian faith.[5]

"How greatly you have delayed us, you one-eyed [rascal]! We've been wait-ing for you forever," Jamila exclaimed when Jucef de Quatorze walked through the door, according to Pere's second confession. Jucef turned directly to Pere and, having been apprised of the situation on the way over by Salomon, he moaned, "Wretched man! How could you err so greatly as to renounce the law of Moses, the law of the one, true, and immortal God, and accept an empty, dead, and pernicious law, through which no one can be saved?"[6]

Then, according to Pere's second confession, Jucef de Quatorze set about mocking Christianity at length, focusing on Christian beliefs in the virginity of Mary and the divinity of Christ, by narrating the following version of a widespread Jewish satire of the Gospels known as the *Toledot Yeshu*:

On a great festivity of the Jews, Mary's husband, Joseph, left the house while it was still night to hear morning prayers at the Temple. He shut the door behind him and left the key in a hole next to the gate, leaving Mary indoors. As soon as Joseph was out of sight, a Jew who had been spying on him and had seen where he had put the key, snatched the key, entered the house, lay with Mary, and impregnated her with a son.

A few years later, when the boy was four or five, he was playing with other boys one day with a hoop before the doors of the Temple. At the entrance of the Temple there were two lions who were put there so that, if someone wanted to enter the Temple, they would be too afraid of the lions to read the name *Semhammeforas* [*Shem ha-meforash*], which is the name of God and is so powerful that the first to read it would perform great miracles. As the boys were playing, the hoop of Mary's son fell before the steps of the Temple, and when the boy went after his hoop, he raised his eyes and saw the aforementioned name of God, *Semhammeforas* [*Shem ha-meforash*], written on the lintel of the Temple in golden letters. He memorized the name and, with dust and spit, wrote it on his hand, lest he should forget it on account of fear of the lions. Afterward, he wrote the name on a thin piece of parchment, folded it, and sewed it under the skin of his right shin.

Thereafter, by the power of this name, the boy performed wonders and many miracles. For example, he rode on a ray of the sun and hung from it, he made live sparrows out of clay, and he cured all those who were sick. He grew up refined, clever, and pleasant, and by means of the miracles that he performed, he turned people's hearts to him and made himself adored as the son of God. In this way he deceived the world, until the doctors of the law and the high priests condemned him to death as a fraud.[7]

The Jews' position was clear. Christianity was a false and laughable creed. Pere had sinned grievously by embracing it and rejecting the one true faith. What is more, his soul was in jeopardy. The situation needed to be remedied. Pere had to return to Judaism.

Pere was beginning to tremble, Miriam Navarro later testified, when the Jews made a fearsome announcement. Pere would not be able simply to renounce Christianity and rejoin the Jewish community, as some repentant apostates are known to have done in the medieval Crown of Aragon. In fact, the Almulis and Jucef de Quatorze never mentioned the possibility that Pere might resume life as a Jew. Instead, Pere would have to die at the stake, "in the law in which he had been born," in order to save his soul. Seven years earlier, they added, they had convinced the apostate Abadia to follow this advice. Challenging Pere to emulate Abadia, they pointed out that Abadia had become a Jewish martyr and, as a result, his soul was "safe with God."[8]

The Jews gave Pere specific instructions for getting condemned to the stake. Pere was to go to the home of the *justicia* of Calatayud on the Callegia Nova, and he was to ask the *justicia* to have him burned for having committed "so great a crime" as to have "renounced the law of the one God, accepted the empty and dead law of the Christians, and been baptized."[9] The Jews also told Pere what to do if his galling demand did not have the desired effect. If the *justicia* were to tell Pere to go away, for example, Pere was to provoke him further by requesting that the fingers with which he had made the sign of the cross be amputated, the skin of his forehead that had come into contact with chrism be ripped off, and the skin of his knees on which he had knelt before the crucifix—"displaying honor for [the crucifix]"—be flayed.[10] In addition, Pere could threaten to have a notary document the *justicia*'s refusal to condemn a Christian apostate to death, putting the *justicia* in peril of censure. Or he could break into public blasphemy, declaring to the *justicia* "and those around him" that "the law of the Christians was empty and dead" and that "Christ, whom Christians worship, is not God, nor was he ever God, or else he would not have died; instead, he was an accursed bastard and the son of the greatest whore."[11] The Jews assured Pere that if he did these things, the *justicia* would have him executed without delay.

Here, the Jews stopped for breath, having laid out their entire plan. According to Pere's first confession, Pere "was silent, not knowing how to respond," and according to Salomon Navarro, Pere requested time to think. But the crackling kitchen fire—an ominous harbinger of Pere's impending fate—must have been audible for only a moment, for the Jews hastened to redouble their efforts. According to Miriam, Velida commanded Pere, "Do as you are told!" The Jews assured Pere that the "temporal punishment [of burning at the stake would] pass quickly," and they repeated that, by embracing death, Pere "would acquire eternal life and be a martyr before God."[12] According to Salomon Navarro, the Jews responded to Pere's hesitation by pressuring him "extremely strongly" to renounce the Christian faith. And, according to Pere's first confession, Janto resumed blaspheming against Christianity, repeating his slurs "three or four times," and then he began to repeat everything else that he had already said until finally he "turned Pere away to the Jewish superstition and to his advice." Thus, the Jews "Judaized" (*judayçaverunt*) Pere, and they "made him renounce the Catholic faith." To celebrate, Jamila gave everyone a cup (*cifum*), and they all drank wine.[13]

The charges that Pere and the Navarros leveled against the Almulis and Jucef de Quatorze signaled deep Jewish horror at apostasy to Christianity, illustrated by the Jews' condemnation of Pere's baptism and their insistence that Pere's soul was in danger. These charges also, however, suggested a certain ambivalence with regard to the treatment of apostates. The Jews did not want to readmit Pere into their earthly community, and they prescribed a terrible death as a "temporal punishment" for his sin. Yet they insisted that it was imperative that Pere renounce Christianity and die as a Jew, and they professed to want to help ensure his salvation. The impulse to reject was thus in tension with the desire to rehabilitate, and the perceived need for punishment with the possibility of expiation.

In the two chapters that follow, we shall examine these impressions in light of a range of contemporary sources, including royal and episcopal letters and rabbinic *responsa*. In exploring the causes, expressions, and consequences of a variety of medieval Jewish responses to apostasy, we shall focus first on Jewish repudiation of apostates and then on efforts to bring apostates back to Judaism. In so doing, we shall continue to consider the ways in which the experiences of Jewish apostates illumine the state of Jewish-Christian relations in the medieval Crown of Aragon prior to 1391, and we shall note additional continuities across medieval Western Europe.

Chapter 5

Apostasy as Scourge: Jews and the Repudiation of Apostates

> It is beyond our obligation to be kind [to an apostate]. He is not our brother, and we do not have mercy upon him—on the contrary, we cast [him] down [*moridin*].
> —Rabbi Solomon ben Avraham ibn Aderet (Rashba),
> c. 1233–1310[1]

In the eyes of medieval Jews, apostasy was a heinous sin. It involved the abandonment of a God, a people, and a promised destiny. Going over to Christianity, moreover, was uniquely egregious. Christianity was not merely, to quote Jucef de Quatorze, "empty, erroneous, and false," but, in some ways, it was antithetical to Judaism.[2] The doctrines of the Trinity, the Incarnation, and the Virgin Birth, for example, were viewed as flagrant breaches of Judaism's most sacred precepts, and medieval Jewish polemicists—including the philosopher and legal scholar Hasdai Crescas of Barcelona (c. 1340–1410/11)—thus railed against these dogmas at length.[3]

Furthermore, on account of the panoply of Christian devotional images that confronted Jews on a daily basis—on the exteriors of churches and other buildings and during processions, for example—Christianity seemed idolatrous, and, as such, a violation of the second commandment. In fact, no less a figure than Maimonides deemed Christianity a form of idolatry.[4] Likewise, Rashba and Ritva referred to apostasy to Christianity as apostasy to "idol worship" (*avodah zarah*).[5] Undoubtedly speaking for many of his co-religionists, a Jew is said to have declared during the Mallorca Disputation (1286): "I wonder at you Christians . . . [for you] fashion and adore idols and images that neither feel nor hear, and you [thereby] act against God!"[6] In his *Practica inquisitionis*, Bernard Gui explained, not implausibly, that when, in the Aleinu prayer, Jews daily asked God to "cause the idols to pass away from the earth," they referred to "the images that the Christians of the land adore[d] in honor of Christ."[7] The implications of the view that Christianity was idolatrous were particularly grave. According to the Babylonian Talmud, idolatry was one of three sins—together with murder and severe sexual misconduct, such as adultery or incest—so grievous that one was to embrace death rather than commit them.[8]

Jews considered apostasy to Christianity an outrage not only on account of the nature of Christian beliefs and practices, however, but also because of a long history of Christian abuse of Jews. As we have seen, even though Jews and Christians in the Crown of Aragon often interacted positively, Jews remained epic villains in the eyes of Christians, and relations between the groups were laced with animosity. Jews lived at the mercy of Christians, and Christians taunted and humiliated Jews, spread noxious rumors about them, stoned Jewish quarters during Holy Week, prosecuted Jews for crimes against Christians and the Christian faith, and sometimes even forcibly baptized Jews, heightening Jews' loathing of the sacrament of baptism. Going over to Christianity, then, could be tantamount to joining the ranks of a cruel oppressor.

Finally, as the history of tensions between Christians and Jews was predicated on a theological jostling for preeminence, apostasy to Christianity also involved capitulation to an age-old rival. Christians claimed that Christ fulfilled the promises of Jewish scriptures and that their faith had superseded Judaism, and they maintained also that they had replaced the Jews as God's "chosen people." For their part, Jews denied that Christ was the Messiah, and they kept faith in the election of Israel. Indeed, some Jews even envisioned an End of Days when Christians would convert to Judaism.[9]

As apostasy involved subscribing to beliefs and practices that violated Judaism, forsaking the Jewish people for its persecutors, and capitulating to Jews' theological adversaries, it amounted to the worst imaginable form of treason. As a result, over the course of the Middle Ages, Jews gave their lives—and the lives of their children—to avoid it and, instead, "sanctify the name of God" through martyrdom. This was the case most famously during the Rhineland massacres of the First Crusade.[10] In the midst of anti-Jewish riots in fourteenth-century France, Jewish women reportedly also hurled their children into fire and leaped in after them rather than apostatize to Christianity.[11] And, in Iberia, during the massacres of 1391, there were also Jews who chose martyrdom. Indeed, in the wake of this violence, Hasdai

Crescas wrote of his son, who died rather than convert: "I have offered him up as a burnt offering. I will vindicate the judgment [of heaven] and be comforted with the goodliness of his portion and the pleasantness of his fate."[12]

In the pages that follow, we shall examine how Jews in the medieval Crown of Aragon expressed their hostility toward apostates and delve deeper into the roots and consequences of this antagonism. I shall argue that, just as Christians shunned converts not merely because of ideas about the immutability of Jewishness—potent though these may have been—but also because of individual converts' problematic pasts, patent ulterior motives in seeking baptism, and objectionable behavior following baptism, so, too, Jews repudiated apostates not merely because of apostates' treachery—great though it was felt to be—but also because apostates terrorized Jewish communities and tore apart Jewish families. In other words, daily realities played a key role in shaping Christian and Jewish attitudes. To Jews, apostates represented imminent danger. The injuries they wrought were so severe that Shem Tov ibn Shaprut described these, in the preface to the *Even bohan*, as divine retribution for Jews' sins.[13]

Expressions of Repudiation

Abhorrence for the sin of apostasy to Christianity translated naturally into loathing for the sinner, and thus, many Jews repudiated apostates. Indeed, it was widely believed—in spite of influential Jewish legal rulings to the contrary—that apostates had ceased to be Jews.[14] Writing under Muslim rule in the twelfth century, Maimonides declared that "the apostate to idolatry [wa]s like a non-Jew in all respects," and, during the first half of the fourteenth century, the Iberian polemicist Isaac Polgar gave voice to this opinion, too, when he signed a letter to the apostate Alfonso of Valladolid thus: "All my days, and still with all my power and being, [I, Isaac, as opposed to you, apostate Alfonso, remain] a Jew."[15] The terminology used to designate apostates attests to this view, as well. The common Hebrew term for "apostate," *meshumad*, is from the root *shmad*, meaning annihilation and implying the obliteration of the apostate from the Jewish community.[16] According to Nahmanides, apostates were even worse than non-Jews. Cradle Christians merely followed "what [they had] heard all of [their] days." Apostates, by contrast, knowingly transgressed.[17]

Jews expressed their hostility toward apostates in numerous ways. Some of these were internal to the Jewish community. For example, it was customary for Jews to refrain from mentioning apostates' names in liturgical contexts. Thus, when, in synagogue in thirteenth-century Marseilles, the son of an apostate father was called to the *bimah*, this boy was referred to not as the son of his apostate father but as the son of his Jewish grandfather.[18] In addition, in the Crown of Aragon, as in northern European communities, when "one who separate[d] himself from the community" (*mi she-piresh mi-darkhei tsibur*) died, Jews were not to tear their clothes, arrange for a Levirate marriage, or eulogize him, as they would upon the death of a faithful Jew.[19] Moreover, Bernard Gui pointed out—as some medieval Hebrew texts indicate, as well—that Jews prayed for the destruction of apostates three times every day in the twelfth benediction of the Amidah, known as the Birkhat ha-minim. The version of the prayer that Gui recorded in his *Practica inquisitionis* reads as follows: "Let there be no hope for the lost, for converts to the faith of Christ, for all heretics and unbelievers, for informers and the double-tongued, for all such traitors. Let the moment come, let them in a moment be lost, let all enemies of thy people Israel be swiftly slain and the kingdom of iniquity be in an instant driven to madness, be smashed and broken, till it falls and more than falls swiftly, speedily, in our own day. Blessed art thou, God, who destroyeth enemies and casteth down the wicked."[20]

Other Jewish expressions of hatred for apostates were directed at apostates themselves. For example, Jews publicly jeered at apostates. In 1294, for instance, a Jew from Huesca named Avraham Abingavet reportedly spat at an apostate named Martí Pere and, in 1296, King Jaume agreed to protect three converts in Valencia against the "abusive words" of local Jews.[21] Along similar lines, Rashba told in a *responsum* of Jews who allegedly insulted an apostate by calling him a *meshumad*, which the apostate translated (when he denounced these Jews to Christians) as "renegade" or "heretic."[22] Jews also taunted apostate preachers. Thus, for example, in 1320, the Infant Alfons ordered his officials to protect Juan of Huesca from Jewish mockery lest, "on account of so much jeering," he and his fellow converts should change their minds about their conversions.[23] It is possible that reports overstated the degree to which Jews harassed Juan. The fact that Jews apparently did mock him, however, and that the Infant thought that Jewish scorn might discourage convert preachers, casts new light on the dynamics involved in convert preaching. Jewish apostates who became Christian preachers certainly tormented and endangered Jews. But perhaps they were vulnerable to their audiences, as well.[24]

Jews ridiculed Jewish apostates north and southwest of the Crown of Aragon, too, such that continuities in the experiences of Jewish apostates across

Western Europe pertained not only to apostates' behavior and Christian attitudes toward converts, but also to Jewish responses to apostasy. In neighboring Castile, for example, the *Siete partidas* forbade Jews from "dishonoring" apostates and lamented that "many men live[d] and die[d] in foreign beliefs who would love to be Christians, were it not for the . . . insults of word and deed that they s[aw] others who became Christian receive, calling them 'turncoats' and insulting them in many other bad ways."[25] About 1376 in Rheims, a Jew named David (whose parents and eleven siblings had left Catalonia to be baptized in France and had settled in Laon) confided in a visiting Iberian Jew that he, too, wanted to be baptized. The Iberian Jew attempted to dissuade David from being baptized, and he derisively called David's father "a false Christian." David was so angered by these words that he killed the Iberian Jew.[26]

In the Crown of Aragon, and in northern Europe, too, Jews often deprived apostates of their inheritances, in accordance with an established, although not unanimous, tradition that Rashba cited: "An apostate does not inherit from his Jewish father, for an apostate is separated from the holiness of Israel and from the holiness of his father."[27] In or before 1311, the family of a Jew from Zaragoza named Salomon disowned him when he was baptized.[28] In 1382, an apostate from Calatayud named Juan Martín de Malvenda accused his father of having squandered "out of hatred" the inheritance that Juan's late mother had left him. Also in the 1380s, an apostate from Zaragoza named Alienor de Palau, who had been baptized as a young girl, turned to King Pere III to demand her inheritance when her parents and siblings died.[29] In spite of royal decrees that converts should be allowed to retain their inheritances, Pere III sometimes sided with Jews against converts. In 1383, for instance, when the Jews of Calatayud petitioned him to revoke a promise that the Infant Joan had made to local converts, guaranteeing that their Jewish relatives would not be allowed to dispose of goods to which the converts might someday lay a claim, Pere III acquiesced, likely in exchange for a monetary inducement.[30]

On very rare occasions, Jews in the Crown of Aragon physically attacked apostates. During the first quarter of the fourteenth century, a Jew named Joan Ferrand, who previously had apostatized and then returned to Judaism, killed a recent apostate, and in 1363, the Jews of Puigcerdà were prosecuted for the murder of the apostate preacher Nicolau de Gràcia.[31] We do not know what motivated these murders. Yet here again, evidence from north and southwest of the Crown of Aragon suggests a pattern. In 1290, Jews in England murdered an apostate named William of Oxford, who was collecting taxes from Jews,[32] and the *Siete partidas* warned that Jews who could be shown to have murdered, or to have solicited the murder of, a prospective convert or a baptized Jew would burn at the stake.[33]

By shaming apostates, withholding their inheritances, and sometimes physically attacking them, Jews added to the general misery of many apostates. In the words of an apostate from late thirteenth-century Ferrara, on account of persecution by Jews, apostates "could not live without fear."[34]

Apostates and Communal Security

Hostile Jewish acts toward apostates were driven by anger not merely at apostates' decision to apostatize, with its implications of sin, betrayal, heresy, and treason, but also at the ways in which apostates afflicted Jews daily. Surely Jews perceived apostates as spiritually endangering their communities, through their example and especially through their sermons. Apostates also, however, threatened Jews' physical security. As we saw in Chapter 4, apostates extorted money from Jews, subjected them to humiliating harangues, and denounced them to Christian authorities, just like dreaded Jewish *malshinim*, or informers.[35] In 1327, in an effort to protect his community from such harm, the secretary of the *aljama* of Barcelona, Bonsenyor Gracià, paid King Alfons III to guarantee that a particular apostate, who had been excommunicated for physically attacking Bonsenyor, would not harm any Jews from his *aljama*.[36] Indicating that some Jews feared apostates' malicious denunciations in northern Europe, too, in 1383, Jews from the French dioceses and provinces of Sens, Rouen, Rheims, and Lyons petitioned Pope Clement VII to prohibit converts from accusing their former co-religionists of any crimes whatsoever.[37]

As inquisitors were known to construe any kind of encounter between an apostate and a Jew as "tasting of heresy," apostates endangered Jews also merely by interacting with them, even when apostates might have meant no harm. An episcopal missive from 1317 describes a Jewish woman's fear on account of her relationship with an apostate. Conort had followed her apostate husband, Pere d'Avinyó, to Tripoli, where he returned to Judaism. Then, however, Pere had died, and Conort "doubted that she should [return to Catalonia] because she had joined and remained with her husband after his holy baptism and [subsequent] apostasy [to Judaism]." Conort may have been concerned about having engaged in forbidden sexual relations with a baptized Christian, but she also seems to have worried that she would be suspected of having encouraged her husband to return to Judaism. Indeed, in a letter promising protection to Conort and her children, Bishop Ponç de Gualba of Barcelona specifically addressed this concern, explaining that he "deemed it entirely appropriate to guide and safeguard" Conort's family, since it did not seem that Conort or any of her sons or daughters "bore guilt in the aforesaid matters."[38]

Some Jews in the Crown of Aragon were so concerned that they might be accused of conspiring with repentant apostates that they denounced apostates—and suspected apostates—to Christian authorities. In Vilafranca del Penedès in 1325, a boy (*puer*) who claimed to be a Jew from Chartres named Aquinet, and who was not wearing the circular red—or half red and half yellow—cloth badge required of local Jews, entered a synagogue one day. Suspecting that he might be an apostate, the secretaries of the *aljama* denounced Aquinet to the bailiff, Ferrer Oller. The bailiff held the boy for three days and "asked him whether he was a Christian or a Jew and whether he was baptized." When Aquinet responded that he was a Jew and that he had never been baptized, however, and "it was found that he had been circumcised," the bailiff released him, upon the advice of the jurist Guillem Luppeti.[39] During the 1370s, in the diocese of Girona, a Jew by the name of en Saltel denounced to the local inquisition three repentant apostates who had been baptized *in Provincia* and were now "living as Jews" in Catalonia.[40]

In 1335, members of the Jewish *aljama* of Vilafranca del Penedès again appealed to Christian authorities when they feared that an apostate might bring the wrath of the inquisition upon them. An eighteen-year-old apostate named Bertran, who claimed to have a preaching license, had assembled Jews in the church of the Friars Minor and unexpectedly launched into an incendiary rant against Christianity. The Jewish audience was so afraid that it would be accused of collaborating with Bertran that the leaders of the *aljama* asked the secretaries of the Jewish *aljama* of Barcelona to report Bertran to the bishop of Barcelona for uttering words that were "infamous and false and derogatory to the Catholic faith." The bishop informed the vicar general of the bailiff of Vilafranca del Penedès, Guillem de Torrelles, that he was writing to the deacon of Vilafranca del Penedès to have Bertran arrested, and he requested that Guillem aid him in determining how Bertran "felt in the faith."[41]

Apostates and Family Life

In addition to endangering Jewish communities, apostates wreaked havoc in the private sphere. Apostasy often destroyed marriages, for example. Some time before 1343, for instance, a Jew named David de Ripoll chose to be baptized, taking the name Jaume Pallars. His wife, Tolrana, whom he had married in 1337, refused to apostatize. Jaume claimed that he tried to bring Tolrana with him into the Christian faith, but Tolrana ignored his pleas, "stubbornly wishing to stay and remain in Jewish blindness." Tolrana was lucky in that Jaume gave her a *get*, or bill of divorce. Thus, in a notarized document from November 7, 1343, Tolrana acknowledged that "Jaume Pallars, formerly a Jew, but now a neophyte," had completed part of the divorce process, paying the fifty-five hundred Barcelona sous specified in the "marriage contract . . . written with Hebrew letters, which among Jews is commonly called a *ketubah*." Two days later Jaume agreed, "in accordance with Jewish custom," to give Tolrana or her representative "the bill of repudiation that in Hebrew and among Jews is commonly called a *get*." In closing, Jaume referred to Tolrana as "the Jewess who was formerly my wife" and promised that he had not done, nor would he do, anything to hinder the concession of the *get*.[42]

The promise not to hinder the concession of Tolrana's *get* may have been formulaic. However, it may nevertheless attest to widespread concern about apostate husbands whom Jewish communal pressures could no longer affect. Even though Rashba advised the Jewish wives of apostates to run away from their husbands "as one runs away from a snake," these women still were considered legally married.[43] As a result, women whose husbands left without giving them a *get* became *agunot*, "chained ones," who could not remarry.[44] Conort's apostate husband, Pere d'Avinyó, may have failed to give Conort a *get*. In a letter that Conort sent to Bishop Ponç de Gualba about 1317, she explained that she had felt "rudely abandoned" by her husband following his conversion to Christianity.[45]

Apostasy sometimes deprived children of a parent. For instance, Pablo Christiani brought his children into the Catholic faith with him, leaving his wife bereft. Years later, a former acquaintance reminded him, in a letter ostensibly meant to dissuade him from continuing to harm Jews, how greatly Pablo's wife had suffered from the loss of her children. The author of the letter berated Pablo as follows: "You have not had mercy on your wife, your faultless pigeon [allusion to Song of Songs 5:2]. While she still nested on her chicks, you took her children [from] under her wings and removed them from their tradition. You shaved them, and you changed their garments. All of this [your wife's] eyes saw and her ears heard. Woe to her eyes that saw this! Woe to her ears that heard this! . . . Who shall console [her]?"[46]

Similar episodes occurred outside the Crown of Aragon. In 1229, Pope

Gregory IX ruled, in a letter to the bishop of Strasbourg, in favor of an apostate who demanded custody of his four-year-old son. Gregory explained that, since the boy was over the age of three, it would be "to the greatest advantage of the Christian faith" to grant custody to his father. The pope indicated that it was more important that the boy be reared among Christians than cared for by his mother, who "might easily mislead him into the error of infidelity." Gregory's verdict was incorporated into canon law.[47]

Some Jews went to great lengths to spare mothers such agony. In or before 1341, for example, the son-in-law of a Jew named David de Ripoll (David may have been the father of Tolrana's husband, who was also named David de Ripoll) was baptized in Barcelona, and he brought his two daughters, who were "between the ages of three and nine," to live with him. Fearing that he might lose his daughter and granddaughters in addition to his son-in-law, David took all three away "to other parts." When David's apostate son-in-law discovered the disappearance of his daughters, he requested that the bishop of Barcelona, Ferrer d'Abella, and the inquisitor fra Bernat de Puigcercós return them to him. The bishop agreed that this would be the proper thing to do "in accordance with canonical sanctions," and he ordered the arrest of David, his daughter, and his granddaughters. The bishop further decreed that David's possessions were to be confiscated until he should appear before the bishop and make satisfaction for his deeds in accordance with canon law. In the meantime, no one was to pay debts they owed to David or return anything they had borrowed from him. We do not know whether the fugitives were apprehended.[48]

In a similar case, in 1309 in Morvedre, an apostate named Francesc de Vilario reported that his Jewish brother-in-law, Jacob Aldoctori, was preventing his children, Astruc and Stella, from being baptized, even though the children wanted to convert. Jacob may have been acting on behalf of his sister, the children's Jewish mother. King Jaume II ruled that the local *justicia* should determine whether the children truly desired baptism. If they did not, they were to be allowed to remain Jews.[49]

Unlike Pablo Christiani, the son-in-law of David de Ripoll, and Francesc de Vilario, other apostate fathers left their children to be raised by their Jewish mothers. The recorded text of the Mallorca Disputation (1286) suggests that this happened frequently, as it portrays the Christian Genoese merchant Inghetto Contardo as having told a Jew whom he was trying to convert that he understood that love for his children held him back from accepting baptism.[50] Several examples confirm Inghetto's concern. When an apostate who took the name Pere de la Mercè was baptized some time in or prior to 1339, for example, he left his wife and children behind. Similarly, the apostate father of the boy who was called to the *bimah* in thirteenth-century Marseilles, mentioned above, clearly left his son in the Jewish community. Another abandoned son of an apostate appeared in court in Avignon in 1365 with his Jewish grandmother.[51]

In northern France in the 1390s, an act of apostasy deprived four children of both of their parents. In this case, the provost of Paris ordered the seizure of the four children of a Jewish woman named Lionne de Cremi and an apostate named Denis Machaut, who was accused of relapsing into Judaism. Lionne appealed the decree, but her plea was rejected. By August 1394, the three older children—ages eleven, nine, and five—were being held at the prison of the Châtelet, and the one-year-old baby was being cared for by a Christian nurse.[52]

The ways in which apostates shattered peace at home—by abandoning spouses, relegating wives to the status of *agunah*, and separating children from parents—can only have strengthened Jewish convictions about apostates' wickedness. Indeed, together with the ways in which apostates endangered entire communities, these offenses may have loomed particularly large in the minds of the Jews who—in northern Europe and Christian Spain—jeered at apostates, withheld their inheritances, and, on rare occasions, attacked them physically. Apostates were not only heretics, rejecters of Jewish tradition, and traitors to the Jewish people, but they were also informers, attractors of inquisitorial suspicion, and unscrupulous spouses and parents.

Murder in Calatayud?

The intensity of medieval Jewish antagonism toward apostates raises new questions about Pere's case. If the Almulis, Jucef de Quatorze, or any of the other Jews accused of involvement in the alleged re-Judaizations of Pere and Abadia were more or less guilty as charged, might they have acted as they did in order to punish apostates? And if Pere fabricated his accusations against the Almulis and Jucef de Quatorze, did he conceive of the conspiracy as having a punitive dimension?

Several assertions that were made during the course of the trials of the Almulis and Jucef de Quatorze support these possibilities. For instance, fra Bernat de Puigcercós asked Jucef de Quatorze whether it was true that Abadia had acknowledged that he "deserved" to burn at the stake "because he had taken on the Christian law."⁵³ This question shows that fra Bernat, for one, believed that Abadia had viewed his burning as a form of punishment. It suggests also that someone—presumably either Pere or Salomon or Miriam Navarro—had told fra Bernat that Abadia had said this, such that this person, too, might have believed that the case involved an effort to chasten apostates. In addition, it is noteworthy that, according to Miriam Navarro, the Almulis and Jucef de Quatorze assured Pere on the night of January 4, 1341 that the "temporal *penalty* [*pena*] [of burning at the stake] would pass quickly" (emphasis mine).⁵⁴

A desire to make apostates suffer and die for their sins, however, fails fully to account for the Jews' alleged actions in Pere's case. Indeed, if the Jews' goal had been mere punishment, surely they would have devised a safer course of action, one that did not require the participation of Christian authorities and unfold before a Christian audience. Whether in actuality or merely in Pere's mind, then, something more was afoot.

Chapter 6

Recruiting Repentance: The Re-Judaization of Apostates

And this is a great *mitzvah*: to save a Jewish soul from the
desecration of idol worship and bring it back in repentance.
—Rabbi Yom Tov ben Avraham Ishbili (Ritva), 1250–1330[1]

In spite of the intensity with which many Jews repudiated apostates, relations
between Jews and apostates in the Crown of Aragon were not uniformly antagonistic. Some Jews continued to interact productively with apostates, for
example, by lending them money at interest. On the basis of Deuteronomy
23:21, taking interest was forbidden between Jews. To the extent that apostates no longer were considered full-fledged Jews, however, Jews could lend to
them. Thus, in late thirteenth-century Mallorca, Jews lent money at interest to
an apostate named Guillem Godor, and, in fourteenth-century Vic, Jews lent
money at interest to an apostate named Mateo de Camprodon.[2]

If some Jews had commercial interactions with apostates, others under-
took the dangerous work of helping apostates return to Judaism. They did so
at enormous risk to themselves and their communities and in the face of internal Jewish opposition. Nevertheless, these Jews achieved some success. During
the first quarter of the fourteenth century, for example, Jews in Catalonia referred to the repentant apostate Joan Ferrand as a *baal teshuvah*—a "repentant
one" or "returnee"—a title that suggests that the Jewish community had reac-
cepted this individual.[3] Inquisitors' fears about Jews re-Judaizing apostates,
then, although perhaps exaggerated, were not unfounded.

In this chapter, as we delve into the ambivalence and complexity of medieval Jewish attitudes toward apostates, we shall first examine the identities and motivations of the Jews who assisted repentant apostates and then focus on the ways in which re-Judaization efforts reflected Jewish attitudes toward Christianity. As we saw in Chapter 5, Jewish repudiation of apostates in part reflected Jewish disdain for Christianity and resentment of Christian abuses of Jews. Attempts to bring apostates back to Judaism were part of this same constellation of medieval Jewish expressions of scorn and anger.[4] In fact, turning a straying Jew away from Christianity and back toward Judaism proclaimed in a particularly bold way that Judaism was the true and superior religion.

The Re-Judaizers

In his *Practica inquisitionis*, Bernard Gui informed inquisitors that the Jews who reached out to apostates were often "those connected [to apostates] by blood or marriage."[5] In fact, in medieval Western Europe, apostates' relatives frequently were accused of bringing apostates back to Judaism. In late thirteenth-century Manosque, for example, Avraham de Grassa and his wife, Rosa, were charged with bringing Rosa's daughter, Agnes (formerly Belia), who had lived *in ordine beguinarum* in Lausanne for more than five years, back to Judaism. Similarly, in 1311, seven relatives, including the brother, Cecri, of an apostate from Zaragoza named Salomon Abenbeli were accused of making Salomon "renounce his baptism." A register kept by the vicar general of the inquisitor general of the Crown toward the end of the fourteenth century notes that a Jew named Aaron was accused of helping his baptized relative, Jucef Mosse, "live as a Jew" in Besalú.[6] In addition, as we have seen, there existed close connections between Pere and the Jews who may have been involved in his re-Judaization. Pere may have been related to Mosse Camariel. Pere's father was an old friend of the Navarros, and Pere had known the Almulis for years.[7] Similar examples emerge from northern Europe. In France in 1307, for example, an apostate named Prote told inquisitors that his brother had convinced him to return to Judaism. Later, perhaps to undo the harm he had caused his brother, Prote changed his story, explaining that he had implicated his brother only because the latter owed him money.[8] It would have made sense for apostates' close associates and relatives to have been involved in efforts to re-Judaize their estranged friends and kin. Presumably, these individuals feared for apostates' welfare. Perhaps they even hoped to lessen the disgrace that they personally might have incurred on account of the apostasy of their relations.[9]

Personal ties were not the only driving force behind Jewish efforts to re-Judaize apostates. A sense of religious duty appears to have been an important motivating factor, as well. Indeed, the Jews involved in efforts to rehabilitate apostates must have drawn inspiration from Rashi, who famously applied the talmudic dictum, "even though he sinned, he remains a Jew" to apostates.[10] The view that apostates were still legally Jews (and thus, for example, their Jewish wives required a *get* to remarry) stood in tension with the popular perception that apostates had excluded themselves from the Jewish fold (and thus, for example, Jews were permitted to lend to them at interest).[11] Yet, medieval rabbinic authorities widely accepted Rashi's position, if to varying degrees, and Jewish scholars in Barcelona were no exception.[12] In the beginning of the fourteenth century, for instance, Rashba cited the *Yoreh deah* section of the *Arbaah turim* (*The Four Rows*) of Rabbi Jacob ben Asher (who was born in Cologne c. 1269 and died in Toledo c. 1343) to the effect that "a Jew who became an apostate because of fear" (*she-nishtamed mahmat yirah*) was still a Jew.[13]

The view that apostates were obligated to return to Judaism went hand in hand with the view that it was Jews' pious duty to facilitate apostates' repentance. Indeed, unless repentant apostates moved to a new location and attempted to return to Judaism incognito, as some did, apostates could not hope to return to Judaism without Jewish support.[14] As the re-Judaization of apostates had important spiritual implications as well as potentially grave repercussions for communal security, the responsibility for helping apostates formally return to Judaism appears to have fallen on the shoulders of communal leaders, of the kind who were singled out in Pere's case. Janto Almuli, whom Pere initially described as the leader of his re-Judaization and who allegedly was involved in bringing Abadia back to Judaism, as well, was a prominent member of his community. King Jaume II considered him so valuable that in 1323 he reduced his taxes. Janto's son, Jucef Almuli, worked for King Pere III.[15] Jucef de Quatorze, whom Pere described in his second confession as having directed his re-Judaization and who allegedly was involved also in the circumcision of a Christian boy in 1326 and in Abadia's return to Judaism, was the son of Sanson de Quatorze, an *adelantado*, or executive officer, of the Jewish *aljama* of Calatayud, who was appointed to the important post of tax collector in 1286. In addition, in 1327, Jucef de Quatorze was chosen to represent the Jewish *aljama* of Calatayud before King Jaume II.[16] Rabbi Salomon Amnalguer, whom Janto denounced as the ringleader in Abadia's re-Judaization, whom Pere also listed as present at Abadia's re-Judaization, and whom Jucef de Quatorze listed as present at the circumcision of 1326, was a scribe and tax collector. Aaron and Mosse Abenafia, two ancestors of Aaron Abenafia (who was present at Abadia's re-Judaization according to Pere, Salomon Navarro, and Jucef de Quatorze, and who allegedly was present also at the circumcision of 1326), were trusted royal functionaries whom King Pere II sent on a mission to Valencia in 1284.[17] Isaach Avenlaut, who was allegedly present at the circumcision of 1326, was considered a valuable source of income by the Infanta María.[18] An ancestor of Jafuda del Calvo, whom Jucef de Quatorze claimed was present at Abadia's re-Judaization, served as an *adelantado* of Calatayud and was appointed tax collector in 1286.[19]

Elsewhere in medieval Western Europe, Jewish communal leaders also appear to have been associated with re-Judaization of apostates. In the thirteenth-century Rhineland, for instance, the *Sefer hasidim* (*Book of the Pious*) described an apostate who made it known to "the important people . . . and the sages in the town" that he wanted to return to Judaism. In thirteenth-century Apulia, the Dominican friar Bartolomeo de Aquila fined a Jewish notable from Naples for causing a convert to return to Judaism. During the first quarter of the fourteenth century, Bernard Gui noted in his *Practica inquisitionis* that when Christians were made Jewish, they were required to carry a certificate with the names of all of the rabbis (*magistrorum*) who had facilitated the process. In northern France in 1395, the Jews who allegedly persuaded Denis Machaut to return to Judaism included the prominent talmudic scholar Rabbi Yohanan de Trêves of Paris. Beyond our period, in 1465, in Huesca, local leaders, including Rabbi Isaach Bivach, Master Isaach Arrondi, Rabbi Avraham Almosino, and Rabbi Isaach Cocumbriel, reportedly were involved in the circumcision of a Castilian apostate to Judaism named Juan de Ciudad.[20]

Divergent Jewish attitudes regarding the treatment of apostates may have contributed to the fractious internal dynamics of Jewish communities in and around the medieval Crown of Aragon, which were characterized by deep tensions between rich and poor. Jews of humble means had particular reason to dread inquisitorial investigations that could result from re-Judaization efforts. Indeed, even though, as we saw in Chapter 2, poor Jews, like the Navarros, sometimes extricated themselves from inquisitorial proceedings, the poor suffered disproportionately when inquisitors imposed communal penalties, confiscating property and levying fines. They easily could lose the little they owned. It was easier for the rich, who had reserves of capital, to bear inquisi-

torial confiscations and fines. The participation of some of the more powerful members of society in re-Judaization efforts thus may have constituted
an additional grievance of the poor. Indeed, these observations may help us
understand why, according to Avraham de Grassa of Manosque, "some Jewish paupers" once denounced him to inquisitors on the grounds that he had
sheltered "many baptized apostates" who subsequently returned to Judaism.[21]

Deprecating Christianity

The descriptions of the re-Judaizations of Pere and Abadia that are preserved
in the records of the trials of the Almulis and Jucef de Quatorze provide a rich
account of some of the rhetorical tools that Jews used to persuade apostates
to return to Judaism. In particular, they convincingly show how, in recruiting
apostate repentance, Jews drew upon a variety of expressions of Jewish hostility toward Christianity. Most striking, perhaps, was the pièce de résistance of
the evening of Thursday, January 4, 1341, namely, Jucef de Quatorze's narration
of the anti-Christian satire, the *Toledot Yeshu*. Portraying Mary as an adulteress
and Christ as an illegitimate child who stole the *Shem ha-meforash*—the ineffable name of God—from the Temple and tricked the world into worshipping
him, this narrative lambasted Christianity.

Whether or not Jucef de Quatorze actually recounted the *Toledot Yeshu*
before Pere in January 1341, it is clear that the tale did circulate among Jucef's
Jewish contemporaries. The *Even bohan* of Shem Tov ibn Shaprut echoed elements of the *Toledot Yeshu*, and the shorter *Keshet u-magen* (*Bow and Shield*)
that Shimon ben Tzemah Duran of Mallorca composed in 1423 contained a
description of Mary's adultery.[22] In the thirteenth century, the Catalan Dominican polemicist Ramon Martí included a Latin translation of a version of
the *Toledot Yeshu* in his compendium of anti-Jewish and anti-Muslim polemic,
the *Pugio fidei*, and, toward the end of the fourteenth century, the Catalan
Franciscan writer Francesc Eiximenis, who was familiar with the *Pugio fidei*,
strongly condemned the *Toledot Yeshu* in his *Vita Christi*, which circulated
widely among the Christian laity. As we mentioned in the Introduction, it has
even been suggested that Eiximenis composed the *Vita Christi* specifically in
order to combat the claims of the *Toledot Yeshu*.[23]

Pere's depiction of the intimate context in which Jucef de Quatorze allegedly gave voice to the *Toledot Yeshu*—at night, in the kitchen, by the fire,
among friends and family—suggests that the narrative typically may have

been recounted in the privacy of Jewish homes. Indeed, an inquisitorial dossier from the second half of the fifteenth century similarly portrays the *Toledot Yeshu* as the stuff of fireside lore. One century after Pere's case, in a neighboring Aragonese village, a Jewish convert to Christianity named Salvadora Salvat allegedly sat by the fire and told her children that "while Joseph was out of the house, an iron-monger entered, and lay with Mary, and that's where Jesus came from." Moreover, Salvadora explained that she had heard this story from her father, and she believed it.[24] Presumably, just as Salvadora claimed, the narrative was passed orally among Jews, from generation to generation. As an internal form of anti-Christian polemic, it granted Jews a sense of moral and intellectual superiority to Christians, buttressing them psychologically against the allures of Christian culture and arming them against the claims of Christian preachers.

Sources beyond the records of the trials of the Almulis and Jucef de Quatorze also suggest, however, that, in addition to serving as a form of internal Jewish anti-Christian polemic, the *Toledot Yeshu* was used in re-Judaization efforts. First, in his *Vita Christi*, Francesc Eiximenis remarked: "I have heard that this book of the devil is [found] in the large *aljamas* of Spain and that it is read there among [Jews] in order to bring back [to Judaism] those [Jews] who dare to make themselves Christians."[25] Eiximenis may have been familiar with Pere's case. If so, then his comment may indicate that Pere's story was widely disseminated and created a general sense that Jews employed the *Toledot Yeshu* in re-Judaization efforts. If Eiximenis heard about the practice elsewhere, however, then there must have existed additional allegations that Jews used the *Toledot Yeshu* to bring apostates back to Judaism. Second, the confession of a Jewish convert named Francesco Colonna, who was tried by the Venetian Inquisition in 1553, suggests that the Jewish practice of using the *Toledot Yeshu* in re-Judaization efforts actually may have been widespread. According to Francesco, Jews sought to make him renounce Christianity by saying "many horrible things against Christ and the Virgin Mary," including "that [Christ] was a bastard and a fraud, that he had entered the Holy of Holies and taken the name of God and sewn it in his side, and that it was on account of this that he performed miracles."[26]

We can observe with confidence, in any case, that the *Toledot Yeshu* could be a powerful tool in an enterprise whose aim was to convince apostates to abandon Christianity. Since Jews commonly were raised on the *Toledot Yeshu*, the narrative might have reminded apostates of the rejection of Christian principles as it had figured in their earliest memories, triggering nostalgia and guilt. More importantly, the *Toledot Yeshu* would have embarrassed apostates by mocking the Christian tenets to which they had subscribed.

In light of these observations, it is remarkable that the version of the *Toledot Yeshu* that Jucef de Quatorze reportedly recounted actually was relatively gentle. Indeed, although the narrative plainly stated that Christianity was based on deception, it depicted the Christian faith as more pathetic than evil. Unlike some later attestations of the *Toledot Yeshu*, it did not describe Mary as menstruating (and therefore ritually impure) at the time of Jesus' conception; it portrayed Jesus' discovery of the ineffable name of God as accidental; and it noted that Jesus "grew up refined, clever, and pleasant."[27] Moreover, this version of the *Toledot Yeshu*, unlike others, barely referred to Jesus' trial and death. It seems, then, that Jews may have tailored the *Toledot Yeshu* to suit particular occasions. When confronting vacillating apostates, they may have deemed it wise to focus on undermining central Christian claims, rather than to cast aspersions on Jesus and Mary at length and dwell on historical details. The goal, after all, was to cajole apostates into coming home.

In addition, the mildness of the version of the *Toledot Yeshu* that Pere put in the mouth of Jucef de Quatorze suggests that Pere did not fabricate his testimony in order to destroy the Almulis and Jucef de Quatorze. If this had been Pere's aim, Pere likely would have given a far more vitriolic rendition of the tale. This observation, in turn, strengthens the likelihood that the *Toledot Yeshu* actually was recounted, as recorded, in an effort to re-Judaize Pere.

Pere alone mentioned the *Toledot Yeshu* before the tribunals of either fra Sancho de Torralba or fra Bernat de Puigcercós, but other defendants and witnesses intentionally may have omitted reference to the tale in the hope of escaping any association with this blasphemy of blasphemies. Jamila Almuli said that she did not know which "other words" were spoken on the night of January 4, 1341, as she had been coming and going from the room. Janto maintained that, because he had been very sick, he could not remember whether Pere had been instructed to tell the *justicia* of Calatayud that "Christ whom Christians worship is not God, nor was he [ever] God or else he would not have died; instead, he was an accursed bastard and the son of the greatest whore." Janto added that he did not remember which "words" Jucef de Quatorze had said to Pere.[28]

In the process of seeking to convince Pere and Abadia to return to Judaism, Jews allegedly drew upon another form of Jewish anti-Christian polemic, in addition to the *Toledot Yeshu*. They are said to have insisted that the law of Moses alone granted salvation, whereas Christianity "grant[ed] not life but

eternal death to those who kep[t] it, such that all those who live[d] in it [we]
re damned and lost."[29] The view that Christianity was unable to save souls
was not uncommon among medieval Jews.[30] Indeed, Bernard Gui noted in
his *Practica inquisitionis* that, in the Aleinu prayer, Jews praised God for not
making them like "the nations of the world," who worshipped "vanity and
emptiness and pray[ed] to a god *who c[ould] not save*" (emphasis mine).[31]
Recited three times daily, surely these words became deeply engrained. In
twelfth-century Barcelona, Rabbi Avraham bar Hiyya warned in his *Higayon
ha-nefesh ha-atsuvah* (*The Meditation of the Sad Soul*) that only Jews and "those
who believe[d] in Torah [and took] shelter beneath the wings of the *Shekhinah*"—that is, converts to Judaism—would be spared destruction at the End
of Days.[32]

Sources that preserve the views of fourteenth-century Jews—albeit
through a Christian filter—also document the belief that the law of Moses was
uniquely salvific. In 1314, for example, the tribunal of Bernard Gui recorded
that an apostate named Joan of Bretz had returned to Judaism "believing that
he would be able to be saved in the faith and life and ritual and observance
of the Jews." In 1320, the apostate Joan (formerly Baruch) told the tribunal of
Jacques Fournier at Pamiers that he believed that he could be saved only "in
Judaism." In fact, Joan added that, for this reason, it was better to kill oneself
than to convert to Christianity when one knew that it would be impossible
to return to Judaism.[33] By the fifteenth century, the idea that one could be
saved only through the law of Moses would become a cardinal tenet of crypto-
Jewish belief. Thus, in 1464, to cite one example of many, a convert named
Juan de Madrid cried: "I declare that the law of Moses is best, and that by it
[alone] men can be saved!"[34]

In convincing apostates to return to Judaism, Jews would have been likely
to stress that salvation was possible only through the law of Moses because
Christians had long warned Jews of precisely the opposite, namely, that there
was no salvation outside the church (*extra ecclesiam nullus salvus*). Indeed,
in his final sentence for the Almulis and Jucef de Quatorze, fra Bernat de
Puigcercós declared that Jews lived "a wicked life of damnation."[35] During
the Mallorca Disputation, Inghetto Contardo allegedly urged a Jew: "Do not
delay accepting baptism for . . . your soul shall be saved!" And, according to
Pere's second confession, on the evening of January 4, 1341, Pere proclaimed: "I
accepted the Catholic faith . . . and through it I believe I shall be saved."[36] By
insisting that salvation was possible only through Judaism, then, Jews deliber-

ately made use of concepts that Judaism shared with Christianity in order to counter the claim that salvation was possible only through Christ.

Purifying Returnees

The explicitly anti-Christian nature of re-Judaization efforts is observed in a broader range of sources when one turns from the techniques that Jews used to convince apostates to abandon Christianity and return to Judaism to the methods that Jews adopted to effect the readmission of repentant apostates into the Jewish community.

A range of opinions existed regarding appropriate re-Judaization proce- dure. In twelfth-century Ashkenaz, Rabbi Elazar ben Yehudah of Worms rec- ommended that repentant apostates wear hair shirts, engage in mourning and suffering, wash only minimally, refrain from meat and wine, avoid celebrations, and accept insults.[37] At the turn of the fourteenth century in Barcelona, Rashba and Ritva likewise demanded that returning apostates perform public penance. Thus, for example, Rashba wrote that an apostate who wished to return to Judaism deserved lashes for his transgressions and should undergo public ad- monition, and Ritva noted that an apostate had to accept rabbinic discipline before a court. Rashba explained that public repentance served to reinstate the trust that had been broken when the repentant apostate was baptized.[38]

Acts of public penance demonstrated the contrition of repentant apos- tates, but many Jews felt that they did not adequately address Jewish concerns about the specific consequences of apostasy to Christianity. As a result, in both northern Europe and Spain, there developed a popular rite for rehabilitating apostates that centered on ritual immersion.[39] Six descriptions of this rite of re-Judaization survive from, or refer to, the environs of the medieval Crown of Aragon.[40] The most detailed of these texts appears in the *Practica inquisitionis* of Bernard Gui and was repeated in the *Directorium inquisitorum* of Nicolau Eimeric. It reads as follows:

> He who is to be re-Judaized is summoned and asked by one of the Jews
> present whether he wishes to submit to what is called *tymla* [*tevilah*]
> in Hebrew, which in Latin means whether he wishes to take a bath or
> washing in running water, in order to become a Jew. He replies that he
> does. Then, the Jew who presided says to him in Hebrew *baaltussuna*

[*baal teshuvah*], which means in Latin, "you are reverting from the
state of sin." After this, he is stripped of his garments and is sometimes
bathed in warm water. The Jews then rub him energetically with sand
over his entire body, but especially on his forehead, chest, and arms,
that is, on the places which, during baptism, received the holy chrism.
Then, they cut the nails of his hands and feet until they bleed. They
shave his head, and afterward put him in the waters of a flowing stream,
and plunge his head in the water three times. After this immersion they
recite the following prayer: "Blessed be God, the Lord eternal, who has
commanded us to sanctify ourselves in this water or bath which is called
tymla [*tevilah*] in Hebrew." This done, he emerges from the water, dons
a new shirt and breeches, and all the attending Jews kiss him and give
him a name, which is usually the name he had before baptism. He who
is thus re-Judaized is required to confess his belief in the law of Moses,
to promise to keep and observe it, and to live henceforth according
to it. Similarly, [he is to promise] that he renounces baptism and the
Christian faith, and that henceforth he will neither keep nor serve it,
and he promises to observe the law, and he repudiates baptism and the
Christian faith. Afterward, they give him a certificate or testimonial
letter to all other Jews so that they may receive him, trust him, and assist
him. From then on, he lives and acts as a Jew and attends the school, or
synagogue, of the Jews.[41]

This rite of re-Judaization may have functioned, in part, as a ceremony
of conversion back to Judaism. Thus, it may have aimed to satisfy Jews who
believed that apostates had ceased to be Jews. Indeed, like proselytes—and
unlike Jews who immersed only for the purpose of ritual purification—the repentant apostates described by Bernard Gui recited the requisite blessing after
immersing, and not before. At least one medieval Jewish scholar acknowledged the association between this rite of re-Judaization and the ritual for receiving proselytes. The thirteenth-century German rabbinic authority, Rabbi
Eliezer ben Yoel ha-Levi ("Rabiah"), wrote that the repentant apostate needed
to shave and immerse, just like a convert (*ka-ger*).[42]

This rite of re-Judaization was understood also as cleansing apostates,
and thus it strove to appease Jews who believed that apostates had been contaminated by baptism and life among Christians. Twelfth-century Ashkenazi
texts referred to baptism as pollution (*tinuf*) or defilement (*shemets*),[43] and, in
1320, the convert Joan (formerly Baruch) told the tribunal of Jacques Fournier

that, during the rite of re-Judaization, the entire body of the apostate was washed in running water, the nails of the hands and feet were cut, and the head was shaved because "[Jews] believe[d] that baptism pollute[d] those who receive[d] it."[44] In addition, apostates' participation in activities forbidden by Jewish law may have contributed to the sense that apostates had had been contaminated. In early thirteenth-century Germany, Rabbi Simhah of Speyer cited the case of a Jewish woman captive who was required to immerse after she was released, in order to purify her from, among other things, the sin of eating non-kosher food. Thirteenth-century Ashkenazi rabbis repeatedly described ritual immersion as a means of removing the general contamination (zuhamah) of Christianity.[45]

According to the version of the rite of re-Judaization recorded by Bernard Gui and Nicolau Eimeric, the purification of repentant apostates was to be effected not only by means of immersion, but also by shaving hair, paring nails, and rubbing sand on parts of the body that had come into contact with baptismal chrism. Shaving hair and paring nails removed possible obstructions to the penetration of water and were customary practices in conjunction with ritual immersion. The rubbing of sand, however, was novel in the context of ritual immersion. Other medieval references to the practice of symbolically removing chrism suggest that the ritual had penitential significance. Medieval Christians engaged in the symbolic removal of chrism when they wished to undo some form of consecration. Thus, in 1398 in Paris, the fingers of two condemned monks were scrubbed to remove the chrism used at their ordinations, and these individuals were declared to have lost all ecclesiastical authority.[46]

The records of the trials of Janto and Jamila Almuli and Jucef de Quatorze describe the symbolic removal of chrism as part of an elaborate ritual that involved punishing the body parts that had participated in several Christian practices. Pere and the Navarros claimed that the Almulis and Jucef de Quatorze told Pere and Abadia to ask the justicia of Calatayud to have the fingers with which they had made the sign of the cross amputated, the skin of their knees on which they had knelt before the crucifix flayed, and *the skin of their foreheads that had come into contact with baptismal chrism torn off*.[47] These prescriptions are reminiscent of the advice of the mid-thirteenth-century Catalan moralist Jonah ben Avraham Gerondi (d. 1263), who advocated doing good with the bodily organs with which one had sinned.[48] They also call to mind a story first attested in Ashkenaz around 1400 about the imaginary Rabbi Amnon of Mainz, who was said once to have suggested that his tongue should be cut off for having expressed doubt about Judaism.[49] Rubbing sand on the parts of apostates' bodies that had come into contact with baptismal chrism, then, may have been a way of marking these body parts for the sins in which they had participated, and punishing and purifying them.

Insofar as the rite of re-Judaization was intended to purify repentant apostates from the effects of their encounter with Christian culture, it recalls Christian efforts to purge Jewish converts of lingering Jewishness. Both Christians and Jews washed incomers in water—Christians using a baptismal font and Jews, a *mikveh*. Moreover, just as, according to Bernard Gui, Jewish returnees changed their names and received new clothes, so, too, did converts to Christianity.[50] Fearing that incomers still, in one way or another, embodied their previous identities, both Christians and Jews developed rituals to signify a rupture with a problematic past.

Among Jews as among Christians, however, the power of these acts was limited. Just as the bishops of Barcelona and Girona granted begging licenses to Jewish converts in which they insisted on converts' Christian piety in order to ease converts' way among Christians, so, too, according to Bernard Gui, did Jews furnish returnees with a certificate of re-Judaization that was intended to establish returnees' integrity as Jews. The need for such documents indicates that, in spite of carefully crafted rituals, many Jews and Christians remained suspicious of individuals who had traversed the boundary between Judaism and Christianity. Indeed, Gui noted that if returnees did not carry their certificate of re-Judaization with them, Jews would not eat or drink with them.[51]

In the medieval Crown of Aragon, as well as in northern Europe, many Jews taunted apostates, cut them off financially, and even threatened them physically, yet other Jews—including some communal leaders—took great risks in order to rehabilitate apostates. All of these responses to apostasy were informed in part by Jewish hostility toward Christians and Christianity. In repudiating apostates, Jews expressed anger at a society that persecuted Jews and disdain for a faith they viewed as idolatrous. Re-Judaization efforts, however, displayed Jewish defiance at its most muscular. In fulfillment of inquisitors' fears, these efforts turned individual apostates into the objects of a contest between Christians and Jews.

Martyrdom in Calatayud?

Unlike other known medieval re-Judaization efforts, the alleged plans to re-Judaize Pere and Abadia were not intended to help apostates rejoin the Jewish community, at least not in this world. Instead, they led apostates to a horrific end. It is conceivable that Pere's case points to the existence of a religious sensibility in the environs of Calatayud during the second quarter of the fourteenth century that favored martyrdom—and specifically martyrdom by fire—as a salvific act for apostates. Presumably, according to the putative proponents of this view, neither rabbinic discipline nor the popular rite of re-Judaization could atone adequately for apostates' sins or render apostates fit for re-entry into the Jewish community. The sooner apostates perished by fire, however, the sooner they would "be with God," so Salomon Navarro said he had heard Abadia say.[52]

No other cases of apostate martyrdom have come to light from this period in the Crown of Aragon, yet this possibility is not without resonance in northern Europe. In the *Sefer hasidim*, for instance, a Jew remarked of a repentant apostate who was in danger of discovery by Christian authorities that, if Christians should kill him, his death would "be a penance" for his sins.[53] The idea even surfaced that death by fire—with its connotations of religious sacrifice, purgation, hell, and divine light—was a particularly appropriate way to atone for apostasy. The twelfth-century *Chronicle of Solomon bar Samson*, for example, which tells of the massacres of the First Crusade, recounts the story of a man referred to as "the righteous Master Isaac," who chose to burn to death after having been baptized, and who thereby atoned for the sin of his apostasy. "I shall repent and be fully whole hearted with the Lord God of Israel until I repay him with my life and fall by His hand," Master Isaac allegedly declared.[54] Closer to our period, in Paris in 1306, an apostate named Jean (formerly Mutlot) confessed that he had declared in front of the Châtelet that he wished to expiate by fire "the sin he had committed by water," that is, baptism.[55] It is possible that knowledge of episodes such as these inspired the reported deeds of the Almulis, Jucef de Quatorze, and their alleged associates, or that it sparked Pere's imagination.

Even if the Almulis, Jucef de Quatorze, and their alleged associates shared—or were imagined to share in—this approach to apostasy, however, this still would not explain why Jews would have wanted apostates to burn at the stake, that is, at the hands of Christians and before a Christian audience. Here, the strength of Jewish anti-Christian sentiments in the medieval Crown of Aragon presents an alternative possibility. Perhaps these Jews convinced—or were imagined to have convinced—Abadia and Pere to burn at the stake not only, or even primarily, in order to punish these apostates or save their souls, but in order to confront Christians with what Salomon Navarro called Jewish "contempt for the Christian faith."[56] Death at the stake would publicize widely the return to Judaism and martyrdom of apostates, displaying the triumph of Judaism over Christianity. It would also create Jewish martyrs to compete with Christian martyrs, such as Saint Peter, for example—Pere's namesake and the patron saint of the Dominican monastery of Calatayud—who was said to have been crucified head down by the Romans. Moreover, Jews might derive pleasure from using Christians, such as the *justicia* of Calatayud, as unwitting accomplices in their anti-Christian scheme.[57] According to this interpretation, Pere and Abadia were instruments of Jewish revenge against Christians.

Fra Sancho de Torralba and fra Bernat de Puigcercós certainly understood the alleged actions of the Almulis, Jucef de Quatorze, and their supposed associates as a scandalous affront to Christianity. According to Guillem de Roca, the townspeople of Calatayud shared this view. They warned that Pere had been influenced by "certain enemies of the Christian faith," and that, "unless the truth were uncovered and a remedy applied," these developments would lead to "a strengthening of [the Jewish] sect and doubt regarding [the faith] of Christians since, among Jews, such [martyrs as Abadia and Pere] would be, and are, reputed to be holy."[58]

The history of the Jewish *aljama* of Calatayud may help to explain what could have motivated such an elaborate and perilous scheme. Jewish-Christian relations had long been particularly volatile around Calatayud. Tensions flared in previous generations, for example, in 1279, when Christians broke into the Jewish quarter while Jews were attending a compulsory Christian sermon in synagogue.[59] In addition, the community had a record of problems with apostates. As we discussed in Chapter 4, in 1324, an apostate named Ramon blackmailed a local Jewish scribe named Judah Hochon, extorting money from Judah's wife and leading to Judah's imprisonment.[60] Moreover, inquisitors harassed the community during the 1320s. Fra Guillem Costa charged members of the *aljama* with having circumcised two Christians, and he accused two relatives of Jucef de Quatorze—Sulema and Ora de Quatorze—of having helped a baptized Jewish woman from France return to Judaism.[61] When Jucef de Quatorze reminisced about this period during his trial, he intimated that a number of baptized Jewish refugees from France had taken shelter in Calatayud.[62]

As a result of inquisitorial investigations in the 1320s, the Jewish *aljama* of Calatayud had been "destroyed and devastated." Jews were imprisoned, and their property was confiscated. During his trial, Jucef de Quatorze lamented that "many men of his lineage lost all of their goods." King Jaume II gave some of the Jewish books that were seized—including the Hebrew Bible, David Qimhi's *Sefer ha-shorashim* (*Book of Roots*), and some talmudic tractates—to the Franciscan friar Ramon de Miedas. In addition, major fines were levied, and two houses of study were slated to be destroyed, presumably in accordance with the inquisitorial custom of demolishing the houses of heretics, which were believed to have been contaminated by heresy. (These houses of study ultimately were spared because Jaume II intervened, warning fra Guillem Costa in December 1326 that this measure would utterly ruin the community.) These experiences may have led some Jews in Calatayud to take a particularly provocative and aggressive stance toward Christians and apostates.[63]

As fact, fabrication, or a combination of the two, the charges that Pere and the Navarros leveled against the Almulis and Jucef de Quatorze stand as striking evidence of the vigor of mutual hostility between Christians and Jews in the Crown of Aragon, nearly a decade before the anti-Jewish riots that followed the outbreak of the Black Death in 1348, and half a century prior to the massive violence of 1391. If true, these charges demonstrate the extremes to which Jewish antagonism toward Christians could lead and the unique potency of repentant Jewish apostates as Jewish instruments of revenge against Christians. If fabricated, they reveal what Christians believed Jews to be capable of and how deeply Christians cared about keeping Jewish converts in the Christian fold to prevent reversals in the Christian campaign against Jews and Judaism.

The Road to the Stake

The records of the trials of the Almulis and Jucef de Quatorze provide three conflicting accounts of Pere's departure from La Almunia de Doña Godina following the gathering at the Almulis' home. According to Pere's first confession, Pere met with the Almulis on the morning of Friday, January 5, 1341 (and not on the evening of Thursday, January 4), and he departed for Calatayud immediately thereafter, with the intention of accomplishing everything that the Almulis had instructed him to do.[1]

According to Pere's second confession and the testimonies of Salomon and Miriam Navarro, however, the Almulis and Jucef de Quatorze allowed Pere to sleep on his decision to become a Jewish martyr. These accounts describe how, on the evening of Thursday, January 4, 1341, after agreeing in the Almulis' kitchen to renounce Christianity and burn at the stake, Pere went home with the Navarros and spent the rest of the night at their house. According to Pere's second confession and the testimony of Miriam Navarro, Pere stood firm in his decision when he awoke, and he headed to Calatayud on Friday morning.[2]

Finally, according to Salomon Navarro, Pere met with the Almulis and Jucef de Quatorze on Thursday evening, and then he went home with the Navarros, but, the next morning, he returned with the Navarros to the Almulis' home. There, upon "seeing that Pere [still] wanted to go to Calatayud, [Janto Almuli] again told Pere how firm he would have to stand and that he should be sure to accomplish what he set out to do." Then, Janto, Jamila, and Velida asked Pere whether he wanted anything. Pere responded that he desired "nothing but bread for the road." So "they gave him some bread, [and he] accepted [it] . . . and [then] he tore down the road toward Calatayud to have himself burned."[3]

In his first confession, Pere told the tribunal of fra Sancho de Torralba that along the way he saw "many Jews" but did not stop to discuss his plans with any of them. He did, however, ask one of Janto Almuli's relatives for alms, receiving six denarii and one obolo.[4]

Pere's encounter with the *justicia* of Calatayud is not described in detail. At the end of his first confession, Pere explained that, upon arriving in Calatayud, he went to the home of the *justicia* without any delay, and "he did each and every thing" that the Jews had told him to do. He "asked to be burned," and "the *justicia* condemned him to death by fire."[5]

In addition, at the start of the records of the trial of Jucef de Quatorze, Guillem de Roca wrote the following:

[On January 5, 1341,] there was a great racket in the town of Calatayud in the diocese of Tarazona, for it was rumored that the [Christian] neophyte Pere, who was a native of the town, had arrived . . . and had personally approached Juan Martínez de Benies, the representative of the local *justicia*, Miguel de Gorrea, and told him that he was a Jew, and that he had had himself baptized and had undertaken the Christian faith. [Pere] had insisted, however, that, in so doing, he had greatly erred, for the law and faith of the Jews is good and, through it, it is possible to be saved, whereas the law and faith of the Christians is false . . . and through it, one cannot be saved. Therefore, [Pere] asked said representative of the local *justicia* to have him burned . . . because he wanted to die by fire in the faith of the Jews. It was also rumored in the town that, for the aforesaid reason, the representative of the local *justicia* had condemned Pere to be consumed by flames and die, in accordance with his own petition and request.[6]

Guillem de Roca did not cite the source of these rumors. Perhaps Juan Martínez de Benies and the individuals who witnessed his encounter with Pere spread the news. We know only that Pere was, by all accounts, condemned to the stake in Calatayud in January 1341, seven years after Abadia, and that, when Pere was unbound from the pyre by command of fra Sancho de Torralba and Bernardo Duque, what might have been the wretched end of one man's tumultuous journey became the start of an even greater human drama.

Conclusion

Inspired by the story of Pere, this book has explored Jewish conversion and the inquisitorial prosecution of Jews and converts in the Crown of Aragon during the century prior to 1391. In so doing, it has highlighted Christian suspicion of Jews who converted to Christianity and Jewish suspicion of apostates who returned to Judaism, sentiments that stemmed both from general perceptions of converts' and returnees' ties to their previous faiths and also from disdain for these individuals' behavior. The present work also has shown, however, that, in spite of widespread distrust of converts and returnees, Christians and Jews deemed converts and returnees valuable testaments to the superiority of their respective faiths. Thus, Christian authorities encouraged Jewish conversion and some Jews sought to recruit apostate repentance, such that some converts became the objects of a contest between Christians and Jews. Converts, then, not only suffered rejection on account of Jewish-Christian tensions, but their presence could galvanize religious conflict, as well. Both of these dynamics point to the strength of mutual antagonism between Christians and Jews and to the ways in which converts were a focus of Jewish-Christian hostility in the medieval Crown of Aragon.

In the process of illustrating these dynamics, this book has considered three discrete historical contexts. First, it has explored how medieval inquisitors, whose mandate was to eradicate Christian heresy, prosecuted Jews and converts in the Crown of Aragon, starting more than two centuries prior to the establishment of the Spanish Inquisition. Medieval inquisitors prosecuted Jews because they were convinced that Jews sought to harm Christians and undermine Christianity, especially by re-Judaizing converts. When they investigated Jewish converts, it was usually because these converts were accused of backsliding. Inquisitorial activity in the medieval Crown of Aragon thus illustrates the importance of Jewish conversions to the church. Inquisitorial trials also constituted a serious threat to the security and prosperity of Jews, as they wreaked havoc on the lives of individual Jews and on the morale and finances of entire communities.

Second, this book has examined the experiences of Jewish converts who lived in the Crown of Aragon prior to the massacres and forced conversions of 1391. Many of these men and women used baptism as a means of escaping from difficult personal circumstances, often stemming from conflicts within the Jewish community. Christians continued to view converts as Jews, in spite of efforts to purge them of Jewishness, and many Jews repudiated their brethren who went over to Christianity. In fact, some Jews were unwilling even to reaccept apostates who professed repentance. As a result, many converts were relegated to a no-man's land. Some became wandering beggars—the reality of their daily existence a cruel reflection of their social and religious homelessness—and some turned back toward their former co-religionists seeking revenge.

Third, this book has examined Jewish responses to apostasy in the medieval Crown of Aragon, especially as they related to Jewish antagonism toward Christians and Christianity. Jewish disdain for Christianity and resentment of Christian abuses of Jews contributed to fueling Jewish anger at apostates. These sentiments also, however, sustained and shaped the efforts of some Jews to bring apostates back to Judaism. The enterprise of re-Judaizing apostates was inherently a powerful polemical statement. Moreover, in seeking to convince apostates to return to Judaism, Jews mocked Christianity and refuted Christian beliefs, and a popular rite of re-Judaization shows that Jews sought to cleanse repentant apostates of the pollution they were believed to have incurred through baptism and life among Christians.

The conclusions of this study are not without caveats. The sources upon which they are based are fragmentary, and many stones have yet to be unturned. It is my hope, however, that, by beginning to outline broad characteristics of the worlds of Jews, converts, and inquisitors in the medieval Crown of Aragon, and by starting to trace the links between these worlds, this study will contribute to laying the groundwork for further investigation.

This exploration of Jewish conversion and inquisition in the medieval Crown of Aragon bears upon several related subjects. First, similarities between the experiences of Jewish and Muslim converts to Christianity in the Crown of Aragon—especially the tendency to seek baptism as a means of escaping hardships such as debt and punishment—indicate that the history of Jewish conversion in the medieval Crown should be understood within the broader framework of majority-minority relations. The Jews and the Muslims of the Crown of Aragon typically are studied separately. The two groups had contrasting histories and socioeconomic profiles, and they elicited different concerns among Christians. Yet both Jews and Muslims were infidels who lived at the mercy of Christians, and both were the objects of Christian missionary aspirations. The similar circumstances under which some Jews and Muslims were baptized reveal that, in addition, some Jews and Muslims developed similar responses to the temptations and opportunities conferred by Christian dominance.

Significant parallels in the experiences of Jewish converts to Christianity, and in Jewish and Christian attitudes toward converts, across the Crown of Aragon, Castile, and northern Europe, demonstrate that the history of Jewish conversion in the medieval Crown belongs also to a larger narrative about Jewish conversion in medieval Western Europe. In northern Europe and Christian Spain, baptism served as an escape route for disaffected Jews; converts became beggars, informers, and preachers; and some sought to return to Judaism. In both realms, too, Christians aspired to convert Jews but rejected most actual converts, and Jews expressed horror at apostasy yet sometimes facilitated apostates' return to Judaism.

These commonalities should not surprise for, in important ways, northern Europe and Christian Spain comprised an organic, if variegated, whole. Northern Europe shared with Christian Spain the institutional and ideological dominance of the Catholic Church, such that Jews in both realms faced similar pressures. Moreover, there was extensive contact across the Pyrenees. Jews from northern lands poured into Spain following expulsions, and Jewish merchants and scholars regularly journeyed and corresponded between Germany, France, Catalonia, and Castile. Indeed, Rashba and Ritva based some of their rulings regarding apostates on the teachings of Ashkenazi authorities. In addition, bishops and inquisitors, all subject to one pope until the schism of 1378, were in touch across political boundaries and even returned suspected Jewish *relapsi* to each other's lands for trial. Finally, converts themselves created ties across medieval Western Europe. In order to be baptized, in the course of begging and preaching, and in order to return to Judaism, converts traveled between Portugal, Castile, Aragon, Catalonia, France, and Germany. Because of similarities in the experiences of converts and in attitudes toward converts across Western Christendom, then, and also because of travel and communication between far-flung regions, the study of converts deepens our understanding of common characteristics of medieval Jewish life in Western

Christendom as a whole, while making it possible to analyze regional differences from a more informed perspective.

Finally, the conclusions of this study regarding Jewish conversion and inquisition in Iberia prior to 1391 are not without relevance to the subsequent chapter in Iberian history. The year 1391 constituted a major turning point in the history of Sephardic Jewry. In that year, some one hundred thousand Jews were murdered, another one hundred thousand were forcibly converted, and thousands more fled to Muslim lands.[1] The sheer number of Jewish converts in the aftermath of 1391 created unprecedented conditions that led to significant social, political, religious, economic, intellectual, and institutional developments that manifested in different ways across Iberia. In spite of so much rupture, however, important continuities bridged the periods before and after 1391. In fact, in some ways, the events of the late fourteenth and fifteenth centuries magnified Jewish and Christian competition for, and repudiation of, Jewish converts, intensifying preexisting behaviors and patterns of thought.

Throughout the course of the fifteenth century, for example, Christians continued to make a concerted effort to convert Jews. Vincent Ferrer waged vigorous conversionary campaigns early in the fifteenth century. The Tortosa Disputation of 1413–14 produced additional Jewish conversions. And, even as they issued the edict of expulsion in 1492, the Catholic Monarchs implemented an intensive preaching program aimed at converting Jews at the last hour.[2]

Also as prior to 1391, some Jews in fifteenth-century Spain endeavored to bring converts back to Judaism. They provided converts with kosher food and instruction in Jewish law, and they circumcised converts' children. In Morvedre in the 1450s, some Jews even proselytized converts who were vacillating between Christianity and Judaism. One Jewish man persuaded a convert named Pere de la Rosa "that the law of Moses was the true one" and that he would achieve salvation through performing Jewish ceremonies. Another Jew convinced a convert named Ursula Forcadell that "the law of Moses . . . [wa]s the only law, and that she should not believe that there [wa]s a Trinity but [should believe] that there [wa]s only one God who created the heavens, stars, sea, and sands."[3] Furthermore, several leading Jewish authorities, including Rabbi Isaac ben Sheshet Perfet (b. 1326), Rabbi Shimon ben Tzemah Duran (1361–1444), his son Rabbi Shlomo ben Shimon Duran (c. 1400–1467), his son, Tzemah—who coined the phrase "Israel, even uncircumcised, is circumcised"—and Tzemah's brother, Shimon II (1438–after 1510), defended the Jewishness of some of the converts of their day.[4] During the second half of the fifteenth century, the chief Rabbi of Granada, Saadiah ben Maimon ibn Danan, declared: "When it comes to lineage, all the people of Israel are brethren. We are all the sons of one father, the rebels and the criminals, the apostates and the forced converts, and the proselytes. . . . All of these are Israelites. Even if they left God or denied Him, or violated his law, the yoke of that law [would] still [be] upon their shoulders and [it] will never be removed from them."[5] Similarly, Rabbi Isaac Abarbanel (d. 1509) maintained that forced converts and their descendants who still clung to Judaism remained a part of the Jewish people and would be redeemed when the Messiah came.[6]

In contrast to conditions prior to 1391, individuals who converted in, or shortly after, 1391 were not predominantly marginalized individuals desperate to escape personal predicaments. Instead, they more fully represented a cross-section of Jewish society. Moreover, early in the fifteenth century, many converts fared well. Emboldened by their numbers and usually still in possession of their property, converts took advantage of the equality to which they were entitled, as well as of Christian society's growing need for literate men. They entered monasteries, universities, and municipal government and married into "old Christian" families, including noble ones.

As before 1391, however, Jewish and Christian attitudes toward converts were conflicted, and, as the fifteenth century progressed, they generally soured, to converts' great detriment. Some Jews denounced apostates to inquisitors, and rabbis became increasingly reluctant to re-embrace repentant apostates and their descendants.[7] Moreover, Christian suspicion of converts—now deepened by converts' economic success and the magnitude of the perceived threat they posed on account of their numbers—had consequences that were previously unfathomable. In 1449, riots broke out against converts in Toledo, and statutes of purity of blood were enacted, denying individuals with Jewish ancestry access to positions of power. As we have seen, Christians had long suspected that converts were still, in some sense, Jews. Now, however, the stigma was reflected in law, and it officially applied to converts' descendants, as well.[8]

By 1480, the wheels of the Spanish Inquisition were in motion on the tracks laid down by medieval inquisitors. Initially dedicated almost exclusively to eradicating crypto-Judaism, Spanish inquisitors condemned nearly one thousand Jewish converts to the stake between 1480 and 1530.[9] Spanish inquisitors shared their predecessors' concern about Jewish efforts to re-Judaize converts. In fact, the belief that Jews were corrupting converts directly influenced the Catholic Monarchs' decision to expel the Jews from Spain in 1492. In the edict of expulsion, Ferdinand and Isabella explained as follows:

> We have been informed that, in these our kingdoms, there were
> some wicked Christians who Judaized and apostatized from our holy
> Catholic faith, the great cause of which was interaction between Jews
> and these Christians . . . [for] Jews . . . seek always and by whatever
> means and ways they can to subvert and to steal faithful Christians
> from our holy Catholic faith and to separate them from it, and to
> draw them to themselves and subvert them to their own wicked belief
> and conviction . . . persuading them as much as they can to hold and
> observe the law of Moses, convincing them that there is no other law or
> truth except for that one.[10]

These words echoed those of Bernard Gui with which we opened Chapter
1, warning medieval inquisitors in 1323 that Jews were intent on bringing
converts back to Judaism. This resonance reminds us that the events of the
fifteenth century had an important prehistory and that, in order fully to ap-
preciate their novelty, we must grapple with their antecedents.

Spanish inquisitors themselves were aware of the precedents for their
work that we have examined. In fact, in 1503, the inquisitor general, fra Diego
de Deza (successor to Tomás de Torquemada), requested a copy of the final
sentence for Janto and Jamila Almuli and Jucef de Quatorze.[11] In conformity
with inquisitorial protocol, this sentence opened with a summary of the entire proceedings, and it is likely that Deza hoped to mine the document for
information useful to his own work. Pere's case thus lived on in the minds of
later inquisitors, an additional link across the generations. It is my hope that
it will live on for many generations yet, as an invitation to probe more deeply
the world from which it emerged, the worlds that followed, and also our own.

Abbreviations

ACA	Barcelona, Arxiu de la Corona d'Aragó
ACB	Barcelona, Arxiu de la Catedral de Barcelona
ACF	Vic, Arxiu de la Curia Fumada (within AEV series)
ADB	Barcelona, Arxiu Diocesà de Barcelona
ADG	Girona, Arxiu Diocesà de Girona
ADT	Tarazona, Archivo Diocesano de Tarazona
ADV	Valencia, Arxiu Diocesà de Valencia
ADZ	Zaragoza, Archivo Diocesano de Zaragoza
AEV	Vic, Arxiu Episcopal de Vic
AHCB	Barcelona, Arxiu Històric de la Ciutat de Barcelona
ARV	Valencia, Arxiu del Regne de Valencia
Baer, *Urkunden*	Yitzhak Baer, *Die Juden im christlichen Spanien: Urkunden und Regesten* (2 vols., Berlin, 1936)
BC	Barcelona, Biblioteca de Catalunya
BG	Batllia General (within ACA and ARV series)
BUB	Biblioteca de la Universitat de Barcelona
C	Còdex (within ACB series)
Canc.	Cancelleria Reial (within ACA series)
Cortes	*Cortes de los antiguos reinos de Aragón y de Valencia y principado de Cataluña* (Madrid, 1896–1903)
CR	Cartes Reials (within ACA series)
Directorium inquisitorum	Nicolau Eimeric, *Directorium inquisitorum R. P. F. Nicolai Emerici, Ordinis Praedicatorum S. Theol. Mag. Inquisitoris haereticae pravitatis in Regnis Regis Aragonum . . . cum scholiis seu annotationibus eruditissimis D. Francisci*

	Pegnae hispani, s. theologiae et iuris utriusque doctoris (Rome, 1578)
Finke	Heinrich Finke, ed., *Acta Aragonensia: Quellen zur deutschen, italienischen, französischen, spanischen, zur Kirchen- und Kulturgeschichte aus der diplomatischen Korrespondenz Jaymes II (1291–1327)*, 3 vols. (Berlin, 1908–22)
HTR	*Harvard Theological Review*
Jacobs	Joseph Jacobs, ed., *Inquiry into the Sources of the History of the Jews of Spain* (London, 1894)
JQR	*Jewish Quarterly Review*
LT	Llibres de Tesorería (within ACA series)
Rashba	Rabbi Solomon ben Avraham ibn Aderet, *Sheelot u-teshuvot, The Responsa Project* 16.0, CD-ROM (Ramat Gan, Israel, 2008)
RC	Registra Communium (within ADB series)
RCT	*Revista Catalana de Teologia*
Reg.	Registro (within ACA series)
Régné, *History*	Jean Régné, comp., *History of the Jews in Aragon: Regesta and Documents (1213–1327)*, edited by Yom Tov Assis (Jerusalem, 1978)
REJ	*Revue des Études Juives*
RG	Registra Gratiarum (within ADB series)
Ritva, *Sheelot u-teshuvot*	Rabbi Yom Tov ben Avraham Ishbili, *Sheelot u-teshuvot, The Responsa Project* 16.0, CD-ROM (Ramat Gan, Israel, 2008)
RP	Reial Patrimoni (within ACA series)
UB	Barcelona, Universitat de Barcelona
Vincke	Johannes Vincke, *Zur Vorgeschichte der Spanische Inquisition: Die Inquisition in Aragon, Katalonien, Mallorca und Valencia während des 13. und 14. Jahrhunderts* (Bonn, 1941)
VP	Visites Pastorals (within ADB, ADG, and AEV series)
X	*Decretales Gregorii IX*

Notes

INTRODUCTION

1. "Journey from Islam: Incipient Cultural Transition in the Conquered Kingdom of Valencia (1240–1280)," *Speculum* 35 (1960): 338.

2. The Crown of Aragon was a confederation comprised of Aragon, Catalonia, and Valencia, Mediterranean islands such as Mallorca, and some territories north of the Pyrenees. For a succinct introduction to its political and economic history, see Thomas N. Bisson, *The Medieval Crown of Aragon: A Short History* (Oxford, 1986). In 1391, thousands of Jews across Iberia were slaughtered and thousands more baptized by force.

3. On the "golden age" of Jewish culture in the medieval Crown of Aragon, see, for example, Yom Tov Assis, *The Golden Age of Aragonese Jewry: Community and Society in the Crown of Aragon, 1213–1327* (London, 1997). For a discussion of scholarship that explores the limits, and questions the utility, of the vexed notion of *convivencia*, often understood as the harmonious "living together" of Jews, Muslims, and Christians in medieval Spain, see Maya Soifer, "Beyond *Convivencia*: Critical Reflections on the Historiography of Interfaith Relations in Christian Spain," *Journal of Medieval Iberian Studies* (2009): 19–35.

4. ACB, C126, fols. 2r, 23r, 25r, 40r, 47v.

5. ACB, C126, fols. 39r–v, 42r, 43r, 50r.

6. ACB, C126, fols. 90r, 91v–92v. Josep Perarnau i Espelt published an introductory analysis of these trials in "El procés inquisitorial barceloní contra els jueus Janto Almuli, la seva muller Jamila i Jucef de Quatorze (1341–1342)," *RCT* 4 (1979): 309–53. He discusses them also in "L'autodifesa nella parola di tre ebrei davanti all-inquisitore," in *La parola all-accusato*, ed. Jean-Claude Maire Vigueur et al. (Palermo, 1991), 74–84. Also see Kristine T. Utterback, "'Conversi' Revert: Voluntary and Forced Return to Judaism in the Early Fourteenth Century," *Church History* 64 (1995): 16–28; and Robin Vose, *Dominicans, Muslims and Jews in the Medieval Crown of Aragon* (Cambridge, 2009), 188–91.

7. I refer to "medieval inquisitions" in the plural, for medieval inquisitors were never integrated into a unified, centralized organization. See the discussion in Edward Peters, *Inquisition* (Berkeley, Calif., 1989), 67–71.

8. On other extant transcripts of medieval inquisitorial trials involving Jews and converts, see Joseph Shatzmiller, *Recherches sur la communauté juive de Manosque au moyen âge* (Paris, 1973), 54–63; Jacques Fournier, *Le registre d'inquisition de Jacques Fournier*, ed. Jean Duvernoy (Toulouse, 1965), 1:177–90, translated with analysis by Solomon Grayzel in "The Confession of a Medieval Jewish Convert," *Historia Judaica* 17 (1955): 89–120; Josep

Hernando i Delgado, "El procés contra el converso Nicolau Sanxo, ciutadà de Barcelona, acusat d'haver circumcidat el seu fill (1437–1438)," *Acta Historica et Archaeologica* 13 (1992): 75–100; and Mark D. Meyerson, "Seeking the Messiah: *Converso* Messianism in Post-1453 Valencia," in *The Conversos and Moriscos in Late Medieval Spain and Beyond*, ed. Kevin Ingram (Leiden, 2009), 51–82.

9. See, for example, Yosef H. Yerushalmi, "The Inquisition and the Jews of France in the Time of Bernard Gui," *HTR* 63 (1970): 317–76; Joseph Shatzmiller, "L'inquisition et les juifs de Provence au XIIIe s.," in *Histoire de la Provence et civilization medieval: Études dédiées à la mémoire d'Edouard Baratier*, Provence Historique 23 (Marseille, 1973), 327–38; Solomon Grayzel, "Popes, Jews, and Inquisition, from *Sicut* to *Turbato*," in *The Church and the Jews in the Thirteenth Century*, 2 vols. (New York, 1989), 2:3–45; Maurice Kriegel, "La juridiction inquisitoriale sur les juifs à l'époque de Philippe le Hardi et Philippe le Bel," in *Les juifs dans l'histoire de la France*, ed. Myriam Yardeni (Leiden, 1980), 70–77; Maurice Kriegel, "Prémarranisme et inquisition dans la Provence des XIIIe et XIVe siècles," *Provence Historique* 29 (1978): 313–23; and Yom Tov Assis, "The Papal Inquisition and Aragonese Jewry in the Early Fourteenth Century," *Medieval Studies* 49 (1987): 391–410.

10. Studies of Jewish conversion in Iberia prior to 1391 include Paola Tartakoff, "Jewish Women and Apostasy in the Medieval Crown of Aragon, c. 1300–1391," *Jewish History* 24 (2010): 7–32; and Alexandra Guerson, "Seeking Remission: Jewish Conversion in the Crown of Aragon, c. 1378–1391," *Jewish History* 24 (2010): 33–52.

11. On inquisitorial record production, see James Buchanan Given, *Inquisition and Medieval Society: Power, Discipline, and Resistance in Languedoc* (Ithaca, N.Y., 1997), 25–51.

12. David Nirenberg, *Communities of Violence: Persecution of Minorities in the Middle Ages* (Princeton, N.J., 1996), 26–27. On the history of Jews in the Crown of Aragon from 1213 to 1327, see Assis, *The Golden Age*. On Jewish life in the fourteenth-century Crown, see David Romano, "Les juifs de la Couronne d'Aragon avant 1391," *REJ* 41 (1982): 169–82; and Romano, "Els jueus en temps de Pere el Cerimoniós," in *Pere el Cerimoniós i la seva època* (Barcelona, 1989), 123–29.

13. Maurice Kriegel has argued that, for the purposes of medieval Jewish history, Iberia and southern France may be treated as a coherent cultural unit. See his *Les juifs à la fin du moyen âge dans l'Europe méditerranéenne* (Paris, 1979), 11.

14. See, for example, Assis, *The Golden Age*. Mark D. Meyerson argues for a "golden age" of only thirty or forty years in *Jews in an Iberian Frontier Kingdom: Society, Economy, and Politics in Morvedre, 1248–1391* (Leiden, 2004). For an overview of Jewish life in Iberia during the Reconquista, see Jonathan Ray, *The Sephardic Frontier: The Reconquista and the Jewish Community in Medieval Iberia* (New York, 2006).

15. ACB, 1-6-3475, trans. Elka Klein and published in *Internet Medieval Source Book*, http://www.fordham.edu/halsall/sbook1.asp, accessed on October 16, 2011; Nirenberg, *Communities of Violence*, 39; Yom Tov Assis, "The Jews of Spain in Gentile Courts (XIIIth–XIVth Centuries)" (in Hebrew), in *Tarbut ve-Historia*, ed. Y. Dan (Jerusalem, 1989), 121–45; Robert I. Burns, *Jews in the Notarial Culture: Latinate Wills in Mediterranean Spain, 1250–1350* (Berkeley, Calif., 1996), 30; AEV, VP 1200/2, fol. 40v. On Jews and Christian wet nurses, see Simcha Emanuel, "The Christian Wet Nurse during the Middle Ages: *Halakhah*

and History" (in Hebrew), *Siyyun* 73 (2008): 21–40; and Rebecca Lynn Winer, "Conscripting the Breast: Lactation, Slavery and Salvation in the Realms of Aragon and Kingdom of Majorca, c. 1250–1300," *Journal of Medieval History* 34 (2008): 164–84.

16. Josep Baucells i Reig, *Vivir en la edad media: Barcelona y su entorno en los siglos XIII y XIV (1200–1344)* (Barcelona, 2004–7), 2:1717; Jean Régné, "Rapports entre l'inquisition et les juifs d'après le mémorial de l'inquisiteur d'Aragon," *REJ* 53 (1906): 232–33.

17. Nirenberg, *Communities of Violence*, 140; Meyerson, *Jews*, 83. On interfaith sex in medieval Iberia, also see David Nirenberg, "Conversion, Sex, and Segregation: Jews and Christians in Medieval Spain," *American Historical Review* 107 (2002): 1065–93 and "Love Between Muslim and Jew in Medieval Spain: A Triangular Affair," in *Jews, Muslims, and Christians in and around the Crown of Aragon: Essays in Honour of Professor Elena Lourie*, ed. Harvey J. Hames (Leiden, 2004), 127–55.

18. See Meyerson, *Jews*, 61–62.

19. Chazan, *The Jews of Medieval Western Christendom, 1000–1500* (Cambridge, 2006), 61; Meyerson, *Jews*, 63–78.

20. Shlomo Simonsohn, ed., *The Apostolic See and the Jews: Documents; 492–1404* (Toronto, 1988), 460 (#434) (hereafter cited as Simonsohn, *Documents*).

21. On Holy Week violence, see Nirenberg, *Communities of Violence*, 200–230. As David Nirenberg has shown, in order fully to understand Holy Week violence and other hostilities, one must carefully consider local contexts.

22. Meyerson, *Jews*, 92; Nirenberg, *Communities of Violence*, 108–10. On host desecration, see Miri Rubin, *Gentile Tales: The Narrative Assault on Late Medieval Jews* (Philadelphia, 1999), 109–15; Joaquín Miret i Sans, "El procés de les hosties contra'ls jueus d'Osca en 1377," *Anuari de l'Institut d'estudis catalans* 4 (Barcelona, 1911): 79–80; and Meyerson, *Jews*, 90–91. On ritual murder, see Yitzhak Baer, *A History of the Jews in Christian Spain*, trans. L. Schoffman et al., 2 vols. (Philadelphia, 1961), 2:6–7; Elena Lourie, "A Plot Which Failed? The Case of the Corpse Found in the Jewish *Call* of Barcelona (1301)," *Mediterranean Historical Review* 1 (1986): 187–220; and Meyerson, *Jews*, 90.

23. Meyerson, *Jews*, 93–94.

24. On the Pastoureaux in Aragon, see Jaume Riera i Sans, *Fam i fe: L'Entrada dels Pastorells (juliol de 1320)* (Lleida, 2004); and Nirenberg, *Communities of Violence*, 69–92. On the violence of 1348, see Nirenberg, *Communities of Violence*, 231–49; and Mark D. Meyerson, "Victims and Players: The Attack of the Union of Valencia on the Jews of Morvedre," in *Religion, Text, and Society in Medieval Spain and Northern Europe: Essays in Honor of J. N. Hillgarth*, ed. Thomas Burman et al. (Toronto, 2002), 70–102.

25. Yerushalmi, "The Inquisition and the Jews," 354–63; Israel Yuval, *Two Nations in Your Womb: Perceptions of Jews and Christians in Late Antiquity and the Middle Ages* (Berkeley, Calif., 2006), 115–34.

26. See Jeremy Cohen, *The Friars and the Jews: The Evolution of Medieval Anti-Judaism* (Ithaca, N.Y., 1982), 156–63.

27. Shem Tov ben Isaac ibn Shaprut, *Even bohan/La piedra de toque: Una obra de controversia judeo-cristiana; Introducción, edición crítica, traducción y notas al libro I*, ed. José-Vicente Niclós, Bibliotheca Hispana Bíblica 16 (Madrid, 1997), 9. On informal dis-

putations between Jews and Christians in twelfth-century Ashkenaz, see David Berger, "Mission to the Jews and Jewish Christian Contacts in the Polemical Literature of the High Middle Ages," *American Historical Review* 91 (1986): 585–91.

28. Meyerson, *Jews*, 89–90; Nirenberg, *Communities of Violence*, 91–92. For reflections on the historiography of Jewish violence, see Elliot Horowitz, *Reckless Rites: Purim and the Legacy of Jewish Violence* (Princeton, N.J., 2006), 187–212.

29. See Yerushalmi, "The Inquisition and the Jews," 354–63.

30. David Viera, "The Evolution of Francesc Eiximenis's Attitudes toward Judaism," in *Friars and Jews in the Middle Ages and Renaissance*, ed. Steven J. McMichael et al. (Leiden, 2004), 153–55, 157; AEV, MS 172, fol. 34r.

FOUR ARRESTS

1. ACB, C126, fol. 39v.

2. Fra Sancho de Torralba was named inquisitorial commissary by fra Bernat de Puigcercós on June 14, 1338. Bernardo Duque was also the deacon of the church of Santa María Mayor in Calatayud (ACB, C126, fols. 38v–40r, 43r).

3. The officials present included the inquisitorial scribe and notary Guillem de Roca; a canon of the Church of Santa María de Pina named Juan Pedro de Agrada; the assessor of the representative of the *justicia*, Alfonso Pedro de Agreda; and the inquisitor's public scribe, Nicolás Martín de Trasobares.

4. It was probably for this reason that, in 1264, in the town of Manosque, a Jewish convert to Christianity named Raymbauda chose to swear as a Christian in a Christian court, even though she had lived as a Jew for the past fourteen years, married a Jewish man, and borne six children (Shatzmiller, *Recherches*, 57).

5. ACB, C126, fol. 39v.

6. ACB, C126, fols. 39v–43r.

7. ACB, C126, fol. 49r.

8. Pere said that Jucef de Quatorze listed the following Jews: Aaron Abenafia, Rabbi Mahir Amnalguer the elder, Rabbi Mahir's son Rabbi Salomon, Avraham Mocatil, Salomon Passariel, "and many others whose names Pere could not remember" (ACB, C126, fol. 50r).

9. ACB, C126, fols. 49r–51r, 90v.

10. ACB, C126, fols. 80v–81v. On the inquisitorial prosecution of the Jewish *aljama* of Calatayud during the 1320s, see Assis, "The Papal Inquisition," 402–3 and *The Golden Age*, 58, 61–62.

11. ACB, C126, fol. 51v. Guillem de Roca was a notary public of Barcelona (ACB, C126, fols. 93v–94r).

CHAPTER I. DEFENDING THE FAITH

1. Gui, *Practica inquisitionis heretice pravitatis*, ed. Célestin Douais (Paris, 1886), 288.

2. Ramon de Penyafort, *Summa de paenitentia* (c. 1225), quoted in Christine Caldwell Ames, *Righteous Persecution: Inquisition, Dominicans, and Christianity in the Middle Ages* (Philadelphia, 2009), 151.

3. See Edward Peters, *Torture* (Philadelphia, 1996), 62–67; Ames, *Righteous Persecution*, 169–90, 211–24; Given, *Inquisition and Medieval Society*, 74–75; and Henry Charles Lea, *A History of the Inquisition of the Middle Ages*, 3 vols. (New York, 1888; repr., 1955), 1:553.

4. Eufemià Fort i Cogul, *Catalunya i la inquisició* (Barcelona, 1973), 1–119 provides a basic introduction to medieval inquisitions in the Crown of Aragon. Johannes Vincke, *Zur Vorgeschichte der Spanischen Inquisition: Die Inquisition in Aragon, Katalonien, Mallorca und Valencia während des 13. und 14. Jahrhunderts* (Bonn, 1941) remains the most sophisticated historical analysis of the institution. On inquisitorial activity in the Crown of Aragon, also see Lea, *A History of the Inquisition of the Middle Ages*, 2:162–80; and Vose, *Dominicans, Muslims and Jews*, 85–88.

5. Jaume Puig i Oliver, "El pagament dels inquisidors a la Corona d'Aragó, segles XIII i XIV," *Arxiu de Textos Catalans Antics* 22 (2003): 177.

6. See Yerushalmi, "The Inquisition and the Jews," 350; and Hyam Maccoby, ed. and trans., *Judaism on Trial: Jewish-Christian Disputations in the Middle Ages* (London, 1982), 19–38.

7. See Francisco Diago, *Historia de la provincia de Aragón de la Orden de Predicadores* (Barcelona, 1599; repr., Valencia, 1999), fols. 29r–30r; the annals of the Dominican monastery of Barcelona, Santa Caterina, known as the *Lumen domus* (BUB, MS 1005, fol. 49r); and ACB, C126, fol. 88r.

8. See Régné, *History*, 54 (#2926); Finke, 3:111–12 (#49); Assis, *Golden Age*, 60; and Assis, "The Papal Inquisition," 408–9 (#4–6).

9. Vincke, 84–85 (#48); Ramon de Alós, "El Cardenal de Aragón, fray Nicolás Rossell: Ensayo bio-bibliográfico," *Cuadernos de trabajo de la Escuela Española de Arqueología e Historia en Roma* 1 (1912): 37 (#17); Eduard Pérez i Pons, ed., *Fonts per a l'estudi de la comunitat jueva de Mallorca* (Barcelona, 2005), 160 (#637).

10. See Baer, *Urkunden*, 1:204–6 (#166) (=Régné, *History*, 546 [#2952]), 1:207–8 (#168); Baer, *A History of the Jews*, 2:10–11; Assis, "The Papal Inquisition," 400–401; and Jorge Maíz Chacón, *Los judíos de Baleares en la baja edad media* (Oleiros, Spain, 2010), 72–73.

11. ACB, C126, fol. 82r; Assis, *The Golden Age*, 62; Vincke, 75 (#31).

12. See Vincke, 84–91 (#48–51, 54–57).

13. See Louis Finkelstein, *Jewish Self-Government in the Middle Ages* (New York, 1924), 337–38.

14. *X* 5.7.10, published in *Corpus iuris canonici*, ed. Emil Friedberg (Leipzig, 1881), 2:782–83.

15. See Gui, *Practica inquisitionis*, 39–40; and Vittore Colorni, *Judaica minora: Saggi sulla storia dell'ebraismo Italiano dall'antichità all'età moderna* (Milan, 1983), 161.

16. ACB, C126, fol. 85v.

17. Régné, *History*, 218–19 (#1206); Baer, *Urkunden*, 1:148–49 (#133), 1:360–61 (#256), 1:475 (#322); Asunción Blasco, "La inquisición y los judíos en Aragón en la segunda mitad del siglo XIV," in *Aragón en la edad media*, Estudios de economía y sociedad 7 (Zaragoza, 1987), 92 (#2); Vincke, 123 (#112); Mark D. Meyerson, "Samuel of Granada and the Dominican Inquisitor: Jewish Magic and Jewish Heresy in Post-1391 Valencia," in *Friars and Jews*, 176.

18. Josep Perarnau i Espelt: "El *Tractatus brevis super iurisdictione inquisitorum contra infideles fidem catholicam agitantes* de Nicolau Eimeric," *Arxiu de Textos Catalans Antics* 1 (1982): 114 (lines 155–66), 118 (lines 230–32). Eimeric summarized his position in his *Directorium inquisitorum*, 244–50. On medieval Jews as heretics, see Jeremy Cohen, *Living Letters of the Law: Ideas of the Jew in Medieval Christianity* (Berkeley, Calif., 1999), 147–66.

19. ACB, C126, fol. 2r–v. On Jewish oaths taken in medieval Christian courts, see Joseph Ziegler, "Reflections on the Jewry Oath in the Middle Ages," in *Christianity and Judaism: Papers Read at the 1991 Summer Meeting and the 1992 Winter Meeting of the Ecclesiastical History Society*, ed. Diana Wood (Oxford, 1992), 209.

20. ACB, C126, fols. 16r–v, 32v.

21. See, for example, Jaume Riera i Sans, "Un procés inquisitorial contra els jueus de Montblanc per un llibre de Maimònides," *Aplec de Treballs* 8 (1987): 59–73 and chapter 2.

22. See Puig i Oliver, "El pagament dels inquisidors," 178–80.

23. *Directorium inquisitorum*, 389.

24. Perarnau, "El *Tractatus*," 96; Puig i Oliver, "El pagament dels inquisidors," 181; ACB, C126, fol. 91v.

25. Puig i Oliver, "El pagament dels inquisidors," 200 (#16), 208–9 (#27); Riera i Sans, "Un procés inquisitorial," 67.

26. ACB, C126, fol. 88r–v.

27. ACB, C126, fol. 84v; Grayzel, "Popes, Jews, and Inquisition," 21.

28. ACB, C126, fols. 39r–40v, 84v.

29. During the second half of the fourteenth century, inquisitors prosecuted Jews for a wider range of offenses, including the practice of magic and necromancy and holding theological opinions considered contrary to Jewish and Christian teaching. For an overview of this activity, see Shlomo Simonsohn, ed., *The Apostolic See and the Jews: History* (Toronto, 1991), 359–62 (hereafter cited as Simonsohn, *History*). On the prosecution of Jews for practicing the magical arts, see Meyerson, "Samuel of Granada," 165–68, 176.

30. See Robert Chazan, *Barcelona and Beyond* (Berkeley, 1992); Vose, *Dominicans, Muslims, and Jews*, 144–55, 174; Grayzel, *The Church and the Jews*, 2:92–97 (#24).

31. Yerushalmi, "The Inquisition and the Jews," 326–27.

32. Gui, *Practica inquisitionis*, 291.

33. Jaume Puig i Oliver, "Documents relatius a la inquisició del 'Registrum litterarum' de l'Arxiu Diocesà de Girona (s. XIV)," *Arxiu de Textos Catalans Antics* 17 (1998): 391–92 (#5).

34. See Maccoby, *Judaism on Trial*, 132; and Riera i Sans, "Un procés inquisitorial," 60.

35. ADG, Lletres Episcopals 63, fol. 170r–v (=Puig i Oliver, "Documents relatius a la inquisició," 447–48 [#59]).

36. ACB, C126, fol. 83v.

37. See Elena Lourie, "Complicidad criminal: Un aspecto insólito de convivencia judeo-cristiana," in *Congreso internacional "Encuentro de las tres culturas"* (Toledo, 1988), 99; and Finke, 3:111–12 (#49).

38. Baer, *Urkunden*, 1:360–61 (#256); Régné, "Rapports," 232; Blasco, "La inquisición y los judíos," 93–94 (#3).

39. *Directorium inquisitorum*, 242. On the history and uses of the verb "to Judaize," see Shaye D. Cohen, "Between Judaism and Christianity: The Semicircumcision of Christians According to Bernard Gui, His Sources and R. Eliezer of Metz," *HTR* 94 (2001): 295–300.

40. See Jaume Puig i Oliver, "El *Tractatus de haeresi et de infidelium incredulitate et de horum criminum iudice*, de Felip Ribot, O. Carm., edició i estudi," *Arxiu de Textos Catalans Antics* 1 (1982): 184 (lines 725–37).

41. *Codex Theodosianus* 16.8.19, cited in Amnon Linder, *The Jews in Roman Imperial Legislation* (Detroit, 1987), 258; Simonsohn, *History*, 345–46.

42. See ADB, RC 3, fol. 59r (=Assis, "The Papal Inquisition," 409 [#6]) and ADB, RC 3, fol. 88v. Robin Vose raises the possibility that Jucef Levi converted Stella in order to marry her (*Dominicans, Muslims, and Jews*, 187). On associations between Jews and the devil in the medieval Christian imagination, see Joshua Trachtenberg, *The Devil and the Jews: The Medieval Conception of the Jew and Its Relation to Modern Antisemitism* (New York, 1943).

43. See Joseph Shatzmiller, "Paulus Christiani: Un aspect de son activité anti-juive," in *Hommage à Georges Vajda: Études d'histoire et de pensée juives*, ed. Gérard Nahon and Charles Touati (Louvain, 1980), 208–9, n. 9.

44. Baer, *Urkunden*, 1:204–6 (#166) (=Régné, *History*, 546 [#2952]). See discussion in Vose, *Dominicans, Muslims, and Jews*, 183–86; Assis, "The Papal Inquisition," 400–401; and Maíz Chacón, *Los judíos de Baleares*, 72–73.

45. See Vincke, 84–91 (#48–51, 54–57). On Bernard Gui's claim that when Jews circumcised Christians, "they cut off from them the foreskin halfway from above and not a full circle, as they d[id] to their own Jewish children" (*Practica inquisitionis*, 289–90), see S. Cohen, "Between Judaism and Christianity."

46. See *Decretum Gratiani*, C.28 q.1 c.10, published in *Corpus iuris canonici*, 1:1087.

47. ADB, RC 3, fol. 59r (=Assis, "The Papal Inquisition," 409 [#6]); ACB, C126, fols. 81v, 92r; ACA, Canc., Reg. 434, fol. 136r.

48. See Yom Tov Assis, "Juifs de France réfugiés en Aragon (XIIe–XIVe siècles)," *REJ* 142 (1983): 290–92; Yerushalmi, "The Inquisition and the Jews," 333–35; William Chester Jordan, *The French Monarchy and the Jews: From Philip Augustus to the Last Capetians* (Philadelphia, 1989), 200–251; and William Chester Jordan, "Jews, Regalian Rights and the Constitution in Medieval France," *Association of Jewish Studies Review* 23 (1998): 1–16.

49. Jacobs, 50 (#873) (=Régné, *History*, 624–25 [#3419]); Régné, *History*, 619 (#3389); ACB, C126, fol. 53r.

50. Meyerson, "Samuel of Granada," 175, n. 38; Régné, "Rapports," 225, 229–31.

51. Joaquim Miret i Sans, *Itinerari de Jaume I el Conqueridor* (Barcelona, 1918), 371, 376.

52. Grayzel, "Popes, Jews, and Inquisition," 15.

53. See Grayzel, "Popes, Jews, and Inquisition," 37, n. 92; and Simonsohn, *History*, 234. Pope Nicholas IV reissued this second version in 1290 (Simonsohn, *Documents*, 275 [#266]).

54. Simonsohn, *Documents*, 285–86 (#278).

55. Miquel Pujol i Canelles, *La conversió dels jueus de Castelló d'Empúries* (Castelló d'Empúries, 1997), 34.

56. Lea, *A History of the Inquisition of the Middle Ages*, 2:63, n. 2; Bernard Gui, *Le livre des sentences de l'inquisiteur Bernard Gui 1308–1323*, ed. and trans. Annette Pales-Gobillard (Paris, 2002), 1:805–7, 2:1038–39; Kriegel, "Prémarranisme," 319.

57. See ADG, Lletres Episcopals 64, fol. 92v; 68, fols. 59r–v, 67v, 74v; Puig i Oliver, "Documents relatius a la inquisició," 447–48 (#59); and Vincke, 167 (#11) (=Régné, "Rapports," 229).

58. Grayzel, "Popes, Jews, and Inquisition," 22.

59. ACB, C126, fol. 84r; see *Extravagantes communes*, 1.6 in *Corpus iuris canonici*, 2:1243.

60. 217–18, in Ames, *Righteous Persecution*, 182.

61. Shatzmiller, *Recherches*, 58–60; J. Cohen, *The Friars and the Jews*, 86. In 1298, inquisitors charged the Jews of Rome with "crimes of heresy," which Solomon Grayzel suggested involved bringing converts back to Judaism. A leader of the Jewish community, Elia de Pomis, took the blame upon himself and was burned at the stake (Grayzel, "Popes, Jews, and Inquisition," 23).

62. Régné, *History*, 218–19 (#1206), 548 (#2966), 599 (#3259); Assis, "The Papal Inquisition," 401, 408–9 (#4, 5).

63. See, for example, ADB, RC 3, fols. 91v–92r.

64. *Practica inquisitionis*, 288.

65. On the conversionary fervor of the mid-thirteenth century, see J. Cohen, *The Friars and the Jews*; Robert Chazan, *Daggers of Faith: Thirteenth-Century Christian Missionizing and Jewish Response* (Berkeley, Calif., 1989); Benjamin Z. Kedar, *Crusade and Mission: European Approaches toward the Muslims* (Princeton, N.J., 1984); Robert I. Burns, "Christian-Islamic Confrontation in the West: The Thirteenth-Century Dream of Conversion," *American Historical Review* 76 (1971): 1386–1434; and Vose, *Dominicans, Muslims, and Jews*. On Christians who served as godparents to Jewish converts in the Crown of Aragon, see Chapter 3.

66. On the upsurge in efforts to convert Muslims in the twelfth century, see Kedar, *Crusade and Mission*, esp. 57–74. On Muslim conversion to Christianity in the medieval Crown of Aragon, see Brian Catlos, *The Victors and the Vanquished: Christians and Muslims of Catalonia and Aragon, 1050–1300* (Cambridge, 2004), 249–59; Robert I. Burns, *Muslims, Christians, and Jews in the Crusader Kingdom of Valencia* (Cambridge, 1984), 80–108; Burns, "Journey from Islam"; John Boswell, *The Royal Treasure: Muslim Communities under the Crown of Aragon in the Fourteenth Century* (New Haven, Conn., 1977), 347, 378–81; Meyerson, *Jews*, 61; and Nirenberg, *Communities of Violence*, 184–88.

67. See Vose, *Dominicans, Muslims, and Jews*, 104–15, 161–64; and Catlos, *The Victors and the Vanquished*, 251, n. 186.

68. On a case of return to Islam, see Catlos, *The Victors and the Vanquished*, 254. For a rare and indirect reference to the inquisitorial prosecution of Muslims in the medieval Crown of Aragon, see Puig i Oliver, "El pagament dels inquisidors," 208 (#27).

69. Grayzel, *The Church and the Jews*, 1:222–24 (#85). Similar allusions to Romans 11:24 are found in ADG, Llicències Episcopals 1, fols. 102v–103r, 123v, and 2, fol. 9r–v.

70. In *Obres catalanes*, ed. Miquel Batllori (Barcelona, 1947), 1:234.

71. J. Cohen, *The Friars and the Jews*, 156.

CHAPTER 2. FROM RESISTANCE TO SURRENDER

1. ACB, C126, fol. 54r.

2. ACB, C126, fols. 38r–v, 44r, 51r–52v.

3. Régné, *History*, 599 (#3259); Finke, 2:859–60 (#540) (=Régné, *History*, 602 [#3276]); Simonsohn, *History*, 356–57; Régné, "Rapports," 230.

4. Grayzel, "Popes, Jews, and Inquisition," 22–23; Simonsohn, *Documents*, 254 (#248), 286–87 (#279). It was not always the case, however, that Jews were *impotentes*. About 1376, for example, a Jew from Peratallada named Isaach Vidal arranged for men to kill a certain Pere de Saumana, who had denounced Isaach for blasphemy to fra Guillem Sanguini (Régné, "Rapports," 231–32). Pere de Saumana may have been a convert. See ADG, Lletres Episcopals 68, fols. 59r–v, 67v, 74v (=Puig i Oliver, "Documents relatius a la inquisició," 450–52 [#62, 63]).

5. ACB, C126, fols. 2v, 25r.

6. ACB, C126, fols. 2r–v, 25r–v.

7. ACB, C126, fol. 23r.

8. ACB, C126, fol. 44v.

9. Jaume Riera i Sans, *Els poders publics i les sinagogues segles XIII–XV* (Girona, 2006), 321 (#121), 366 (#172), 367 (#173).

10. ACB, C126, fols. 2v–3r, 21r–v.

11. ACB, C126, fols. 3r, 21r–v.

12. ACB, C126, fol. 21v; *Practica inquisitionis*, 209–33.

13. Régné, *History*, 613–14 (#3353).

14. Régné, *History*, 574–75 (#3115), 586 (#3181), 619 (#3389), 620 (#3396); Baer, *Urkunden*, 1:244 (#184).

15. ACB, C126, fols. 21v–22r.

16. ACB, C126, fol. 22r–v.

17. Baer, *Urkunden*, 1:296–97 (#213).

18. ACB, C126, fols. 44r, 46r, 47v–49r.

19. Riera i Sans comments on this menu in "La conflictivitat de l'alimentació dels jueus medievals (segles XII–XV)," in *Alimentació i societat a la Catalunya medieval, Anuario de Estudios Medievales* 20 (Barcelona, 1988), 295–96.

20. ACB, C126, fols. 45r, 48r–49r. On the alleged participation of Jewish women in related efforts, see also Baer, *Urkunden*, 1:239–41 (#180) (=Régné, *History*, 598–99 [#3256]); Régné, *History*, 619 (#3389), 620 (#3396); ADB, RC 3, fol. 59r (=Assis, "The Papal Inquisition," 409 [#6]); and ADB, RC 3, fol. 88v.

21. ACB, C126, fols. 44v, 45v–46r, 47r.

22. ACB, C126, fol. 47r.

23. ACB, C126, fol. 38r–v.

24. ACB, C126, fols. 21r, 47v; Lea, *A History of the Inquisition of the Middle Ages*, 1:409.

25. ACB, C126, fols. 3v–4r, 5v–6r.

26. ACB, C126, fols. 5v–6r.

27. ACB, C126, fols. 3v–5r, 10v, 46r, 48v, 50r, 68r.

28. ACB, C126, fols. 25v–26v.

29. ACB, C126, fol. 51v.

30. ACB, C126, fol. 53r–v.

31. ACB, C126, fols. 53v–54r, 62r.

32. ACB, C126, fols. 53v–54r.

33. In Pamiers in 1320, the inquisitor Jacques Fournier summoned a respected member of the Jewish community, David of Troyes, to be present at the trial of the convert Joan (formerly Baruch) "so that, if necessary, [David] could translate Hebrew" (Fournier, *Le registre d'inquisition*, 1:177).

34. ACB, C126, fol. 54r–v.

35. See Finkelstein, *Jewish Self-Government*, 338; Simonsohn, *History*, 356, n. 29; Simonsohn, *Documents*, 410–12 (#384–85).

36. Vincke, 64 (#16). Also see Simonsohn, *History*, 348–49, n. 14.

37. Gui, *Practica inquisitionis*, 192–93.

38. ACB, C126, fols. 54v–55r.

39. ACB, C126, fol. 55r.

40. ACB, C126, fol. 55r–v.

41. The witnesses Jucef proposed included Mosse, Salomon, and Sanson Abenforna, Jucef Acrix son of Avraham, Mosse Agradan of Calatayud, Jucef Alpestan, Domingo Andrec, Açecrin Avencresp, Isaach de Exea, Avraham and Isaach de Funes, Mosse German, Jaime Gonzalvez, Juan de Maraig, Sanson Xicus, Jucef Xumiel, and Salema and his son from La Almunia de Doña Godina (ACB, C126, fols. 55v–56r). Those selected were Mosse, Salomon, and Sanson Abenforna, Jucef Acrix son of Avraham, Jucef Alpestan, Açecrin Avencresp, Isaach de Exea, Avraham and Isaach de Funes, Mosse German, and Jucef Xumiel (ACB, C126, fols. 62v–66r).

42. Régné, *History*, 529–30 (#2865), 574–75 (#3115).

43. ACB, C126, fol. 56r.

44. ACB, C126, fols. 6v–8v.

45. ACB, C126, fol. 10v.

46. ACB, C126, fols. 8r–v, 10r–v.

47. ACB, C126, fols. 8r–v, 10r–v.

48. ACB, C126, fols. 10v–11r.
49. ACB, C126, fol. 27r–v.
50. ACB, C126, fol. 56v.
51. ACB, C126, fols. 56v–58r.
52. ACB, C126, fols. 58v–59r.
53. ACB, C126, fol. 60r.
54. ACB, C126, fol. 61r–v.
55. ACB, C126, fols. 61r–62r.
56. ACB, C126, fol. 68r–v.
57. Jucef de Quatorze listed Aaron Abenafia, Mosse Abenforna, Jucef Alcuçentin, Jucef Almedayan, Samuel Alpestan, Mosse Amnalguer, Mosse Avenfalagut, Salomon Avensaprut Ezquierdo, Avraham Azaries, Jucef Havivi, Isaach Habealuz, Avraham Mocatil, Mosse Pasagon, Salomon Passariel, and Isaach Sadoch (ACB, C126, fol. 68r). For Salomon Navarro's list, see p. 39.
58. ACB, C126, fol. 68v.
59. ACB, C126, fols. 68v–69r.
60. ACB, C126, fols. 69v–72v.
61. ACB, C126, fol. 73r–v.
62. ACB, C126, fols. 16r–17r, 32v–33r, 75r–78v.
63. ACB, C126, fol. 80r. On the events of 1326 in Calatayud, see Chapters 1 and 6.
64. Lea, *A History of the Inquisition of the Middle Ages*, 1:457.
65. ACB, C126, fols. 81v–82r.
66. ACB, C126, fols. 82v–83r. Jucef listed Aaron and Mosse Abenafia, Rabbi Salomon Amnalguer, Avraham and Isaach Avenlaut, Jafuda del Calvo, Jucef Nadaya, Galaf Pasagon, Salomon Passariel, Avraham and Sulema de Quatorze, and Jucef and Jafuda el Sage (ACB, C126, fol. 83r).
67. ACB, C126, fols. 84v–85r.

FOUR CONDEMNATIONS

1. ACB, C126, fols. 83v–87v.
2. ACB, C126, fol. 86v. These experts included Pere de Plana; Francesc Despuig, a doctor in canon law; Pere de Casclarí, a doctor of civil law; fra Berenguer de Saltells, a Dominican provincial; fra Bertran Riquer, the prior of the Dominican monastery of Barcelona; fra Bartomeu Ferrer, the Dominican lector at Barcelona; fra Pere de Molins, the Dominican lector at Lleida; fra Bernat Llull, the archdeacon of Santa María del Mar; and four Franciscan friars: Arnau de Canyelles; Francesc Gener; Francesc Batlle, the guardian at Barcelona; and Guillem de Vallseca, the noted jurist and lector at Girona.
3. ACB, C126, fols. 17r–v, 86v–87v. These distinguished lawyers and theologians included Bernat Llull and Pere de Plana, as well as three canons from Barcelona: Guerau Celorri, Bernat de Ruvira, and Guillem Pere-Pallarès.
4. ACB, C126, fols. 91r–92v.

5. ACB, C126, fols. 12v, 76v–78v, 86v, 91r, 93r–v. The five *consellers* present were Guillem Nagera, Arnau Duzay, Francesc de Trilea, Bernat de Ruvira, and Guillem de Vallseca.

6. ACB, C126, fols. 88r, 90r.

7. This description is based on Lea, *A History of the Inquisition of the Middle Ages*, 1:551–52.

ALATZAR AND ABADIA, BAPTIZED

1. ACB, C126, fols. 23r, 25r, 47v.

2. ACB, C126, fols. 2r, 23r, 40r–v. In spite of ecclesiastical pronouncements recommending otherwise, it was the custom in Catalonia, until at least 1370, for every catechumen to have two sets of godparents—godparents "of catechesis," who were supposed to instruct the Christian-to-be, and godparents of the baptism proper, who were to play a special role at the ceremony. See Baucells i Reig, *Vivir en la edad media*, 1:641; and Perarnau i Espelt, "El procés inquisitorial barceloní," 336, n. 47.

3. ACB, C126, fols. 10v, 58v.

CHAPTER 3. BETWEEN DOUBT AND DESIRE

1. ACB, C126, fol. 40r.

2. On Vincenç Esteve, see Régné, *History*, 532 (#2881); and Antoni Cardoner, "Muestra de protección real a físicos judíos españoles conversos," *Sefarad* 12 (1952): 378–80. I am grateful to Jaume Riera i Sans for sharing the information about Romeu and Pere de Pal. On Pere de Gràcia, see Jaume Riera i Sans, "Les llicències reials per predicar als jueus i als sarraïns (Segles XIII–XIV)," *Calls* 2 (1987): 122–23. On Jaume de Faro, see ADG, Lletres Episcopals 64, fol. 92v, published in Tartakoff, "Jewish Women and Apostasy," 19 (#2). On Juan Sánchez de Calatayud, see Baer, *Urkunden*, 1:610 (#390); and Baer, *A History of the Jews*, 2:92–94.

3. ACB, C126, fol. 58v; ADB, RC 3, fol. 140v; Vincke, 180 (#132).

4. In 1279, for example, King Pere II lamented the fact that "some Jews" had been baptized "in spite of themselves" amid the tumult of compulsory mendicant conversionary sermons, and in 1327, the regent of Mallorca had to prohibit baptizing Jews under the age of seven against their will (Régné, *History*, 135–36 [#747]; Antonio Pons i Pastor, *Los judíos del Reino de Mallorca durante los siglos XIII y XIV* [Mallorca, 1984], 2:261 [#76]). In addition, the French Pastoureaux converted some Jews at sword's point in Montclús in 1320 (see Nirenberg, *Communities of Violence*, 78; and Riera i Sans, *Fam i fe*, 133–34). Finally, according to an ordinance that was drafted by Jewish representatives from Catalonia and Valencia in 1354, during the riots that followed the outbreak of the Black Death in 1348, additional Jews, who were unable to withstand these trials, "cross[ed] over the bridge in their distress" (see paraphrase and translation in Finkelstein, *Jewish Self-Government*, 336).

5. ADG, Lletres Episcopals 22, fol. 149r; ADG, Llicències Episcopals 1, fol. 123v.

6. See Chapter 1.

7. See *Las siete partidas del rey Don Alfonso el Sabio*, ed. Real Academia de la Historia (Madrid, 1807), 672–73 (7.24.6); Robert C. Stacey, "The Conversion of Jews in Thirteenth-Century England," *Speculum* 67 (1992): 267–68, 279; Jordan, *The French Monarchy*, 149–50; Grayzel, *The Church and the Jews*, 1:19, n. 36; Norman Golb, *Les juifs de Rouen au moyen âge: Portrait d'une culture oubliée* (Rouen, 1985), 373–78; and Salo W. Baron, *A Social and Religious History of the Jews*, 18 vols. (New York, 1957), 9:72.

8. The full text of the statutes Jaume I issued at the Council of Lleida is preserved in a bull of Pope Innocent III published in Grayzel, *The Church and the Jews*, 1:254–56 (#105). The full text of the decree of 1296 is published in Antoni Rubió i Lluch, ed., *Documents per l'història de la cultura catalana migeval* (Barcelona, 1921), 2:110–11. The full text of the decrees of 1300 and 1311 can be found in *Cortes*, 1:171, 217–18.

9. Régné, *History*, 615 (#3363); Pons i Pastor, *Los judíos del Reino de Mallorca*, 2:289 (#112); Guerson, "Seeking Remission," 37.

10. See Assis, *The Golden Age*, 293–94; and Baron, *A Social and Religious History*, 11:35–36.

11. Guerson, "Seeking Remission," 33, 36–37.

12. Baron, *A Social and Religious History*, 11:36–37. Also see Elena Lourie, "Anatomy of Ambivalence: Muslims under the Crown of Aragon in the Late Thirteenth Century," in *Crusade and Colonisation: Muslims, Christians and Jews in Medieval Aragon* (Aldershot, 1990), 58–59. On this practice in early modern Germany and baptism as an escape from it, see Elisheva Carlebach, *Divided Souls: Converts from Judaism in Germany, 1500–1750* (New Haven, Conn., 2001), 39–42.

13. See Pons i Pastor, *Los judíos del Reino de Mallorca*, 2:240; and Lourie, "Complicidad criminal," 102.

14. Pons i Pastor, *Los judíos del Reino de Mallorca*, 1:208 (#2).

15. Baer, *Urkunden*, 1:204–6 (#166) (=Régné, *History*, 546 [#2952]).

16. ADG, Lletres Episcopals 68, fols. 59r–v, 67v, 74v (=Puig i Oliver, "Documents relatius a la inquisició," 450–52 [#62, 63]); Puig i Oliver, "Documents relatius a la inquisició," 452–53 (#64).

17. See Vose, *Dominicans, Muslims, and Jews*, 133–64.

18. On King Henry III of England serving as a godfather to Jewish converts, see Stacey, "The Conversion of Jews," 269. On Louis IX of France, see Nicholas Vincent, "Jews, Poitevins, and the Bishop of Winchester, 1231–1234," in *Christianity and Judaism*, ed. Wood, 132; Jordan, *The French Monarchy*, 150; Louis Rabinowitz, *The Social Life of the Jews of Northern France in the XII–XIV Centuries as Reflected in the Rabbinical Literature of the Period* (New York, 1972), 103; and Roger Kohn, *Les juifs de la France du nord dans la seconde moitié du XIVᵉ siècle* (Paris, 1988), 187.

19. Augustí Altisent, *L'almoina reial a la cort de Pere el Cerimoniós* (Poblet, 1969), 8, 122, 145, 159.

20. Ibid., 117–18.

21. Ibid., 253, 255, 257, 288, 290, 294, 297, 299, 301, 303, 308, 312, 314, 316, 319, 321, 323, 326, 328, 330.

22. Perarnau i Espelt, "El procés inquisitorial barceloní," 336, n. 47; ADB, RG 7, fol. 123r; ADG, Llicències Episcopals 1, fols. 84v–85r; ADB, RG 8, fol. 196r; Shatzmiller, *Recherches*, 57.

23. ADB, RG 7, fol. 123r; ADG, Llicències Episcopals 1, fols. 84v–85r; ADB, RC 3, fol. 140v.

24. On the currency of this practice in northern Europe, see Jonathan Elukin, "From Jew to Christian? Conversion and Immutability in Medieval Europe," in *Varieties of Religious Conversion in the Middle Ages*, ed. James Muldoon (Gainesville, Fla., 1997), 174. On the term "ex-Jew," see "Minutes notariales de Bonanat de Gradu," in José María de Mas y Casas, *Ensayos históricos sobre Manresa* (Manresa, 1882), 153–54.

25. *Directorium inquisitorum*, 504, 748.

26. Catlos, *The Victors and the Vanquished*, 258–59.

27. Canon 70, published in Norman P. Tanner, ed., *Decrees of the Ecumenical Councils* (Washington, D.C., 1990), 267.

28. ADG, Lletres Episcopals 68, fol. 67v (=Puig i Oliver, "Documents relatius a la inquisició," 452 [#63]).

29. Guerson, "Seeking Remission," 38.

30. Grayzel, "Popes, Jews and Inquisition," 18, 40, n. 18.

31. See Karl F. Morrison, *Understanding Conversion* (Charlottesville, Va., 1992), xii; and Elukin, "From Jew to Christian?" 179.

32. Simonsohn, *Documents*, 54–55 (#52); Riera i Sans, "Les llicències," 133 (#2); ACA, Canc., Reg. 9041, fol. 104r–v.

33. Elukin, "From Jew to Christian?" 173.

34. On the association of "cultural" anti-Judaism with pre-modernity and "biological" anti-Semitism with modernity, see David Nirenberg, "Was There Race before Modernity? The Example of 'Jewish' Blood in Late Medieval Spain," in *The Origins of Racism in the West*, ed. Miriam Eliav-Feldon et al. (Cambridge, 2009), 232–64. On the relationship between Jewish and Christian conceptions of lineage in late medieval Spain, see David Nirenberg, "Mass Conversion and Genealogical Mentalities: Jews and Christians in Fifteenth-Century Spain," *Past and Present* 174 (2002): 3–41. On doubts about the efficacy of baptism for Jews in early modern German culture, see Carlebach, *Divided Souls*, 35–37.

35. Assis, *The Golden Age*, 156–57.

36. Ritva, *Sheelot u-teshuvot*, #159.

37. ACA, Canc., Reg. 428, fols. 12v–13r.

38. Ritva, *Sheelot u-teshuvot*, #159. On Christianity as idol worship, see Chapter 6.

39. See Baer, *A History of the Jews*, 2:61–62.

40. See Joseph Shatzmiller, "Jewish Converts to Christianity in Medieval Europe, 1200–1500," in *Cross Cultural Convergences in the Crusader Period: Essays Presented to Aryeh Grabois on His Sixty-Fifth Birthday*, ed. Michael Goodich et al. (New York, 1995), 306.

41. Ritva, *Sheelot u-teshuvot*, #179.

42. Simonsohn, *History*, 263.

43. *X* 4.19.9, in *Corpus iuris canonici*, 2:724–25.

44. Rashba, sec. 5, #240.

45. ADG, Lletres Episcopals 70, fol. 86v.

46. ADB, RC 42, fol. 177v, published in Tartakoff, "Jewish Women and Apostasy," 20–21 (#4).

47. On the solemnization of marriages in fourteenth-century Barcelona, see Baucells i Reig, *Vivir en la edad media*, 1:704–6.

48. For a more comprehensive discussion of this case, see Tartakoff, "Jewish Women and Apostasy," 15–16.

49. Assis, *The Golden Age*, 292–93.

50. ACB, C126, fols. 4v, 5r, 23r, 46r, 68r.

51. Régné, *History*, 574–75 (#3115), 529–30 (#2865).

52. Shatzmiller, "Jewish Converts," 306.

53. Ibid., 307, n. 42. On the maltreatment of Jewish wives in the medieval Crown of Aragon, see Assis, *The Golden Age*, 258–59.

54. Meyerson, *Jews*, 249–50.

55. See Romano, "Les juifs de la Couronne d'Aragon," 176; Prim Bertran i Roigé, "Els jueus en els llibres de batlle i cort de Cervera (1354–1357)," *Ilerda* 44 (1983):193; and Meyerson, *Jews*, 164–74.

56. Meyerson, *Jews*, 81, n. 61. For Jews who had sunk into poverty from positions of higher social standing, conversion may have been a way to escape embarrassment and disgrace. As Christ and his apostles had rejected wealth, and Christian society generally respected voluntary poverty, conversion might have presented a way for bankrupt Jews to bear their plight with dignity, by becoming "the poor of Christ."

57. See the beginning of Chapter 3. Yitzhak Baer characterized Juan Sánchez de Calatayud as "a new type of apostate" whose conversion was "prompted by political considerations, serving as an 'admission ticket' to a world that was wholly secular and to a career in the civil and political bureaucracy." The grandson of Juan Sánchez was Gabriel Sánchez, a distinguished official of the Catholic Monarchs (Baer, *A History of the Jews*, 2:93–94).

58. ADB, RG 8, fol. 196r; Pujol i Canelles, *La conversió dels jueus*, 61; ADG, Llicències Episcopals 1, fols. 81v–82r, 104r–105v; ACB, C126, fol. 40v; Baron, *A Social and Religious History*, 10:134.

59. See, for example, ADG, Lletres Episcopals 3, fol. 181r; 10, fol. 91v; 22, fol. 149r–v.

60. Shatzmiller, *Recherches*, 56–57; Simonsohn, *Documents*, 423–25 (#398–99).

61. Jacques Fournier, *Le registre d'inquisition*, 1:185.

62. Pujol i Canelles, *La conversió dels jueus*, 61; ADG, Llicències Episcopals 1, fols. 81v–82r.

63. ADG, Lletres Episcopals 16, fol. 37r–v; 21, fols. 73v–74r; 33, fol. 187r; Enrique Claudio Girbal, "Conversiones de judíos en Girona y su obispado," *Revista de Girona* 18 (1894): 35; Llicències Episcopals 1 fol. 90r; ADB, RG 8, fol. 196r.

64. Kohn, *Les juifs de la France du nord*, 187; ADB, RG 7, fol. 123r.

65. Burns, "Journey from Islam," 342; Catlos, *The Victors and the Vanquished*, 252, 254–58.

66. See Vivian D. Lipman, *The Jews of Medieval Norwich* (London, 1967), 109.

67. Simonsohn, *History*, 279.

68. See Carlebach, *Divided Souls*, 30. Also see Alfred Haverkamp, "Baptised Jews in German Lands during the Twelfth Century," in *Jews and Christians in Twelfth-Century Europe*, ed. Michael A. Signer et al. (Notre Dame, Ind., 2001), 267–73; and Stacey, "The Conversion of Jews," 278.

69. Stacey, "The Conversion of Jews," 270–71; Joshua Starr, "The Mass Conversion of Jews in Southern Italy (1290–1293)," *Speculum* 21 (1946): 203–11.

70. See, for example, Gerson D. Cohen, "Messianic Postures of Ashkenazim and Sephardim," in *Studies of the Leo Baeck Institute*, ed. Max Kreutzberger (New York, 1967), 117–58.

71. On responses to forced baptism, see, for example, Elisheva Carlebach, "Between History and Hope: Jewish Messianism in Ashkenaz and Sepharad," Third Annual Lecture of the Victor Selmanowitz Chair of Jewish History, Graduate School of Jewish Studies, Touro College, May 17, 1998; Ram Ben-Shalom, "*Kiddush ha-Shem* and Jewish Martyrdom in Aragon and Castile in 1391: Between Spain and Ashkenaz" (in Hebrew), *Tarbiz* 70 (2001): 227–82; and Abraham Gross, *Struggling with Tradition: Reservations about Active Martyrdom in the Middle Ages* (Boston, 2004). On "voluntary" conversion, see David Malkiel, "Jews and Apostates in Medieval Europe: Boundaries Real and Imagined," *Past and Present* 194 (2007): 3–34; Kenneth R. Stow, "Conversion, Apostasy, and Apprehensiveness: Emicho of Flonheim and the Fear of Jews in the Twelfth Century," *Speculum* 76 (2001): 911–33; Haverkamp, "Baptised Jews," 255–310; William Chester Jordan, "Adolescence and Conversion in the Middle Ages," in *Jews and Christians in Twelfth-Century Europe*, ed. Michael A. Signer et al. (Notre Dame, Ind., 2001), 77–93; and Stacey, "The Conversion of Jews," 263–83.

72. Simonsohn, *History*, 239.

73. Robert Chazan, *Church, State and Jew in the Middle Ages* (New York, 1980), 25.

74. Ibid., 64.

75. See Burns, "Journey from Islam," 342; and Catlos, *The Victors and the Vanquished*, 254–55.

76. On the confiscation of converts' goods, see Baron, *A Social and Religious History*, 9:20–22; Grayzel, *The Church and the Jews*, 1:19, n. 36; and Simonsohn, *History*, 248–53. Léon Bardinet likened the king's treatment of Jewish converts to a lord's treatment of rebellious serfs ("De la condition civile des juifs du Comtat Venaissin pendant le séjour des papes à Avignon (1309–1376)," *Revue Historique* 12 [1880]: 14). On the manumission price that the owners of Muslim slaves exacted from slaves who chose baptism and consequently were to be freed, see Catlos, *The Victors and the Vanquished*, 254–58; and David Abulafia, "The Servitude of Jews and Muslims in the Medieval Mediterranean: Origins and Diffusion," *Mélanges de l'École Française de Rome (moyen âge-temps modernes)* 112 (2000): 687–714.

77. Simonsohn, *History*, 249.

78. Simonsohn, *Documents*, 419–21 (#394).

79. ADG, Lletres Episcopals 16, fols. 37v–38r; Grayzel, *The Church and the Jews*, 1:97–99 (#8).

80. Baron, *A Social and Religious History*, 9:20; Grayzel, *The Church and the Jews*, 1:19, n. 36; Simonsohn, *Documents*, 423–24 (#398). On the use of the verb *dimittere*, compare, for example, Pujol i Canelles, *La conversió dels jueus*, 248; ADG, Llicències Episcopals 1, fols. 18v–19r; and ADB, RG 1371, fol. 100r.

81. These converts included Martí de Peralta (1326, ADG, Lletres Episcopals 2, fol. 18r), Joan de Planils and his sons Pere and Bernat (1326, ADG, Lletres Episcopals 2, fol. 2v), Guillem de Belloc (1328, ADG, Lletres Episcopals 3, fol. 181r), Jucef Cohen/Joan (1346, ADG, Lletres Episcopals 10, fol. 91v), Iomtov/Pere (1347, ADG, Lletres Episcopals 11, fol. 86r), Guillem de Llinyola (1350, ADG, Lletres Episcopals 16, fols. 37v–38r), Joan Serra, Pere de Terre de Fraga, Bernat de Palaciolo of Tarazona, and Ramón Esquert of Valadorit (1350, ADG, Lletres Episcopals 16, fol. 37r–v), Francesc de Papiolo (1352, ADG, Lletres Episcopals 21, fols. 73v–74r), Joan García (1352, ADG, Lletres Episcopals 15, fol. 130r), Daniel de Verger (1353, ADG, Lletres Episcopals 22, fol. 149r–v), Tomás of Girona (1359, ADG, Lletres Episcopals 33, fol. 187r), Blanca, her family, and eighty unnamed others (1371, ADB, RG 4, fol. 100r), Juan Pérez de Benabarre (1372, ADG, Llicències Episcopals 1, fols. 42v–43r), Joan Sord (1375, ADG, Llicències Episcopals 1, fols. 66v–67r), Pere Rodes, his wife Joana, and son Joan (1375, ADG, Llicències Episcopals 1, fols. 67v–68r), Joan de Ruibech (1378, ADB, RG 7, fol. 123r), Pere Alfons (1379, ADG, Llicències Episcopals 1, fol. 90r), David Gerson/Marc Moner, Mosse Valensí/Joan Turon, and Isaach Biton/Joan Estrader (1381, ADG, Llicències Episcopals 1, fols. 81v–82r), and Tonsanus and three companions (1381, ADG, Llicències Episcopals 1, fols. 104r–105v).

82. See ADG, Llicències Episcopals 1, fols. 90r, 104r–105v. On baptismal customs in medieval Barcelona, see Baucells i Reig, *Vivir en la edad media*, 1:611–46; and Perarnau i Espelt, "El procés inquisitorial barceloní," 336, n. 47.

83. See, for example, ADG, Lletres Episcopals 16, fols. 37v–38r; ADG, Llicències Episcopals 1, fol. 123v; and ADG, Llicències Episcopals 1, fols. 18v–19r.

84. See, for example, ADG, Llicències Episcopals 1, fols. 104r–105v; and ADG, Lletres Episcopals 22, fol. 149r–v.

85. Prim Bertran i Roigé, "l'Almoina pontifícia d'Avinyó: Els seus inicis (1316–1324) en temps de Joan XXII," *Acta Historica et Archaeologica Mediaevalia* 25 (2004): 314, n. 143.

86. ADB, RG 7, fol. 123r; ADG, Llicències Episcopals 1, fols. 84v–85r; and Shatzmiller, *Recherches*, 57.

87. See Karl F. Morrison, *Conversion and Text: The Cases of Augustine of Hippo, Herman-Judah, and Constantine Tsatsos* (Charlottesville, Va., 1992), 109. On the disputed authorship of this narrative, see Morrison, *Conversion and Text*, 39–42; Avrom Saltman, "Hermann's *Opusculum de conversione sua*: Truth or Fiction?" *REJ* 147 (1988): 31–56; and Jean-Claude Schmitt, *La conversion d'Hermann le juif: Autobiographie, histoire et fiction* (Paris, 2003).

88. See, for example, ADB, RG 8, fol. 196r; ADG, Lletres Episcopals 3, fol. 181r; ADG, Lletres Episcopals 2, fol. 2v; ADG, Lletres Episcopals 15, fol. 130r; ADG, Lletres Episcopals 16, fol. 37r–v; ADG, Lletres Episcopals 33, fol. 187r; and Riera i Sans, "Les llicències," 136 (#5).

89. ADG, Lletres Episcopals 68, fols. 59r–v, 67v, 74v (=Puig i Oliver, "Documents relatius a la inquisició," 450–52 [#62, 63]).

90. ADB, RG 4, fol. 100r, published in Tartakoff, "Jewish Women and Apostasy," 18–19 (#1); Simonsohn, *Documents*, 423–24 (#398); ADG, Llicències Episcopals 1, fols. 18v–19r; Enrique Claudio Girbal, *Los judíos en Girona* (Girona, 1870), 41–42, n. 2.

91. ADB, RG 4, fol. 100r, published in Tartakoff, "Jewish Women and Apostasy," 18–19 (#1). On medieval Jewish fears about conversion during childbirth, see Elisheva Baumgarten, *Mothers and Children: Jewish Family Life in Medieval Europe* (Princeton, N.J., 2004), 51–52.

92. ADG, Llicències Episcopals 1, fol. 105r. Another miraculous conversion is referred to in ADG, Llicències Episcopals 1, fol. 123v.

93. See Elukin, "From Jew to Christian?" 180–82.

94. ADG, Llicències Episcopals 1, fol. 105r.

CHAPTER 4. HOMEWARD BOUND

1. Ora Limor, ed., *Die Disputationen zu Ceuta (1179) und Mallorca (1286): Zwei antijüdische Schriften aus dem mittelalterlichen Genua* (Munich, 1994), 275. On the Mallorca Disputation, also see Ora Limor, "Missionary Merchants: Three Medieval Anti-Jewish Works from Genoa," *Journal of Medieval History* 17 (1991): 35–51.

2. Jeremy Cohen, "The Mentality of the Medieval Jewish Apostate: Peter Alfonsi, Hermann of Cologne, and Pablo Christiani," in *Jewish Apostasy in the Modern World*, ed. Todd A. Endelmann (New York, 1988), 35–41; José María Coll, "¿Ramon de Tárrega fue formalmente hereje?," *Ilerda* 6 (1948): 7–29.

3. Régné, *History*, 532 (#2881); Baer, *Urkunden*, 1:610 (#390.1).

4. Assis, *The Golden Age*, 56, 228; Régné, *History*, 532 (#2879); Riera i Sans, "Les llicències," 122, 125, 130, n. 38, 131, n. 55. I am grateful to Jaume Riera i Sans for information on the life of Romeu de Pal.

5. Régné, *History*, 528 (#2857), 529 (#2859) (=Baer, *Urkunden*, 1:192–93 [#160]). On the production, sale, and consumption of kosher meat in the medieval Crown, see Assis, *The Golden Age*, 224–29. I am grateful to Jaume Riera i Sans for the information about Romeu de Pal.

6. Coll, "Ramon de Tárrega," 7, 19–20, 23.

7. Rubió i Lluch, *Documents*, 2:59–60 (#63); ADG, Lletres Episcopals 16, fols. 37v–38r; Girbal, *Los judíos en Girona*, 41, n. 2; ADB, RG 4, fol. 100r, published in Tartakoff, "Jewish Women and Apostasy," 18–19 (#1); Simonsohn, *Documents*, 423 (#398); ADG, Llicències Episcopals 1, fols. 18v–19r; ADG, Llicències Episcopals 1, fols. 104r–105v; ADG, Llicències Episcopals 1, fol. 126v. On converts relinquishing their possessions, see Chapter 3.

8. See Chapter 5.

9. Girbal, *Los judíos en Girona*, 41, n. 2. I am grateful to Jaume Riera i Sans for suggesting this interpretation.

10. On destination baptisms, see Chapter 3.

11. See Altisent, *L'almoina reial*, 17, 144, 148, 230; and ADG, Llicències Episcopals 1, fols. 18v–19r, 104r–105v, 123v, 126v. In thirteenth-century England, some destitute converts

found refuge in the Domus Conversorum, a London home for converts founded by King Henry III, while others wandered from monastery to monastery. See Stacey, "The Conversion of Jews," 267–68, 273–78; and Joan Greatrex, "Monastic Charity for Jewish Converts: The Requisition of Corrodies by Henry III," in *Christianity and Judaism: Papers Read at the 1991 Summer Meeting and the 1992 Winter Meeting of the Ecclesiastical History Society*, ed. Diana Wood (Cambridge, Mass., 1992), 133–45.

12. ADB, RG 7, fol. 123r; and ADG, Llicències Episcopals 1, fols. 84v–85r.

13. Simonsohn, *Documents*, 419–21 (#394).

14. On episcopal begging licenses issued to Jewish converts elsewhere in medieval Europe, see Peter Browe, *Die Judenmission im Mittelalter und die Päpste* (Rome, 1942), 197–202. Begging licenses from Girona and Barcelona issued to individual converts include ADG, Lletres Episcopals 2, fols. 2v and 18r; 3, fol. 181; 10, fol. 91v; 11, fol. 86r; 15, fol. 130r; 16, fols. 37v–38r; 21, fols. 73v–74r; 22, fol. 149r–v; 33, fol. 187r; and 64, fol. 92v; and ADG, Llicències Episcopals 1, fols. 42v–43r, 66v–67r, 90r.

15. ADG, Lletres Episcopals 16, fol. 37r–v; ADB, RG 4, fol. 100r, published in Tartakoff, "Jewish Women and Apostasy," 18–19 (#1); ADG, Llicències Episcopals 1, fols. 81v–82r.

16. See Eduard Sierra Valentí, "Captivus de sarraïns: Llicències per a demanar caritat dels bisbes de Girona (1376–1415)," *Anuario de Estudios Medievales* 38 (2008): 386.

17. ADG, Lletres Episcopals 16, fols. 37v–38r; 22, fol. 149r–v.

18. ADG, Lletres Episcopals 64, fol. 92v, published in Tartakoff, "Jewish Women and Apostasy," 19 (#2).

19. ADB, RG 4, fol. 100r, published in Tartakoff, "Jewish Women and Apostasy," 18–19 (#1).

20. Joaquim Sarret Arbós, *Jueus a Manresa* (Manresa, 1917), 47.

21. Guerson, "Seeking Remission," 37; ACA, Canc., Reg. 941, fol. 104r–v.

22. On the kings of France financially supporting Jewish converts, see Kohn, *Les juifs de la France du nord*, 184; Jordan, *The French Monarchy*, 149–50; and Lucien Lazard, "Les juifs de Touraine," *REJ* 17 (1888): 215. On the situation in England, see Stacey, "The Conversion of Jews," 267.

23. Eduardo González Hurtebise, *Libros de tesorería de la casa real de Aragón* (Barcelona, 1911), I, 162 (#719).

24. Altisent, *L'almoina reial*, 43, 117–18, 127, 139, 144, 146.

25. Ibid., 8, 122, 145, 159.

26. Ibid., 253, 255, 257, 288, 290, 294, 297, 299, 301, 303, 308, 312, 314, 316, 319, 321, 323, 326, 328, 330.

27. Mark D. Johnston, "Ramon Llull and the Compulsory Evangelization of Jews and Muslims," in *Iberia and the Mediterranean World of the Middle Ages: Studies in Honor of Robert I. Burns, S.J.*, vol. 1, *Proceedings from Kalamazoo*, ed. Larry J. Simon et al. (Leiden, 1995), 15–16.

28. See paraphrase and translation in Finkelstein, *Jewish Self-Government*, 336.

29. *Even bohan/La piedra de toque*, 5.

30. Assis, *The Golden Age*, 56.

31. See Ricardo del Arco, "Ordenanzas inéditas, dictadas por el concejo de Huesca

(1284 a 1456)," *Revista de Archivos, Bibliotecas y Museos* 29 (1913): 428; and Ricardo del Arco, "La judería de Huesca: Noticias y documentos inéditos," *Boletín de la Real Academia de la Historia* 66 (1915): 321–22.

32. Assis, *The Golden Age*, 56; Rashba, sec. 1 #1091.

33. ADB, RC 3, fol. 33r (=Assis, "The Papal Inquisition," 406–7 [#1]). This Guillem de Belloc may be the same convert who received a begging license in Girona in 1328 (ADG, Lletres Episcopals 3, fol. 181).

34. Finke, 2:861–62 (#542) (=Régné, *History*, 608 [#3314]). On "serial apostates" in medieval Ashkenaz, see Malkiel, "Jews and Apostates," 24–25; and Edward Fram, "Perception and Reception of Repentant Apostates in Medieval Ashkenaz and Premodern Poland," *Association for Jewish Studies Review* 21 (1996): 313–14.

35. Vincke, 180 (#132) (=Régné, "Rapports," 231). On charges of host desecration in the medieval Crown of Aragon, see the Introduction.

36. See Riera i Sans, "Un procés inquisitorial," 60. See Chapter 1.

37. ACA, Canc., 428, fols. 12v–13r.

38. Quoted in Yuval, *Two Nations*, 173. See discussion in Carlebach, *Divided Souls*, 45. On the case in general, see Gavin Langmuir, "Detector of Ritual Murder," *Speculum* 59 (1984): 820–46 and John M. McCulloh, "Jewish Ritual Murder: William of Norwich, Thomas of Monmouth, and the Early Dissemination of the Myth," *Speculum* 72 (1997): 698–740.

39. Limor, *Die Disputationen*, 296; Johnston, "Ramon Llull," 15; Baron, *A Social and Religious History*, 9:19–20, 249, n. 18.

40. See Riera i Sans, "Les llicències," 116–17; and Vose, *Dominicans, Muslims, and Jews*, 153–54.

41. Riera i Sans, "Les llicències," 122–25.

42. Ibid., 120, 132 (#1).

43. Ibid., 120–22, 125, 132–33.

44. Thus, when the hagiographers of Thomas Aquinas described an episode in which the great theologian converted Jews, they specified that these Jews were "rich men and learned in their Law" (Carlebach, *Divided Souls*, 33–34).

45. Riera i Sans, "Les llicències," 136–37 (#5).

46. ADG, Lletres Episcopals 16, fol. 37r–v; 21, fols. 73v–74r.

47. By 1364, Joan Catalan was responsible for the conversions of Peire Regas, Francesc Serra de Guartiminhos, Bartolemi Beniga, Miquel Pagarol de Valencia, Pau Catalan (formerly Jacobet), Loís (formerly Bonhamet), Peire d' Apta (formerly Bonafos), Peire de Pertús, Peire de Cadeneto, Joan Ricard de Manosca, Ramon and Joan d' Apta; their wives, Guillelma (wife of Joan Catalan), Almodia (wife of Pau/Jacobet), Jacoba (wife of Loís), Jacoba (wife of Peire/Bonafos), Caterina (wife of Peire de Pertús), Elena (wife of Joan Ricard), Margarita (wife of Ramon d' Apta); their children, Beatrisina and Joana (of Joan Catalan), Francisca, Jacometa, and Aloyseta (of Pau), Caterina (of Loís), Jacoba, Caterina, and Alumeta (of Peire/Bonafos), and two women, Jacoba de Cadeneto and Caterina Fosseta de Saltu. See Simonsohn, *Documents*, 261 (#398, 399); ADG, Llicències Episcopals 1, fols. 102r–103v.

48. See Régné, *History*, 492 (#2650).

49. *Even bohan/La piedra de toque*, 5.

50. Kohn, *Les juifs de la France du nord*, 34.

51. Isidore Loeb, "Polémistes chrétiens et juifs en France et en Espagne," *REJ* 18 (1889): 226–30.

52. Baer, *Urkunden*, 1:539 (#356.5).

53. ACA, Canc., Reg. 433, fols. 111r–v, 151r; Riera i Sans, "Les llicències," 121, 124–25, 135–38 (#4, 6); Baer, *Urkunden*, 1:541–42. In 1333, the representative of the bailiff of Valencia forbade Jimeno Pérez and Pedro Fernández from preaching to Jews in the cathedral of Valencia (Leopoldo Piles Ros, "Los judíos valencianos y la autoridad real," *Sefarad* 8 [1948]: 78–96).

54. Riera i Sans, "Les llicències," 126, 140–41 (#9).

55. Joseph Shatzmiller, "Converts and Judaizers in the Early Fourteenth Century," *HTR* 74 (1981): 69.

56. See Baron, *A Social and Religious History*, 9:14–15; Roger of Hovenden, *The Annals, Comprising the History of England and of Other Countries of Europe from AD 732 to AD 1201*, tr. Henry T. Riley (London, 1853; repr., New York, 1968), 2:117–19; F. Donald Logan, "Thirteen London Jews and Conversion to Christianity: Problems of Apostasy in the 1280s," *Bulletin of the Institute of Historical Research* 45 (1972): 214–29; Fournier, *Le registre d'inquisition*, 177–90; and Fram, "Perception and Reception," 302–3.

57. Backsliding was known among Muslim converts in the medieval Crown of Aragon, as well. In 1279, the workshop of an unnamed Muslim convert who had allegedly "returned to the sect of Mohammad" was granted to Mahomet de Sale, the magistrate of the *morería* of Valencia (Catlos, *The Victors and the Vanquished*, 254).

58. See Shatzmiller, "Paulus Christiani," 208–9, n. 9; and J. Cohen, "The Mentality of the Medieval Jewish Apostate," 37.

59. See Chapter 5.

60. See Chapter 3.

61. Rashba, sec. 5, #240; Meyerson, *Jews*, 81, n. 61; Assis, *The Golden Age*, 57; ADB, RC 3, fols. 91v–92r, published in Tartakoff, "Jewish Women and Apostasy," 20 (#3). Baucells i Reig reads "Tripoli" as "Reipoll" (*Vivir en la edad media*, 2:1729).

62. Malkiel, "Jews and Apostates," 21–22 and n. 61.

63. Vincke, 95–96 (#65).

64. Simonsohn, *Documents*, 52 (#50).

65. Canon 26, full text in Tanner, *Decrees of the Ecumenical Councils*, 224.

66. Grayzel, *The Church and the Jews*, 1:94–99 (#6, 8).

67. Baron, *A Social and Religious History*, 9:21.

68. See, for example, ADG, Lletres Episcopals 22, fol. 149r–v; and ADG, Llicències Episcopals 1, fol. 105r.

69. On reversion to Judaism and its impact on Christian perceptions of converts and Jews in early modern Germany, see Carlebach, *Divided Souls*, 42–45.

70. See Grayzel, *The Church and the Jews*, 1:100–101 (#11); and *X* 4.19.9 in *Corpus iuris Canonici*, 2:724–25.

TWO CONVERTS, REPENTANT

1. ACB, C126, fols. 45v, 69r.

2. ACB, C126, fols. 40v, 41v. See Chapters 4 and 5.

3. *Directorium inquisitorum*, 295.

4. ACB, C126, fols. 2r, 25r, 40v–41r, 44r, 47v.

5. ACB, C126, fols. 40v–41r.

6. ACB, C126, fols. 41v, 47v.

THE INTERVENTION

1. For an overview of the scholarly controversy concerning the reliability of inquisitorial records for the reconstruction of Jewish history, see Renée Levine Melammed, *A Question of Identity: Iberian Conversos in Historical Perspective* (Oxford, 2004), 28–29.

2. ACB, C126, fols. 41v–42r.

3. ACB, C126, fols. 44r–v, 48r, 49r–v.

4. ACB, C126, fols. 44v, 48r, 49v.

5. ACB, C126, fols. 42r–v, 44v–45r, 48r, 49v.

6. ACB, C126, fols. 49v–50r.

7. ACB, C126, fols. 50r–51r. This attestation of the *Toledot Yeshu* was first brought to light by Riccardo Di Segni in "Due nuovi fonti sulle Toledoth Jeshu," *La Rassegna Mensile di Israel* 55 (1990): 127–32. Also see Yaacov Deutsch, "*Toledot Yeshu* in Christian Eyes," M.A. thesis, Hebrew University of Jerusalem, 1997; and Paola Tartakoff, "The *Toledot Yeshu* and the Jewish-Christian Conflict in the Medieval Crown of Aragon," in *Toledot Yeshu ("The Life Story of Jesus") Revisited*, ed. Peter Schaefer et al. (Berlin, 2011), 297–309. Samuel Krauss, *Das Leben Jesu nach jüdischen Quellen* (Berlin, 1902), remains the most comprehensive work on the *Toledot Yeshu*.

8. ACB, C126, fols. 11r, 42r–v, 48r, 50r.

9. ACB, C126, fols. 8r, 45r.

10. ACB, C126, fols. 50r, 57v.

11. ACB, C126, fols. 8r–v, 45r, 48v. This scenario bears some resemblance to an accusation leveled against a Jew named Isaach Vidal in about 1376. Isaach was said to have called the Virgin Mary a whore in the town square of Peratallada before the *justicia* Bernat de Belloc. Moreover, the *justicia* apparently professed to be unable to punish Isaach out of fear of Isaach's powerful friend, Engalabert (Régné, "Rapports," 231–32).

12. Salomon Navarro's testimony contains a description of an analogous moment during the alleged re-Judaization of Abadia. Salomon recounted how Jews "encouraged [Abadia] to endure the torments and to persevere" (ACB, C126, fol. 46v).

13. ACB, C126, fols. 42v, 44v–45r, 48r–v, 51r.

CHAPTER 5. APOSTASY AS SCOURGE

1. Rashba, sec. 1, #194.

2. ACB, C126, fol. 50r.

3. See Hasdai Crescas, *The Refutation of Christian Principles*, ed. and trans. Daniel J. Lasker (Albany, N.Y., 1992), 37–58.

4. See Maimonides, *Commentary on the Mishnah, Avodah zarah* 1:3; *Mishneh Torah, Hilkhot avodat kohavim* 9:4. On the exceptional perspective of the Provençal scholar Rabbi Menahem ha-Meiri (d. c. 1315), see Jacob Katz, *Exclusiveness and Tolerance: Studies in Jewish-Gentile Relations in Medieval and Modern Times* (West Orange, N.J., 1961), 114–28.

5. See, for example, Rashba, sec. 5, #66; and Ritva, *Sheelot u-teshuvot*, #159.

6. Limor, *Die Disputationen*, 298–90.

7. See Yerushalmi, "The Inquisition and the Jews," 359.

8. Sanhedrin 74a.

9. See David Berger, "On the Image and Destiny of Gentiles in Ashkenazic Polemical Literature" (in Hebrew), in *Facing the Cross: The Persecutions of 1096 in History and Historiography*, ed. Yom Tov Assis et al. (Jerusalem, 2000), 74–91.

10. These deeds are recorded in three Hebrew chronicles edited by Abraham Meir Haberman in *Sefer gezerot Ashkenaz ve-Zarfat* (Jerusalem, 1945). See discussion in Jeremy Cohen, *Sanctifying the Name of God: Jewish Martyrs and Jewish Memories of the First Crusade* (Philadelphia, 2004).

11. Jean de Venette, *The Chronicle of Jean de Venette*, ed. and trans. Richard A. Newhall, Records of Civilization 50 (New York, 1953), 71–72.

12. Quoted in Miriam Bodian, *Dying in the Law of Moses: Crypto-Jewish Martyrdom in the Iberian World* (Bloomington, Ind., 2007), 8. For an overview of scholarship on Jewish martyrdom in medieval Sepharad, see ibid., 4–5, and notes.

13. *Even bohan/La piedra de toque*, 5.

14. On the view that apostates were still Jews, see Chapter 6.

15. Maimonides, *Commentary on the Mishnah, Avodah zarah*, 2:4; Ryan Szpiech, "'Is He Still Israel?' Abner of Burgos on Conversion and Identity in Medieval Castile," paper delivered at the Tauber Institute for the Study of European Jewry at Brandeis University (November 12, 2009), 29, nn. 70, 71.

16. See Carlebach, *Divided Souls*, 12; Solomon Zeitlin, "*Mumar* and *Meshumad*," *Jewish Quarterly Review* 54 (1963): 84–86; and the other sources listed in Malkiel, "Jews and Apostates," 10, n. 16.

17. See discussion in Nina Caputo, *Nahmanides in Medieval Catalonia: History, Community, and Messianism* (Notre Dame, Ind., 2007), 116–17. This perspective is analogous to one that Christians expressed at the Fourth Lateran Council (1215) with regard to Christians who went over to Judaism. Canon 70 stated that "it [wa]s a lesser evil not to know the way of the Lord than to retrace one's steps after it [wa]s known" (published in Tanner, *Decrees of the Ecumenical Councils*, 267).

18. Shatzmiller, "Jewish Converts," 302.

19. Rashba, sec. 1, #763. On this custom in Ashkenaz, see Katz, *Exclusiveness and Tolerance*, 73–74.

20. See discussion and translation in Yerushalmi, "The Inquisition and the Jews," 457.

21. Régné, *History*, 472 (#2529); Meyerson, *Jews*, 81, n. 61.

22. See Assis, *The Golden Age*, 57.

23. This license is published in Riera i Sans, "Les llicències," 132–34 (#2).

24. On Jewish apostates as Christian preachers, see Chapter 4. As Jews mocked Jewish apostates, so, too, did Muslims mock Muslim apostates. In 1281, King Pere II addressed Jews and Muslims together when he warned: "Whatever Jew or Muslim dares to loosen his tongue against the most wholesome faith of the Christians or strike out against a Christian convert in opprobrium of the said faith should be judged for this . . . and punished accordingly" (Catlos, *The Victors and the Vanquished*, 253).

25. *Las siete partidas*, 672–73 (7.24.6), in Dwayne E. Carpenter, *Alfonso X and the Jews: An Edition and Commentary on Siete partidas 7.24 "De los judíos,"* Modern Philology 115 (Berkeley, Calif., 1986), 33–34.

26. Kohn, *Les juifs de la France du nord*, 187.

27. Rashba, sec. 7, #292. In late eleventh-century German lands, Christian charters for Jewish communities specifically prohibited converts from inheriting their parents' estates. In 1249 in England, Josse son of Sampson, the father of a young woman apostate, tried to take back the thirty marks he had given his daughter as a dowry. See Baron, *A Social and Religious History*, 9:20–22; Grayzel, *The Church and the Jews*, 1:18–20; Simonsohn, *History*, 248; Katz, *Exclusiveness and Tolerance*, 72–73; Friedrich Lotter, "Imperial versus Ecclesiastical Jewry Law in the High Middle Ages: Contradictions and Controversies Concerning the Conversion of Jews and Their Serfs," in *Proceedings of the Tenth World Congress of Jewish Studies*, ed. David Assaf (Jerusalem, 1990), 59–60; Lotter, "The Scope and Effectiveness of Imperial Jewry Law in the High Middle Ages," *Jewish History* 4 (1989): 40–41; and Stacey, "The Conversion of Jews," 271.

28. Régné, *History*, 540 (#2919).

29. ACA, Canc., Reg. 824, fol. 189v; Reg. 832, fol. 86r–v. See discussion in Guerson, "Seeking Remission," 40, 42.

30. See Grayzel, *The Church and the Jews*, 1:254–6 (#105); *Cortes*, 1:217–18; ACA, Canc., Reg. 833, fol. 80r–v; and discussion in Guerson, "Seeking Remission," 42.

31. Baer, *Urkunden*, 1:207–8 (#168) (=Régné, *History*, 548 [#2966]); ACA, Canc., Reg. 714, fol. 84r–v, cited in Riera i Sans, "Les llicències," 124.

32. Stacey, "The Conversion of Jews," 280.

33. *Las Siete Partidas*, 672–73 (7.24.6), in Carpenter, *Alfonso X and the Jews*, 33–34.

34. Colorni, *Judaica minora*, 182–83 (#2).

35. On Jewish *malshinim* in the Crown of Aragon, see Assis, *The Golden Age*, 155–56; Elena Lourie, "Mafiosi and Malsines: Violence, Fear and Faction in the Jewish Aljamas of Valencia in the Fourteenth Century," in *Actas del IV congreso internacional "Encuentro de las tres culturas,"* ed. C. Carrete Parrondo (Toledo, 1988), 69–102; and Franciso Bofarull y Sans, "Los judíos malsines," *Boletín de la Real Academia de Buenas Letras de Barcelona* 6 (1911): 207–16.

36. ACA, Canc., 428, fols. 12v–13r.

37. Simonsohn, *Documents*, 485–86 (#457).

38. ADB, RC 3, fols. 91v–92r, published in Tartakoff, "Jewish Women and Apostasy," 20 (#3).

39. Perarnau i Espelt, "El procés inquisitorial barceloní," 323–24, n. 23. On the Jewish badge, see Baucells i Reig, *Vivir en la edad media*, 2:1714; and Meyerson, *Jews*, 84–85.

40. Régné, "Rapports," 229, 231.

41. ADB, RC 6, fol. 172r.

42. Sarret i Arbós, *Jueus a Manresa*, 48–50. The values of the dowries of Christian brides in late thirteenth-century Perpignan ranged from 125 to 17,500 Barcelona sous (Rebecca Winer, *Women, Wealth, and Community in Perpignan c. 1250–1300: Christians, Jews, and Enslaved Muslims in a Medieval Mediterranean Town* [Burlington, Vt., 2006], 25).

43. Rashba, sec. 1, #1162. See Katz, *Exclusiveness and Tolerance*, 70.

44. On the situation in Ashkenaz, see Carlebach, *Divided Souls*, 25–26.

45. ADB, RC 3, fols. 91v–92r, published in Tartakoff, "Jewish Women and Apostasy," 20 (#3).

46. Chazan, *Barcelona and Beyond*, 24–27. The letter was published by Joseph Kobak in *Jeschurun* 6 (1868): Heb. sec., 1–31. The quoted passage corresponds to sec. 22. On this source, also see Kenneth Stow, "Jacob of Venice and the Jewish Settlement in Venice in the Thirteenth Century," in *Community and Culture: Essays in Jewish Studies in Honor of the Ninetieth Anniversary of Graetz College*, ed. Waldman (Philadelphia, 1987), 221–32; also printed in Kenneth R. Stow, *Popes, Church, and Jews in the Middle Ages: Confrontation and Response* (Burlington, Vt., 2007); and Robert Chazan, "The Letter of R. Jacob ben Elijah to Friar Paul," *Jewish History* 6 (1992): 51–63.

47. Grayzel, *The Church and the Jews*, 1:180–82 (#59); X 3.33.2, in *Corpus iuris canonici*, 2:723. Also see Simonsohn, *History*, 253–54; and Baumgarten, *Mothers and Children*, 160–61.

48. ADB, RC 9, fols. 189v–190r, published in Josep Perarnau i Espelt, "Documents de tema inquisitorial del bisbe de Barcelona, fra Ferrer d'Abella (1334–1344)," *RCT* 5 (1980): 467–68 (#9). On the baptism of Jewish children in medieval Europe, see Simonsohn, *History*, 253–57.

49. See the discussion in Meyerson, *Jews*, 81.

50. Limor, *Die Disputationen*, 288.

51. Riera i Sans, "Les llicències," 122; Shatzmiller, "Jewish Converts," 302.

52. Kohn, *Les juifs de la France du nord*, 253–61.

53. ACB, C126, fol. 57r.

54. ACB, C126, fol. 48v.

CHAPTER 6. RECRUITING REPENTANCE

1. Ritva, *Sheelot u-teshuvot*, #159. The term *mitzvah* refers here to a moral deed performed as a religious duty.

2. See Rashba, *Sheelot u-teshuvot*, sec. 1, #242; Katz, *Exclusiveness and Tolerance*, 71–72; the sources cited in Malkiel, "Jews and Apostates," 26, n. 77; Pérez i Pons, *Fonts per a l'estudi de la comunitat jueva de Mallorca*, 79–80 (#265); AEV, ACF, Manuales Anónims 10, fol. 207v.

3. Baer, *Urkunden*, 1:207–8 (#168) (=Régné, *History*, 548 [#2966]). See also Shatzmiller, "Converts and Judaizers," 69.

4. See Chapter 5.

5. *Practica inquisitionis*, 288.

6. Shatzmiller, *Recherches*, 58–60; Baer, *Urkunden*, 1:201–3 (#164); Régné, *History*, 540 (#2919); Baer, *A History of the Jews*, 2:10; Régné, "Rapports," 229.

7. See Chapter 1 and "Two Converts, Repentant."

8. Yerushalmi, "The Inquisition and the Jews," 321–22.

9. In a query addressed to Rabbi Yedidyah ben Samuel of Nuremberg in early fourteenth-century Germany, a Jew articulated the view that apostates tainted their relatives. He wrote: "the world considers [apostates] to be awful, and they do not marry them or their relatives, [even] more so than other sinners" (quoted in Fram, "Perception and Reception," 316).

10. See Katz, *Exclusiveness and Tolerance*, 69–73; and Katz, "Although He Has Sinned, He Remains a Jew" (in Hebrew), *Tarbiz* 27 (1958): 203–17.

11. See Chapter 5.

12. See Ephraim Kanarfogel, "Changing Attitudes toward Apostates in Tosafist Literature of the Late Twelfth and Early Thirteenth Centuries," in *New Perspectives on Jewish-Christian Relations: Studies in Honor of David Berger*, ed. Elisheva Carlebach (forthcoming); and Kanarfogel, "Between Ashkenaz and Sepharad: Tosafist Teachings in the Talmudic Commentaries of Ritva," in *Between Rashi and Maimonides: Themes in Medieval Jewish Thought, Literature, and Exegesis*, ed. Ephraim Kanarfogel and Moshe Sokolow (New York, 2010), 266–70.

13. Rashba, *Sheelot u-teshuvot*, sec. 7, #41. On the extensive influence of medieval Ashkenazi scholarship on Sephardic scholarship, see Avraham Grossman, "Relations between Spanish and Ashkenazi Jewry in the Middle Ages," in *The Sephardi Legacy*, ed. Haim Beinart (Jerusalem, 1992), 1:220–39.

14. On efforts to return to Judaism incognito, see Chapter 4.

15. Régné, *History*, 613–14 (#3353); ACB, C126, fols. 6r, 22r.

16. Régné, *History*, 277 (#1519); ACA, Canc., CR, Jaume II, caixa 86, no. 7.

17. ACB, C126, fols. 1r, 10v–11v, 44v, 50r, 68r, 83r; Régné, *History*, 225–26 (#1248). For more details on the exploits of the Abenafias (or Abinafias), see Meyerson, *Jews*, 13, 30, 33, 69, 77.

18. See ACB, C126, fol. 83r; Baer, *Urkunden*, 1:244 (#184); and Régné, *History*, 621 (#3399).

19. See ACB, C126, fol. 68r; and Régné, *History*, 277 (#1519).

20. Fram, "Perception and Reception," 306; J. Cohen, *The Friars and the Jews*, 86; Gui, *Practica inquisitionis*, 290; Kohn, *Les juifs de la France du nord*, 254; Baer, *A History of the Jews*, 2:385.

21. Shatzmiller, *Recherches*, 59.

22. See George Howard, "A Primitive Hebrew Gospel of Matthew and the Tol'doth Yeshu," *New Testament Studies* 34 (1988): 60–70; and Di Segni, "Due nuovi fonti," 129.

23. Viera, "The Evolution," 152, 157; AEV, MS 172, fol. 34r.

24. See Eleazar Gutwirth, "Gender, History, and the Judeo-Christian Polemic," in *Contra Iudaeos: Ancient and Medieval Polemics between Christians and Jews*, ed. Ora Limor et al. (Tübingen, 1996), 272.

25. AEV, MS 172, fol. 34r.

26. Pier Cesare Ioly-Zorattini, ed., *Processi del S. Uffizio di Venezia contro ebrei e giuda-izzanti (1548–1560)*, Storia dell'Ebraismo in Italia, Studi e testi II, Sezione Veneta I (Florence, 1980), 95–100.

27. See Di Segni, "Due nuovi fonti," 129–30.

28. ACB, C126, fols. 8v, 10r–v, 27r.

29. ACB, C126, fol. 48r.

30. See Berger, "On the Image and Destiny of Gentiles," 74–91.

31. See Yerushalmi, "The Inquisition and the Jews," 359.

32. Quoted in Yuval, *Two Nations*, 111.

33. Gui, *Le livre des sentences*, 2:1038; Fournier, *Le registre d'inquisition*, 1:183–84.

34. Bodian, *Dying in the Law of Moses*, 15. For additional examples, see Encarnación Marín Padilla, *Relación judeoconversa durante la segunda mitad del siglo XV en Aragón: La ley* (Zaragoza, 1986), 89; and Ioly-Zorattini, *Processi del S. Uffizio di Venezia*, 95–100.

35. Limor, *Die Disputationen*, 287–88; ACB, C126, fol. 88r–v.

36. ACB, C126, fols. 44v, 48r, 49v.

37. *Sefer ha-rokeah ha-gadol* (Jerusalem, 1960), 31 (#24).

38. Rashba, sec. 7, #411; Yom Tov ben Avraham Ishbili (Ritva), *Sefer hiddushei ha-Ritva* (on *Yevamot*) (New York, 1960), 29a, trans. Shatzmiller, "Converts and Judaizers," 66.

39. From the late twelfth century, this rite gained the acceptance of some rabbinic authorities in northern France and Germany. In the Crown of Aragon, Ritva acknowledged that, although apostates were not required to immerse "according to the letter of the law," there did exist a rabbinic requirement to do so. See Shatzmiller, "Converts and Judaizers," 66; and Ephraim Kanarfogel, "Returning to the Jewish Community in Medieval Ashkenaz: History and *Halakha*," in *Turim: Studies in Jewish History and Literature; Presented to Dr. Bernard Lander*, ed. Michael Shmidman (New York, 2007), esp. 1:72–73.

40. Gui, *Le livre des sentences*, 2:1038; Gui, *Practica inquisitionis*, 288–89; Nicolau Eimeric, *Directorium inquisitorum*, 243; Felip Ribot, "*Tractatus*," 184; Rashba, sec. 7, #411; Yom Tov ben Avraham Ishbili (Ritva), *Sefer hiddushei ha-Ritva* (on *Yevamot*) (New York, 1960), 29a.

41. *Practica inquisitionis*, 288–89; *Directorium inquisitorum*, 243; Yerushalmi, "The Inquisition and the Jews," 363–64.

42. Kanarfogel, "Returning to the Jewish Community," 86.

43. See ibid., 96 and n. 58.

44. Fournier, *Le registre d'inquisition*, 1:178.

45. See Kanarfogel, "Returning to the Jewish Community," 81, 96.

46. Esther Cohen, *The Crossroads of Justice: Law and Culture in Late Medieval France* (Leiden, 1993), 184.

47. ACB, C126, fols. 8v, 11r, 12r, 14r, 45r, 46v, 48v, 50r, 71v.

48. Jonah ben Avraham Gerondi, *Shaarei teshuvah*, ed. and trans. Shraga Silverstein (Jerusalem, 1971), 49. I am grateful to Bernard Septimus for helping me locate this source.

49. See Ivan G. Marcus, "A Pious Community and Doubt: *Qiddush ha-Shem* in Ashkenaz and the Story of Rabbi Amnon of Mainz," in *Studien zur judischen Geschichte und Soziologie: Festschrift Julius Carlebach* (Heidelberg, 1992), 111–13; and Ivan G. Marcus, "Jews and Christians Imagining the Other in Medieval Europe," *Prooftexts* 15 (1995): 215–16. I am grateful to David Berger for bringing this story to my attention.

50. See Chapter 3.

51. Gui, *Practica inquisitionis*, 289, 290.

52. ACB, C126, fol. 46v.

53. Quoted in Fram, "Perception and Reception," 306.

54. J. Cohen, *Sanctifying the Name of God*, 91–94.

55. Yerushalmi, "The Inquisition and the Jews," 322.

56. ACB, C126, fol. 46v.

57. On the history of connections between Jewish and Christian martyrdom, see Daniel Boyarin, *Dying for God: Martyrdom and the Making of Christianity and Judaism* (Stanford, Calif., 1999), 93–126; and Bodian, *Dying in the Law of Moses*, 6.

58. ACB, C126, fol. 39r–v.

59. Assis, *The Golden Age*, 208; Baer, *A History of the Jews*, 1:168; Régné, *History*, 259 (#736).

60. See Régné, *History*, 608 (#3314); Finke, 2:861–62 (#542); and Assis, *The Golden Age*, 56, n. 29.

61. See ACB, C126, fols. 81v, 92r; Jacobs, 50 (#873) (=Régné, *History*, 624–25 [#3419]); Régné, *History*, 619 (#3389), 620 (#3396); and Assis, *The Golden Age*, 58, 61–62.

62. ACB, C126, fol. 53r.

63. Vincke, 75 (#31); ACB, C126, fols. 53r, 82r; Lea, *A History of the Inquisition in the Middle Ages*, 1:481; Assis, *The Golden Age*, 58, 61–62.

THE ROAD TO THE STAKE

1. ACB, C126, fols. 42v–43r.

2. ACB, C126, fols. 45r–v, 47v, 49r, 51r.

3. ACB, C126, fol. 45v.

4. ACB, C126, fol. 43r.

5. ACB, C126, fol. 43r.

6. ACB, C126, fols. 38v–39r.

CONCLUSION

1. On the massacres and forced conversions of 1391, see Emilio Mitre Fernández, *Los judíos de Castilla en tiempo de Enrique III: El pogrom de 1391* (Valladolid, 1994); Jaume Riera i Sans, "Els avalots del 1391 a Girona," in *Jornades d'història dels jueus a Catalunya* (Girona, 1987), 95–159; Jaume Riera i Sans, "Estrangers participants als avalots contra les jueries de la Corona d'Aragó en 1391," *Anuario de Estudios Medievales* 10 (1980): 577–83; Jaume Riera i Sans, "Los tumultos contra las juderías de la Corona de Aragón en 1391," *Cuadernos de Historia: Anejos de la Revista Hispania* 8 (1977): 213–25; Philippe Wolff, "The 1391 Pogrom in Spain: Social Crisis or Not?" *Past and Present* 50 (1971): 4–18; and Haim Beinart, "The Great Conversion: The Problem of the *Anusim* and Their Fate in the Fifteenth Century" (in Hebrew), in *The Heritage of Spain*, ed. Haim Beinart (Jerusalem, 1992), 280–308.

2. See Melammed, *A Question of Identity*, 42–45.

3. On Morvedre, see Mark D. Meyerson, *A Jewish Renaissance in Fifteenth-Century Spain* (Princeton, N.J., 2004), 200–224. On the circumcision of converts, see Encarnación Marín Padilla, "Relación judeoconversa durante la segunda mitad del siglo XV en Aragón: Nacimientos, hadas, circuncisiones," *Sefarad* 41 (1981): 287–300; and Hernando i Delgado, "El procés contra el convers Nicolau Sanxo." For an overview of scholarship on relations between Jews and converts in fifteenth-century Spain, see Melammed, *A Question of Identity*, 34–42.

4. Nirenberg, "Mass Conversion and Genealogical Mentalities," 20–21.

5. Benzion Netanyahu, *The Marranos of Spain, from the Late 14th to the Early 16th Century, According to Contemporary Hebrew Sources* (Ithaca, N.Y., 1999), 55–57.

6. Shaul Regev, "The Attitude Towards the *Conversos* in 15th- to 16th-Century Jewish Thought," *REJ* 156 (1997): 122–28.

7. See Melammed, *A Question of Identity*, 36; and Netanyahu, *The Marranos of Spain*, 75–76.

8. See Albert A. Sicroff, *Los estatutos de limpieza de sangre: Controversias entre los siglos XV y XVII* (Madrid, 1979).

9. On these statistics, see Melammed, *A Question of Identity*, 23; and Gitlitz, *Secrecy and Deceit: The Religion of the Crypto-Jews* (Albuquerque, N.M., 1996), 73–76.

10. Trans. Edward Peters in Olivia Remie Constable, ed., *Medieval Iberia: Readings from Christian, Muslim, and Jewish Sources* (Philadelphia, 1997), 353–54. For an overview of the factors that propelled the expulsion of the Jews from Spain, see Melammed, *A Question of Identity*, 33–50.

11. ACB, C126, fols. 93v–94r.

Glossary

adelantado (Castilian). An executive official in a Jewish community

agunah (pl. *agunot*) (Hebrew). A Jewish woman whose husband refuses, or is unable, to give her a bill of divorce; literally "chained one"

alatma (Arabic). A lesser form of Jewish excommunication than *herem*

aljama (Arabic). A legally constituted Jewish or Muslim community

avodah zarah (Hebrew). Idolatry

baal teshuvah (Hebrew). Returnee or repentant one

bimah (Hebrew). The elevated platform in a synagogue where a person stands when reading aloud from the Torah

call (Latin or Hebrew). A Jewish quarter

cavaller (Catalan). A knight

converso (Castilian). A Jewish convert to Christianity, especially after 1391

Fueros/Furs (Castilian/Catalan). The law code of the kingdom of Valencia

get (Hebrew). A Jewish bill of divorce

herem (Hebrew). Jewish excommunication

justicia (Castilian). A magistrate in charge of administering justice

ketubah (Hebrew). A Jewish marriage deed detailing the groom's legal and financial obligations as well as the bride's dowry

malshin (pl. *malshinim*) (Hebrew). A Jewish informer

matzah (Hebrew). Unleavened bread that Jews eat during Passover

meshumad (Hebrew). Jewish apostate

mikveh (Hebrew). Bath used for Jewish ritual immersion

mitzvah (pl. *mitzvot*) (Hebrew). A divine commandment or a moral deed performed as a religious duty

morería (Castilian). A Muslim neighborhood

nidui (Hebrew). A lesser form of Jewish excommunication than *herem*

responsum (pl. *responsa*) (Latin). The written answer of a Jewish scholar to a legal question

Shekhinah (Hebrew). The divine presence; literally "dwelling" or "settling"

Shem ha-meforash (Hebrew). The ineffable name of God, the Tetragrammaton

shohet (Hebrew). A Jewish ritual slaughterer
tafureria (Castilian). A gambling house
tevilah (Hebrew). Full body immersion in a *mikveh*
teshuvah (Hebrew). Return or repentance

Bibliography

MANUSCRIPT SOURCES FROM SPAIN

Barcelona, Arxiu de la Catedral de Barcelona, Biblioteca, Còdex 126
Barcelona, Arxiu de la Catedral de Barcelona, Notaria Particular, Bernat Vilarrúbia, Manual
Barcelona, Arxiu de la Corona d'Aragó, Cancellería Reial, Cartes Reials
Barcelona, Arxiu de la Corona d'Aragó, Cancellería Reial, Registres
Barcelona, Arxiu de la Corona d'Aragó, Reial Patrimoni, Llibres de Tesorería
Barcelona, Arxiu Diocesà de Barcelona, Processos
Barcelona, Arxiu Diocesà de Barcelona, Registra Communium
Barcelona, Arxiu Diocesà de Barcelona, Registra Gratiarum
Barcelona, Arxiu Diocesà de Barcelona, Visites Pastorals
Barcelona, Biblioteca de la Universitat de Barcelona, MS 1005–7 [*Lumen domus*]
Girona, Arxiu Diocesà de Girona, Registres de Lletres Episcopals
Girona, Arxiu Diocesà de Girona, Registres de Llicències Episcopals
Valencia, Arxiu del Regne de Valencia, Bailía General, Libros de Privilegios
Vic, Arxiu Episcopal de Vic, Libri Iudeorum
Vic, Arxiu Episcopal de Vic, Manuals Anónims
Vic, Arxiu Episcopal de Vic, Manuscrits, MS 172 [*Vita Christi de Francesc Eiximenis*]
Vic, Arxiu Episcopal de Vic, Processos Civils
Vic, Arxiu Episcopal de Vic, Visites Pastorals
Zaragoza, Archivo Diocesano de Zaragoza, Actos Communes

PRINTED PRIMARY SOURCES

Arnau de Vilanova. *Informació espiritual.* In *Obres catalanes,* edited by Miquel Batllori. Barcelona, 1947.
Baer, Yitzhak (Fritz), ed. *Die Juden im christlichen Spanien.* 2 vols. Berlin, 1936. Reprint, London, 1970.
Bernard Gui. *Le livre des sentences de l'inquisiteur Bernard Gui 1308–1323.* Edited and translated by Annette Pales-Gobillard. Paris, 2002.
———. *Practica inquisitionis heretice pravitatis.* Edited by Célestin Douais. Paris, 1886.
Bernat de Puigcercós. *Quaestio disputata de licitudine contractus emptionis et venditionis*

censualis cum conditione revenditionis. Edited by Josep Hernando i Delgado. In *Acta Historica et Archaeologica Mediaevalia* 10 (1989): 9–98.

Cantigas de Santa María. Edited by Walter Mettmann. Madrid, 1986–88.

Chazan, Robert. *Church, State and Jew in the Middle Ages.* New York, 1980.

Continuationis chronici Guillelmi de Nangiaco. Edited by Hercule Geraud. Publications de la Société de l'Histoire de France 43. Paris, 1843.

Corpus iuris canonici. Edited by Emil Friedberg. 2 vols. Leipzig, 1881.

Cortes de los antiguos reinos de Aragón y de Valencia y principado de Cataluña. Madrid, 1896–1903.

Elazar ben Yehudah. *Sefer ha-rokeah ha-gadol.* Jerusalem, 1960.

Escribà, Gemma, ed. *The Tortosa Disputation: A Regesta of Documents from the Archivo de la Corona de Aragón.* Jerusalem, 1998.

Felip Ribot. *"Tractatus de haeresi et de infidelium incredulitate et de horum criminum iudice."* Edited by Jaume de Puig i Oliver. *Arxiu de Textos Catalans Antics* 1 (1982): 127–90.

Finke, Heinrich, ed. *Acta Aragonensia: Quellen zur deutschen, italienischen, französischen, spanischen, zur Kirchen- und Kulturgeschichte aus der diplomatischen Korrespondenz Jaymes II (1291–1327).* 3 vols. Berlin, 1908–22.

Francesc Eiximenis. *Dotzè llibre del crestià.* Vol. 1. Edited by Xavier Renedo. Girona, 2005.

———. *El tractat d'usura de Francesc Eiximenis.* Edited by Josep Hernando i Delgado. Barcelona, 1985.

Francisco Diago. *Historia de la provincia de Aragon de la Orden de Predicadores.* Barcelona, 1599. Reprint, Valencia, 1999.

Fuero juzgo en latín y castellano cotejado con los más antiguos y preciosos codices. Madrid, 1815.

González Hurtebise, Eduardo, ed. *Libros de tesorería de la Casa Real de Aragón.* Barcelona, 1911.

Hasdai Crescas. *The Refutation of Christian Principles.* Edited and translated by Daniel J. Lasker. New York, 1992.

Huici Miranda, Ambrosio, ed. *Colección diplomática de Jaime I el Conquistador.* 3 vols. Valencia, 1916–1922.

———. *Documentos de Jaime I de Aragón.* 5 vols. Valencia, 1923.

Ioly-Zorattini, Pier Cesare, ed. *Processi del S. Uffizio di Venezia contro ebrei e giudaizzanti (1548–1560).* Storia dell'ebraismo in Italia. Studi e testi II, Sezione Veneta I. Florence, 1980.

Internet Medieval Source Book. http://www.fordham.edu/halsall/sbook1.asp. Last accessed on October 16, 2011.

Jacobs, Joseph, ed. *Inquiry into the Sources of the History of the Jews of Spain.* London, 1894.

Jacques Fournier. *Le registre d'inquisition de Jacques Fournier, evêque de Pamiers [1318–1325].* Edited by Jean Duvernoy. Bibliothèque Méridionale 41. Toulouse, 1965.

Jean de Venette. *The Chronicle of Jean de Venette.* Edited by Richard A. Newhall and translated by Jean Birdsall. Records of Civilization 50. New York, 1953.

Jonah ben Avraham Gerondi. *Shaarei teshuvah.* Edited and translated by Shraga Silverstein. Jerusalem, 1971.

Limor, Ora, ed. *Die Disputationen zu Ceuta (1179) und Mallorca (1286): Zwei antijüdische Schriften aus dem mittelalterlichen Genua.* Munich, 1994.

Linder, Amnon. *The Jews in Roman Imperial Legislation.* Detroit, 1987.

Moses ben Maimon (Maimonides). *Mishneh Torah.* Amsterdam, 1702.

Moses ben Nahman (Nahmanides). "The Disputation at Barcelona." In *Ramban: Writings and Discourses,* 2:656–96. Translated by Charles B. Chavel. 2 vols. New York, 1978.

Muntané Santiveri, Josep Xavier, ed. *Fonts per a l'estudi de l'aljama jueva de Tàrrega: Documents i regesta.* Catalonia Hebraica 8. Barcelona, 2006.

Nicolau Eimeric. *Abrégé du manuel des inquisiteurs.* Edited and translated by André Morellet. Grenoble, 1990.

———. *Directorium inquisitorum R. P. F. Nicolai Emerici, Ordinis Praedicatorum S. Theol. Mag. Inquisitoris haereticae pravitatis in Regnis Regis Aragonum . . . cum scholiis seu annotationibus eruditissimis D. Francisci Pegnae hispani, s. theologiae et iuris utriusque doctoris.* Rome, 1578.

———. "El *Tractatus brevis super iurisdictione inquisitorum contra infideles fidem catholicam agitantes* de Nicolau Eimeric." Edited by Josep Perarnau i Espelt. *Arxiu de Textos Catalans Antics* 1 (1982): 79–126.

Pérez i Pons, Eduard, ed. *Fonts per a l'estudi de la comunitat jueva de Mallorca.* Barcelona, 2005.

Pons i Pastor, Antonio, ed. *Los judíos del Reino de Mallorca durante los siglos XIII y XIV.* 2 vols. Mallorca, 1984.

Ramon Martí. *Pugio fidei adversus mauros et iudaeos.* Leipzig, 1687.

Ramon de Penyafort, O.P. *Summa de iure canonico; summa de paenitentia; summa de matrimonio.* Edited by Javier Ochoa and Luis Diez García. 3 vols. Universa Bibliotheca Iuris 1. Rome, 1975–1978.

Régné, Jean, comp. *History of the Jews in Aragon, Regesta and Documents 1213–1327.* Edited by Yom Tov Assis. Jerusalem, 1978.

Remie Constable, Olivia, ed. *Medieval Iberia: Readings from Christian, Muslim, and Jewish Sources.* Philadelphia, 1997.

Roger of Hovenden. *The Annals, Comprising the History of England and of Other Countries of Europe from AD 732 to AD 1201.* Edited and translated by Henry T. Riley. 2 vols. London, 1853. Reprint, New York, 1968.

Rubió i Lluch, Antoni, ed. *Documents per l'història de la cultura catalana migeval.* Barcelona, 1921.

Sánchez Herrero, José, ed. *Concilios provinciales y sínodos toledanos de los siglos XIV y XV.* La Laguna (Tenerife), 1976.

Sefer gezerot Ashkenaz ve-Zarfat. Edited by Abraham Meir Haberman. Jerusalem, 1945.

Sefer hasidim. Edited by Reuven Margaliot. Jerusalem, 1956.

Shem Tov ben Isaac ibn Shaprut. *Even bohan/La piedra de toque: Una obra de controversia judeo-cristiana; Introducción, edición crítica, traducción y notas al libro I.* Edited and translated into Spanish by José-Vicente Niclós. Bibliotheca Hispana Bíblica 16. Madrid, 1997.

Shlomo ibn Verga. *Shevet Yehudah.* Edited by Yitzhak Baer. Jerusalem, 1947.

Las siete partidas del rey don Alfonso el Sabio. Edited by the Real Academia de la Historia. 3 vols. Madrid, 1807.

Simonsohn, Shlomo, ed. *The Apostolic See and the Jews: Documents; 492–1404.* 7 vols. Toronto, 1988.

Solomon ben Avraham ibn Aderet (Rashba). *Sheelot u-teshuvot (Responsa).* 7 vols. Bnei Brak, 1957–59.

Solomon ben Isaac (Rashi). *Sheelot u-teshuvot (Responsa).* Edited by Israel S. Elfenbein. New York, 1943.

Tanner, Norman, ed. *Decrees of the Ecumenical Councils.* Washington, D.C., 1990.

Tejada Ramiro, Juan, ed. *Colección de cánones y de todos los concilios de la Iglesia de España y de América (en latín y castellano) con notas e ilustraciones.* Madrid, 1859.

Usatges de Barcelona: El codi a mitjan segle XII; Establiment del text Llatí i edició de la versió catalana del manuscrit del segle XIII de l'Arxiu de la Corona d'Aragó de Barcelona. Edited by Joan Bastardas. Barcelona, 1984.

Yom Tov ben Avraham Ishbili (Ritva). *Sefer hiddushei ha-Ritva* (on *Yebamot*). New York, 1960.

———. *Sheelot u-teshuvot (Responsa).* Edited by Yoseph Kapah. Jerusalem, 1959.

Yosef ha-Cohen. *Emek ha-bachah.* Krakow, 1895.

SECONDARY SOURCES

Abulafia, David. "The Apostolic Imperative: Religious Conversion in Llull's *Blanquerna.*" In *Religion, Text, and Society in Medieval Spain and Northern Europe: Essays in Honor of J. N. Hillgarth,* edited by Thomas E. Burman et al., 105–21. Toronto, 2002.

———. "From Privilege to Persecution: Crown, Church and Synagogue in the City of Mallorca, 1229–1343." In *Church and City, 1000–1500: Essays in Honour of Christopher Brooke,* edited by David Abulafia et al., 111–28. Cambridge, 1992.

———. *A Mediterranean Emporium: The Catalan Kingdom of Mallorca.* Cambridge, 1994.

———. "'*Nam iudei servi regis sunt, et semper fisicos regio deputati,*' the Jews of the Municipal *Fuero* of Teruel (1176–7)." In *Jews, Muslims and Christians in and around the Crown of Aragon,* edited by Harvey J. Hames, 97–123. Leiden, 2004.

———. "The Servitude of Jews and Muslims in the Medieval Mediterranean: Origins and Diffusion." *Mélanges de l'École Française de Rome (moyen âge-temps modernes)* 112 (2000): 687–714.

Agus, Irving. *R. Meir of Rothenburg: His Life and His Works as Sources for the Religious, Legal, and Social History of the Jews of Germany in the Thirteenth Century.* Philadelphia, 1947.

Alós, Ramon de. "El cardenal de Aragón, fray Nicolás Rossell: Ensayo bio-bibliográfico." *Cuadernos de trabajo de la Escuela Española de Arqueología e Historia en Roma* 1 (1912): 15–60.

Altisent, Augustí. *L'almoina reial a la cort de Pere el Cerimoniós.* Poblet, 1969.

Ames, Christine Ellen Caldwell. "Does Inquisition Belong to Religious History?" *American Historical Review* 110 (2006): 11–37.

———. *Righteous Persecution: Inquisition, Dominicans, and Christianity in the Middle Ages.* Philadelphia, 2009.

Andreu, Concepción, María Pilar Latorre, and María Carmen Poloc. "Evolución del plano de la Almunia." *Ador* 2 (1996): 21–80.

Arco, Ricardo del. "La judería de Huesca: Noticias y documentos inéditos." *Boletín de la Real Academia de la Historia* 66 (1915): 321–54.

———. "Ordenanzas inéditas, dictadas por el concejo de Huesca (1284 a 1456)." *Revista de Archivos, Bibliotecas y Museos* 29 (1913): 427–52.

Arnold, John H. *Inquisition and Power: Catharism and the Confessing Subject in Medieval Languedoc.* Philadelphia, 2001.

Assis, Yom Tov. *The Golden Age of Aragonese Jewry: Community and Society in the Crown of Aragon, 1213–1327.* London, 1997.

———. "Jewish Diplomats in Muslim Lands in the Service of the Crown of Aragon" (in Hebrew). *Sefunot* 3 (1985): 11–34.

———. "Jewish Moneylenders in Medieval Santa Coloma de Queralt." In *Jews and Conversos: Studies in Society and the Inquisition, Proceedings of the Eighth World Congress of Jewish Studies Held at the Hebrew University of Jerusalem, August 16–21, 1981,* edited by Yosef Kaplan, 21–38. Jerusalem, 1985.

———. "Jewish Physicians and Medicine in Medieval Spain." In *Medicine and Medical Ethics in Medieval and Early Modern Spain: An Intercultural Approach,* edited by S. S. Kottek et al., 33–49. Jerusalem, 1996.

———. *The Jews of Santa Coloma de Queralt at the End of the Thirteenth Century.* Jerusalem, 1987.

———. "The Jews of Spain in Gentile Courts (XIIIth–XIVth Centuries)." In *Tarbut ve-Historia* (in Hebrew), edited by Y. Dan, 121–45. Jerusalem, 1989.

———. "Juifs de France réfugiés en Aragon (XIIe–XIVe siècles)." *Revue des Études Juives* 142 (1983): 285–322.

———. "The Papal Inquisition and Aragonese Jewry in the Early Fourteenth Century." *Medieval Studies* 49 (1987): 391–410.

Baer, Yitzhak (Fritz). *A History of the Jews in Christian Spain.* Translated by L. Schoffman et al. 2 vols. Philadelphia 1961.

Bardinet, Léon. "De la condition civile des juifs du Comtat Venaissin pendant le séjour des papes à Avignon (1309–1376)." *Revue Historique* 12 (1880): 1–60.

Baron, Salo W. *A Social and Religious History of the Jews.* 18 vols. New York, 1957.

Baucells Reig, Josep. *Vivir en la edad media: Barcelona y su entorno en los siglos XIII y XIV (1200–1344).* 4 vols. Barcelona, 2004–7.

Baumgarten, Elisheva. *Mothers and Children: Jewish Family Life in Medieval Europe.* Princeton, N.J., 2004.

Beinart, Haim. "The Great Conversion: The Problem of the *Anusim* and Their Fate in the Fifteenth Century" (in Hebrew). In *The Heritage of Spain,* edited by Haim Beinart, 280–308. Jerusalem, 1992.

Ben-Shalom, Ram. "*Kiddush ha-Shem* and Jewish Martyrdom in Aragon and Castile in 1391: Between Spain and Ashkenaz" (in Hebrew). *Tarbiz* 70 (2001): 227–82.

Berger, David. "Christians, Gentiles and the Talmud: A Fourteenth-Century Response to the Attack on Rabbinic Judaism." In *Religiongespräche im Mittelalter*, edited by Hg. Von B. Lewis et al., 115–30. Wiesbaden, 1992.

———. *The Jewish-Christian Debate in the High Middle Ages: A Critical Edition of the Nizzahon Vetus*. Northvale, N.J., 1996.

———. "Mission to the Jews and Jewish-Christian Contacts in the Polemical Literature of the High Middle Ages." *American Historical Review* 91 (1986): 576–91.

———. "On the Image and Destiny of Gentiles in Ashkenazic Polemical Literature" (in Hebrew). In *Facing the Cross: The Persecutions of 1096 in History and Historiography*, edited by Yom Tov Assis et al., 74–91. Jerusalem, 2000.

Bertran i Roigé, Prim. "L'Almoina pontifícia d'Avinyó: Els seus inicis (1316–1324) en temps de Joan XXII." *Acta Historica et Archaeologica Mediaevalia* 25 (2004): 291–315.

———. "Els jueus en els llibres de batlle i cort de Cervera (1354–1357)." *Ilerda* 44 (1983): 189–205.

Bisson, Thomas N. *The Medieval Crown of Aragon: A Short History*. Oxford, 1986.

Blasco, Asunción. "Alatzar Golluf, regente de la tesorería de la reina de Aragón y su entorno familiar (siglos XIII–XIV)." In *Cristianos y judíos en contacto en la edad media: Polémica, conversión, dinero, y convivencia*, edited by Flocel Sabaté and Claude Denjean, 481–580. Lleida, 2009.

———. "La inquisición y los judíos en Aragón en la segunda mitad del siglo XIV." In *Aragón en la edad media*. Estudios de economía y sociedad 7, 83–96. Zaragoza, 1987.

Blidstein, Gerald. "The Personal Status of Captured and Converted Women in Medieval Halakhah" (in Hebrew). *Shenaton ha-mishpat ha-Ivri* 3–4 (1976–77): 35–116.

Bodian, Miriam. "Death at the Stake as Seen in the Northern Sephardi Diaspora" (in Hebrew). *Pe'amim* 75 (1998): 47–62.

———. *Dying in the Law of Moses: Crypto-Jewish Martyrdom in the Iberian World*. Bloomington, Ind., 2007.

———. "In the Cross-Currents of the Reformation: Crypto-Jewish Martyrs of the Inquisition, 1570–1670." *Past and Present* 176 (2002): 66–104.

Bofarull y Sans, Francisco. *Los judíos en el territorio de Barcelona*. Barcelona, 1910.

———. "Los judíos malsines." *Boletín de la Real Academia de Buenas Letras de Barcelona* 6 (1911): 207–16.

Bohigas, Pere. "Prediccions i profecies en les obres de fra Francesc Eiximenis." In *Franciscalia: Homenatge de les lletres catalanes a sant Francesc amb motiu del setè centenary de son traspàs (1226), de la seva canonització (1228) i quart de l'autoctonia de l'Ordre Caputxí (1528)*, 94–115. Barcelona, 1928.

Bollweg, John August. "Sense of a Mission: Arnau de Vilanova on the Conversion of Muslims and Jews." In *Iberia and the Mediterranean World of the Middle Ages: Studies in Honor of Robert I. Burns, S.J.* Vol. 1, *Proceedings from Kalamazoo*, edited by Larry J. Simon, 50–71. Leiden, 1995.

Boswell, John. *The Royal Treasure: Muslim Communities under the Crown of Aragon in the Fourteenth Century.* New Haven, Conn., 1977.

Boyarin, Daniel. *Border Lines: The Partition of Judaeo-Christianity.* Philadelphia, 2004.

———. *Dying for God: Martyrdom and the Making of Christianity and Judaism.* Stanford, Calif., 1999.

Brann, Ross. *The Experience of Judaism under the Orbit of Medieval Islam.* New York, 1985.

Brodman, James William. *Ransoming Captives in Crusader Spain: The Order of Merced on the Christian-Islamic Frontier.* Philadelphia, 1986.

Bronisch, Alexander Pierre. *Die Judengesetzgebung im katholischen Westgotenreich von Toledo.* Hannover, 2005.

Browe, Peter. *Die Judenmission in Mittelalter und die Päpste.* Rome, 1942.

Brundage, James A. "Intermarriage between Christians and Jews in Medieval Canon Law." *Jewish History* 3 (1988): 25–40.

———. *Law, Sex, and Christian Society in Medieval Europe.* Chicago, 1987.

Bulliet, Richard. *Conversion to Islam in the Medieval Period: An Essay in Quantitative History.* Cambridge, 1979.

———. "Conversion Stories in Early Islam." In *Conversion and Continuity: Indigenous Christian Communities in Islamic Lands, Eighth to Eighteenth Centuries,* edited by Michael Gervers et al., 123–33. Toronto, 1990.

Burns, Robert Ignatius. "Christian-Islamic Confrontation in the West: The Thirteenth-Century Dream of Conversion." *American Historical Review* 76 (1971): 1386–1434.

———. *Diplomatarium of the Crusader Kingdom of Valencia: The Registered Charters of Its Conqueror Jaume I, 1257–1276.* Princeton, N.J., 1985.

———. *Jews in the Notarial Culture: Latinate Wills in Mediterranean Spain, 1250–1350.* Berkeley, Calif., 1996.

———. "Journey from Islam: Incipient Cultural Transition in the Conquered Kingdom of Valencia (1240–1280)." *Speculum* 35 (1960): 337–56.

———. *Muslims, Christians, and Jews in the Crusader Kingdom of Valencia.* Cambridge, 1984.

———. *Society and Documentation in Crusader Valencia.* Princeton, N.J., 1985.

———. *The Worlds of Alfonso the Learned and James the Conqueror.* Princeton, N.J., 1985.

Burrell, David B. "Thomas Aquinas and Islam." *Modern Theology* 20 (2004): 71–89.

Caputo, Nina. *Nahmanides in Medieval Catalonia: History, Community, and Messianism.* Notre Dame, Ind., 2007.

Cardoner, Antoni. "Muestra de protección real a físicos judíos españoles conversos." *Sefarad* 12 (1952): 378–80.

Carlebach, Elisheva. "Between History and Hope: Jewish Messianism in Ashkenaz and Sepharad." Third Annual Lecture of the Victor Selmanowitz Chair of Jewish History, Graduate School of Jewish Studies, Touro College, May 17, 1998.

———. *Divided Souls: Converts from Judaism in Germany, 1500–1750.* New Haven, Conn., 2001.

Carpenter, Dwayne E. *Alfonso X and the Jews: An Edition and Commentary on Siete partidas 7.24 "De los judíos."* Modern Philology 115. Berkeley, Calif., 1986.

Carreras y Candi, Francesch. *L'aljama de juhéus de Tortosa.* Barcelona, 1928.

———. "Evolució histórica dels juheus y juheissants barcelonins." *Estudis Universitaris Catalans* 3 (1909): 498–522.

———. "L'inquisició barcelonina, substituida per l'inquisició castellana (1446–1487)." *Anuari de l'Institut d'estudis Catalans* 3 (1909–10): 130–77.

Castro, Américo. *España en su historia: Cristianos, moros, y judíos.* Barcelona, 1983.

Catlos, Brian. "Cristians, musulmans i jueus a la Corona d'Aragó medieval: Un cas de 'conveniència.' " *L'Avenç* 236 (November 2001): 8–16.

———. "Contexto social y 'conveniencia' en la Corona de Aragón: Propuesta para un modelo de interacción entre grupos etno-religiosos minoritarios y mayoritarios." *Revista d'Història Medieval* 12 (2002): 220–35.

———. *The Victors and the Vanquished: Christians and Muslims of Catalonia and Aragon, 1050–1300.* Cambridge, 2004.

Chabás, Roque. "Estudio sobre los sermones valencianos de San Vicente Ferrer que se conservan manuscritos en al Biblioteca de la Basílica Metropolitana de Valencia." *Revista de Archivos, Bibliotecas y Museos* 6 (1902): 1–6, 155–68; 7 (1902): 131–42, 419–39; 8 (1903): 38–57, 111–26, 291–95; 9 (1903): 85–102.

Chazan, Robert. "An Ashkenazic Anti-Christian Treatise." *Journal of Jewish Studies* 34 (1983): 63–72.

———. *Barcelona and Beyond.* Berkeley, Calif., 1992.

———. *Daggers of Faith: Thirteenth-Century Christian Missionizing and the Jewish Response.* Berkeley, Calif., 1989.

———. *European Jewry and the First Crusade.* Berkeley, Calif., 1987.

———. "The First Crusade as Reflected in the Earliest Hebrew Narratives." *Viator* 29 (1998): 25–38.

———. "From Friar Paul to Friar Raymond: The Development of Innovative Missionizing Argumentation." *Harvard Theological Review* 76 (1983): 289–306.

———. *God, Humanity, and History: The Hebrew First Crusade Narratives.* Berkeley, Calif., 2000.

———. *The Jews of Medieval Western Christendom, 1000–1500.* Cambridge, 2006.

———. "The Letter of R. Jacob ben Elijah to Friar Paul." *Jewish History* 6 (1992): 51–63.

———. "The Persecution of 992." *Revue des Études Juives* 129 (1970): 217–20.

———. *Reassessing Jewish Life in Medieval Europe.* Cambridge, 2010.

Cohen, Esther. *The Crossroads of Justice: Law and Culture in Late Medieval France.* Leiden, 1993.

Cohen, Gerson D. "Messianic Postures of Ashkenazim and Sephardim." In *Studies of the Leo Baeck Institute,* edited by Max Kreutzberger, 117–58. New York, 1967.

Cohen, Jeremy. "Between Martyrdom and Apostasy: Doubt and Self-Definition in Twelfth-Century Ashkenaz." *Journal of Medieval and Early Modern Studies* 19 (1999): 431–71.

———. *Christ Killers: The Jews and the Passion from the Bible to the Big Screen.* Oxford, 2007.

———. "The Christian Adversary of Solomon ibn Adret." *Jewish Quarterly Review* 71 (1980): 48–55.

————. *The Friars and the Jews: The Evolution of Medieval Anti-Judaism*. Ithaca, N.Y., 1982.

————. *Living Letters of the Law: Ideas of the Jew in Medieval Christianity*. Berkeley, Calif., 1999.

————. "The Mentality of the Medieval Jewish Apostate: Peter Alfonsi, Hermann of Cologne, and Pablo Christiani." In *Jewish Apostasy in the Modern World*, edited by Todd A. Endelmann, 20–47. New York, 1988.

————. "Profiat Duran's *The Reproach of the Gentile* and the Development of Jewish Anti-Christian Polemic." In *Shlomo Simonsohn Jubilee Volume: Studies on the History of the Jews in the Middle Ages and Renaissance Period*, edited by Daniel Carpi et al., 71–84. Tel Aviv, 1993.

————. *Sanctifying the Name of God: Jewish Martyrs and Jewish Memories of the First Crusade*. Philadelphia, 2004.

————. "*Synagoga conversa:* Honorius Augustodunensis, the Song of Songs, and Christianity's Eschatological Jew." *Speculum* 79 (2004): 340–406.

Cohen, Mark D. *Under Crescent and Cross: The Jews in the Middle Ages*. Princeton, N.J., 1994.

Cohen, Shaye D. "Between Judaism and Christianity: The Semicircumcision of Christians According to Bernard Gui, His Sources and R. Eliezer of Metz." *Harvard Theological Review* 94 (2001): 285–321.

Coll, José María. "¿Ramon de Tárrega fue formalmente hereje?" *Ilerda* 6 (1948): 7–29.

Colorni, Vittore. *Judaica minora: Saggi sulla storia dell'ebraismo Italiano dall'antichità all'età moderna*. Milan, 1983.

Deutsch, Yaacov. "*Toledot Yeshu* in Christian Eyes." M.A. thesis, Hebrew University of Jerusalem, 1997.

Di Segni, Riccardo. "Due nuovi fonti sulle *Toledoth Jeshu*." *La Rassegna Mensile di Israel* 55 (1990): 127–32.

Dondaine, Antoine. "Le manuel de l'inquisiteur (1230–1330)." *Archivum Fratrum Praedicatorum* 17 (1947): 85–194.

Eidelberg, Shlomo. *The Jews and the Crusaders: The Hebrew Chronicles of the First and Second Crusades*. Madison, Wisc., 1977.

Einbinder, Susan. "On the Borders of Exile: The Poetry of Solomon Simhah of Troyes." In *Medieval Constructions in Gender and Identity: Essays in Honor of Joan M. Ferrante*, edited by Teodolinda Barolini, 69–85. Tempe, Ariz., 2005.

Elukin, Jonathan. "The Discovery of the Self: Jews and Conversion in the Twelfth Century." In *Jews and Christians in Twelfth-Century Europe*, edited by Michael A. Signer and John Van Engen, 63–76. Notre Dame, Ind., 2001.

————. "From Jew to Christian? Conversion and Immutability in Medieval Europe." In *Varieties of Religious Conversion in the Middle Ages*, edited by James Muldoon, 171–89. Gainesville, Fla., 1997.

————. *Living Together, Living Apart: Rethinking Jewish-Christian Relations in the Middle Ages*. Princeton, N.J., 2007.

Emanuel, Simcha. "The Christian Wet Nurse during the Middle Ages: *Halakhah* and History" (in Hebrew). *Siyyun* 73 (2008): 21–40.

Epstein, Isidore. *The "Responsa" of Rabbi Solomon ben Adreth of Barcelona (1235–1310) as a Source of the History of Spain.* London, 1923. Reprinted in *Studies in the Communal Life of the Jews of Spain: As Reflected in the Responsa of R. Solomon b. Adreth and R. Simon b. Zemach Duran.* New York, 1968.

Feliu i Marbres, Eduard. *"Cataluña no era Sefarad: Precisiones metodológicas."* In *La Cataluña judía,* edited by Mariona Companys, 25–35. Barcelona, 2002.

———. *Disputa de Barcelona de 1263.* Barcelona, 1985.

Finkelstein, Louis. *Jewish Self-Government in the Middle Ages.* New York, 1924.

Fita, Fidel. "Los judíos mallorquines y el Concilio de Viena." *Boletín de la Real Academia de la Historia* 36 (1900): 233–58.

———. "Privilegios de los hebreos mallorquines en el Códice Pueyo." *Boletín de la Real Academia de la Historia* 36 (1900): 15–35, 122–48, 185–209, 273–306, 369–402, 458–94.

Foa, Anna. "The Witch and the Jew: Two Alikes That Were Not the Same." In *From Witness to Witchcraft: Jews and Judaism in Medieval Christian Thought,* edited by Jeremy Cohen, 361–74. Wiesbadden, 1996.

Fort i Cogul, Eufemià. *Catalunya i la inquisició.* Barcelona, 1973.

Foster, Kenelm. *The Life of Saint Thomas Aquinas: Biographical Documents.* London and Baltimore, 1959.

Fram, Edward. "Perception and Reception of Repentant Apostates in Medieval Ashkenaz and Premodern Poland." *Association for Jewish Studies Review* 21 (1996): 299–339.

Fredriksen, Paula. *Augustine and the Jews: A Christian Defense of Jews and Judaism.* New York, 2008.

Freidenreich, David M. *Foreigners and their Food: Constructing Otherness in Jewish, Christian, and Islamic Law.* Berkeley, 2011.

Friedlander, Alan. *The Hammer of the Inquisitors: Brother Bernard Delicieux and the Struggle against the Inquisition in Fourteenth-Century France.* Boston, 1999.

Friedman, Jerome. "Jewish Conversion, the Spanish Pure Blood Laws and Reformation: A Revisionist View of Racial and Religious Antisemitism." *Sixteenth Century Journal* 18 (1987): 3–31.

Funkenstein, Amos. "Basic Types of Christian Anti-Jewish Polemics in the Later Middle Ages." *Viator* 2 (1971): 373–82.

Galinsky, Judah. "Jewish Charitable Bequests and the *Hekdesh* Trust in Thirteenth-Century Spain." *Journal of Interdisciplinary History* 35 (2005): 423–40.

Galmés Mas, Lorenzo. "San Ramon de Penyafort y la inquisición en la Alta Catalunya." In *Praedicatores, Inquisitores.* Vol. 1, *The Dominicans and the Medieval Inquisition: Acts of the First International Seminar on the Dominicans and the Inquisition,* edited by Wolfram Hoyer, 85–103. Rome, 2004.

Gampel, Benjamin. "The 'Identity' of Sephardim of Medieval Christian Iberia." *Jewish Social Studies* 8 (2002): 133–38.

———. "Jews, Christians, and Muslims in Medieval Iberia: *Convivencia* through the Eyes of Sephardic Jews." In *Convivencia: Jews, Muslims, and Christians in Medieval Spain,* edited by Vivian B. Mann et al., 11–37. New York, 1992.

———. "A Letter to a Wayward Teacher: The Transformation of Sephardic Culture in

Christian Iberia." In *Cultures of the Jews: A New History*, edited by David Biale, 389–447. New York, 2002.

———. *The Last Jews on Iberian Soil: Navarrese Jewry, 1479–1498*. Berkeley, Calif., 1989.

García y García, Antonio. "Jews and Muslims in the Canon Law of the Iberian Peninsula in the Late Medieval and Early Modern Period." *Jewish History* 3 (1988): 42–50.

Garganta, José María de la. *Biografía y escritos de San Vicente Ferrer*. Madrid, 1956.

Gerber, Jane S. *The Jews of Spain: A History of the Sephardic Experience*. New York, 1994.

Ghéon, Henri. *St. Vincent Ferrer*. New York, 1939.

Gillman, Neil. *The Death of Death: Resurrection and Immortality in Jewish Thought*. Woodstock, Vt., 1997.

Girbal, Enrique Claudio. "Conversiónes de judíos en Girona y su obispado." *Revista de Girona* 18 (1894): 33–37.

———. *Los judíos en Girona*. Girona, 1870.

Gitlitz, David M. *Secrecy and Deceit: The Religion of the Crypto-Jews*. Albuquerque, N.M., 1996.

Given, James Buchanan. *Inquisition and Medieval Society: Power, Discipline, and Resistance in Languedoc*. Ithaca, N.Y., 1997.

———. "A Medieval Inquisitor at Work: Bernard Gui, 3 March 1308 to 19 June 1323." In *Portraits of Medieval and Renaissance Living: Essays in Memory of David Herlihy*, edited by Samuel K. Cohn et al., 207–32. Ann Arbor, 1996.

———. "Social Stress, Social Strain and the Inquisitors of Medieval Languedoc." In *Christendom and Its Discontents: Exclusion, Persecution, and Rebellion, 1000–1500*, edited by Scott L. Waugh et al., 67–85. Cambridge, 1996.

Golb, Norman. *Les juifs de Rouen au moyen âge: Portrait d'une culture oubliée*. Rouen, 1985.

Graetz, Heinrich. *The Structure of Jewish History and Other Essays*. Edited and translated by Ismar Schorsch. New York, 1975.

Graizbord, David. *Souls in Dispute: Converso Identities in Iberia and the Jewish Diaspora, 1580–1700*. Philadelphia, 2004.

Grau i Montserrat, Manuel. "Una familia jueva a Besalú: Aaró Jucef." *Annals de l'Institut d'estudis gironins* 25 (1979–80): 299–307.

———. "Jueus convertits al Cristianisme (Besalú, segles XIV–XV)." *Patronat d'Estudis Històrics d'Olot i Comarca* (1979): 91–115.

Grayzel, Solomon. *The Church and the Jews in the XIIIth Century*. Vol. 1, New York, 1966. Vol. 2, edited by Kenneth R. Stow, New York, 1989.

———. "The Confession of a Medieval Jewish Convert." *Historia Judaica* 17 (1955): 89–120.

———. "Popes, Jews, and Inquisition, from *Sicut* to *Turbato*." In *The Church and the Jews in the Thirteenth Century*, vol. 2, *1254–1314*, edited by Kenneth Stow, 3–45. New York, 1989.

Greatrex, Joan. "Monastic Charity for Jewish Converts: The Requisition of Corrodies by Henry III." In *Christianity and Judaism: Papers Read at the 1991 Summer Meeting and the 1992 Winter Meeting of the Ecclesiastical History Society*, edited by Diana Wood, 133–45. Cambridge, Mass., 1992.

Gross, Abraham. "On the Ashkenazi Syndrome of Martyrdom in Portugal in 1497" (in Hebrew). *Tarbiz* 64 (1994–95): 83–114.

———. *Struggling with Tradition: Reservations about Active Martyrdom in the Middle Ages.* Boston, 2004.

Grossman, Avraham. "Legislation and Responsa Literature." In *The Sephardi Legacy*, edited by Hayim Beinart, 1:199–204. 2 vols. Jerusalem, 1992.

———. *Pious and Rebellious: Jewish Women in Medieval Europe.* Waltham, Mass., 2004.

———. "Relations between Spanish and Ashkenazi Jewry in the Middle Ages." In *The Sephardi Legacy*, 2 vols., edited by Haim Beinart, 1:220–39. Jerusalem, 1992.

Grundmann, Herbert. *Religious Movements in the Middle Ages.* Notre Dame, Ind., 1995.

Guerson, Alexandra. "Seeking Remission: Jewish Conversion in the Crown of Aragon, c. 1378–1391." *Jewish History* 24 (2010): 33–52.

Gutwirth, Eleazer. "Conversions to Christianity amongst Fifteenth-Century Spanish Jews: An Alternative Explanation." In *Shlomo Simonsohn Jubilee Volume: Studies on the History of the Jews in the Middle Ages and Renaissance Period*, edited by Daniel Carpi, 97–121. Jerusalem, 1993.

———. "Gender, History, and Judeo-Christian Polemic." In *Contra Iudaeos: Ancient and Medieval Polemics between Christians and Jews*, edited by Ora Limor et al. Tübingen, 1996.

———. "Toward Expulsion: 1391–1492." In *Spain and the Jews: The Sephardi Experience, 1492 and After*, edited by E. Kedourie, 51–73. London, 1992.

———. "Widows, Artisans, and the Issues of Life: Hispano-Jewish Bourgeois Ideology." In *Iberia and Beyond: Hispanic Jews Between Cultures*, edited by B. D. Cooperman, 143–74. Newark and London, 1998.

Hames, Harvey. *The Art of Conversion: Christianity and Kabbalah in the Thirteenth Century.* Leiden, 2000.

Haverkamp, Alfred. "Baptised Jews in German Lands during the Twelfth Century." In *Jews and Christians in Twelfth-Century Europe*, edited by Michael A. Signer et al., 255–310. Notre Dame, Ind., 2001.

Hernando i Delgado, Josep. "El procés contra el converso Nicolau Sanxo, ciutadà de Barcelona, acusat d'haver circumcidat el seu fill (1437–1438)." *Acta Historica et Archaeologica Mediaevalia* 13 (1992): 75–100.

———. "Un tractat anònim *Adversus iudaeos* en català." In *Paraula i historia: Miscellania P. Basili Rubi.* Barcelona, 1986.

Hertz, Deborah. "Women at the Edge of Judaism: Female Converts in Germany, 1600–1750." In *Jewish Assimilation, Acculturation and Accommodation*, edited by Menachem Mor, 87–109. Lanham, Md., 1992.

Hillgarth, Jocelyn N. Introduction to *The Register Notule Communium.* Toronto, 1983.

———. *Ramon Llull i el naixement del lul.lisme.* Montserrat, 1998.

Horowitz, Elliot. *Reckless Rites: Purim and the Legacy of Jewish Violence.* Princeton, N.J., 2006.

Howard, George. "A Primitive Hebrew Gospel of Matthew and the *Tol'doth Yeshu*." *New Testament Studies* 34 (1988): 60–70.

Idel, Moshe. "Rabbi Moses ben Nahman: Kabbalah, Halakhah and Spiritual Leadership." *Tarbiz* 64 (1994): 535–80.

Isaacs, Abraham Lionel. *The Jews of Mallorca*. Mallorca, 1936.

Johnston, Mark D. *The Evangelical Rhetoric of Ramon Llull*. Oxford, 1996.

———. "Ramon Llull and the Compulsory Evangelization of Jews and Muslims." In *Iberia and the Mediterranean World of the Middle Ages: Studies in Honor of Robert I. Burns, S.J.* Vol. 1, *Proceedings from Kalamazoo*, edited by Larry J. Simon, 3–37. Leiden, 1995.

———. *The Spiritual Logic of Ramon Llull*. Oxford, 1987.

Jordan, William Chester. "Administering Expulsion in 1306." *Jewish Studies Quarterly* 15 (2008): 241–50.

———. "Adolescence and Conversion in the Middle Ages." In *Jews and Christians in Twelfth-Century Europe*, edited by Michael A. Signer et al., 77–93. Notre Dame, Ind., 2001.

———. "Christian Excommunication of the Jews in the Middle Ages: A Restatement of the Issues." *Jewish History* 1 (1986): 31–38.

———. *The French Monarchy and the Jews: From Philip Augustus to the Last Capetians*. Philadelphia, 1989.

———. "Home Again: The Jews in the Kingdom of France, 1315–1322." In *The Stranger in Medieval Society*, edited by Frank Akehurst et al., 27–45. Minneapolis, 1997.

———. Jews, Regalian Rights and the Constitution in Medieval France." *Association of Jewish Studies Review* 23 (1998): 1–16.

Kamen, Henry. "A Crisis of Conscience in Golden Age Spain: The Inquisition against 'Limpieza de Sangre.'" In *Crisis and Change in Early Modern Spain*, essay 7. Aldershot, 1993.

———. *The Spanish Inquisition*. New York, 1965.

———. *The Spanish Inquisition: A Historical Revision*. New Haven, Conn., 1997.

Kanarfogel, Ephraim. "Between Ashkenaz and Sefarad: Tosafist Teachings in the Talmudic Commentaries of Ritva." In *Between Rashi and Maimonides: Themes in Medieval Jewish Thought, Literature, and Exegesis*, edited by Ephraim Kanarfogel and Moshe Sokolow, 237–73. New York, 2010.

———. "Changing Attitudes toward Apostates in Tosafist Literature of the Late Twelfth and Early Thirteenth Centuries." In *New Perspectives on Jewish-Christian Relations: Studies in Honor of David Berger*, edited by Elisheva Carlebach. Leiden, forthcoming.

———. "*Halakha* and *Metziut* (Realia) in Medieval Ashkenaz: Surveying the Parameters and Defining the Limits." *Jewish Law Annual* 14 (2003): 193–224.

———. "Returning to the Jewish Community in Medieval Ashkenaz: History and *Halakha*." In *Turim: Studies in Jewish History and Literature; Presented to Dr. Bernard Lander*, edited by Michael Shmidman, 1:69–97. New York, 2007.

Katz, Jacob. "Although He Has Sinned, He Remains a Jew" (in Hebrew). *Tarbiz* 27 (1958): 203–17.

———. *Exclusiveness and Tolerance: Studies in Jewish-Gentile Relations in Medieval and Modern Times*. West Orange, N.J., 1961.

Kedar, Benjamin Z. *Crusade and Mission: European Approaches toward the Muslims*. Princeton, N.J., 1984.

Klein, Elka. "Good Servants, Bad Lords: The Abuse of Authority by Jewish Bailiffs in the

Medieval Crown of Aragon." In *The Experience of Power in Medieval Europe, 950–1350*, edited by Robert Berkhofer, Alan Cooper, and Adam Kosto, 59–72. Burlington, Vt., 2005.

———. *Jews, Christian Society, and Royal Power in Medieval Barcelona*. Ann Arbor, Mich., 2006.

———. "Splitting Heirs." *Jewish History* 16 (2002): 49–71.

———. "The Widow's Portion." *Viator* 31 (2000): 147–63.

Kohn, Roger. *Les juifs de la France du nord dans la seconde moitié du XIVe siècle*. Paris, 1988.

Kozodoy, Maud. "A Study of the Life and Works of Profiat Duran." Ph.D. diss., Jewish Theological Seminary of America, 2006.

Krauss, Samuel. *The Jewish-Christian Controversy from the Earliest Times to 1789*. Edited by William Horbury. Tübingen, 1995.

———. *Das Leben Jesu nach jüdischen Quellen*. Berlin, 1902.

Kriegel, Maurice. *Les juifs à la fin du moyen âge dans l'Europe méditerranéenne*. Paris, 1979.

———. "La juridiction inquisitoriale sur les juifs à l'époque de Philippe le Hardi et Philippe le Bel." In *Les juifs dans l'histoire de la France*, edited by Myriam Yardeni, 70–77. Leiden, 1980.

———. "Prémarranisme et inquisition dans la Provence des XIIIe et XIVe siècles." *Provence Historique* 29 (1978): 313–23.

———. "La prise d'une décision: L'expulsion des juifs d'Espagne en 1492." *Revue Historique* 260 (1978): 49–90.

Kruger, Steven F. *The Spectral Jew: Conversion and Embodiment in Medieval Europe*. Minneapolis, 2006.

Lambert, Malcolm D. *Medieval Heresy: Popular Movements from Bogomil to Hus*. London, 1977.

Langmuir, Gavin. "Detector of Ritual Murder." *Speculum* 59 (1984): 820–46.

Lazard, Lucien. "Les juifs de Touraine." *Revue des Études Juives* 17 (1888): 210–34.

Lea, Henry Charles. *Chapters from the Religious History of Spain Connected with the Inquisition*. Philadelphia, 1890.

———. *A History of the Inquisition of the Middle Ages*. 3 vols. New York, 1888. Reprint, s.l., 1955.

———. *A History of the Inquisition of Spain*. 4 vols. London, 1906.

———. "El Santo Niño de la Guardia." *English Historical Review* 4 (1889): 229–50.

Levtzion, Nehemia. "Conversion under Muslim Domination: A Comparative Study." In *Religious Change and Cultural Domination*, edited by David N. Lorenzen, 19–38. Mexico City, 1981.

Limor, Ora. "Missionary Merchants: Three Medieval Anti-Jewish Works from Genoa." *Journal of Medieval History* 17 (1991): 35–51.

Linehan, Peter. *The Spanish Church and the Papacy in the Thirteenth Century*. Cambridge, 1971.

Lipman, Vivian D. *The Jews of Medieval Norwich*. London, 1967.

Llop Jordana, Irene. "L'aljama de jueus de Vic al segle XIII: Orígens i consolidació de l'aljama (1231–1315)." Ph.D. diss., Universitat de Barcelona, 2006.

Loeb, Isidore. "Polémistes chrétiens et juifs en France et en Espagne." *Revue des Études Juives* 18 (1889): 43–70, 219–42.

Logan, F. Donald. "Thirteen London Jews and Conversion to Christianity: Problems of Apostasy in the 1280s." *Bulletin of the Institute of Historical Research* 45 (1972): 214–29.

López Asensio, Álvaro. *La judería de Calatayud: Sus casas, calles y barrios.* Zaragoza, 2003.

Lotter, Friedrich. "Imperial versus Ecclesiastical Jewry Law in the High Middle Ages: Contradictions and Controversies Concerning the Conversion of Jews and Their Serfs." In *Proceedings of the Tenth World Congress of Jewish Studies,* edited by David Assaf, 59–60. Jerusalem, 1990.

————. "The Scope and Effectiveness of Imperial Jewry Law in the High Middle Ages." *Jewish History* 4 (1989): 40–41.

Lourie, Elena. "Anatomy of Ambivalence: Muslims under the Crown of Aragon in the Late Thirteenth Century." In *Crusade and Colonisation: Muslims, Christians and Jews in Medieval Aragon,* 1–77. Aldershot, 1990.

————. "Complicidad criminal: Un aspecto insólito de convivencia judeo-cristiana." In *Actas del IV congreso internacional "Encuentro de las tres culturas,"* 93–108. Toledo, 1988.

————. "Jewish Moneylenders in the Local Catalan Community, c. 1300: Vilafranca del Penedès, Besalú, and Montblanc." *Michael* 11 (1989): 33–98.

————. "Mafiosi and *Malsines*: Violence, Fear and Faction in the Jewish Aljamas of Valencia in the Fourteenth Century." In *Actas del IV Congreso Internacional "Encuentro de las Tres Culturas,"* edited by C. Carrete Parrondo, 69–102. Toledo, 1988.

————. "A Plot Which Failed? The Case of the Corpse Found in the Jewish *Call* of Barcelona (1301)." *Mediterranean Historical Review* 1 (1986): 187–220.

Maccoby, Hyam, ed. and trans. *Judaism on Trial: Jewish-Christian Disputations in the Middle Ages.* East Brunswick, N.J., 1982.

MacKay, Angus. *Spain in the Middle Ages: From Frontier to Empire, 1000–1500.* London, 1977.

Madurell Marimon, Josep María. "El arte de la seda en Barcelona entre judíos y conversos: Notas para su historia." *Sefarad* 25 (1965): 247–81.

————. "La contratación laboral judaica y conversa en Barcelona (1349–1416)." *Sefarad* 16 (1956): 33–71, 369–98; 17 (1957): 73–100.

————. "Encuadernadores y libreros barceloneses judíos y conversos." *Sefarad* 21 (1961): 300–338; 22 (1962): 345–72; 23 (1963): 74–103.

————. "Plateros judíos barceloneses." *Sefarad* 27 (1967): 290–98.

Magdalena Nom de Déu, José Ramon. "Delitos y 'calònies' de los judíos valencianos en la segunda mitad del siglo XIV (1351–1384)." *Anuario de Filología* 2 (1976): 181–226.

Maitland, Frederic William. "The Deacon and the Jewess; or, Apostasy at Common Law." In *The Collected Papers of Frederic William Maitland,* edited by Hal Fisher, 1:385–406. Cambridge, 1911.

Maíz Chacón, Jorge. *Los judíos de Baleares en la baja edad media.* Oleiros, Spain, 2010.

Malkiel, David. "Jews and Apostates in Medieval Europe: Boundaries Real and Imagined." *Past and Present* 194 (2007): 3–34.

Marcus, Ivan G. "Hierarchies, Religious Boundaries, and Jewish Spirituality in Medieval Germany." *Jewish History* 1 (1986): 7–26.

———. "Jews and Christians Imagining the Other in Medieval Europe." *Prooftexts* 15 (1995): 209–26.

———. "A Pious Community and Doubt: *Qiddush ha-Shem* in Ashkenaz and the Story of Rabbi Amnon of Mainz." In *Studien zur judischen Geschichte und Soziologie: Festschrift Julius Carlebach*, 97–113. Heidelberg, 1992.

Marín Padilla, Encarnación. *Relación judeoconversa durante la segunda mitad del siglo XV en Aragón: La ley.* Zaragoza, 1986.

———. "Relación judeoconversa durante la segunda mitad del siglo XV en Aragón: Nacimientos, hadas, circuncisiones." *Sefarad* 41 (1981): 273–300; 42 (1982): 59–77.

Marquès, Josep M. "Sis-cents pidolaires (1368–1540): Captius, esclaus i peregrins." *Estudis del Baix Empordà* 13 (1994): 137–65.

Martí Bonet, José M. *Ponç de Gualba obispo de Barcelona (a. 1303–1334).* Barcelona, 1983.

Martínez, María Elena. *Limpieza de Sangre, Religion, and Gender in Colonial Mexico.* Stanford, Calif., 2008.

Mas y Casas, José María de, ed. *Ensayos históricos sobre Manresa.* Manresa, 1882.

McCulloh, John M. "Jewish Ritual Murder: William of Norwich, Thomas of Monmouth, and the Early Dissemination of the Myth." *Speculum* 72 (1997): 698–740.

Melammed, Renée Levine. *A Question of Identity: Iberian Conversos in Historical Perspective.* Oxford, 2004.

Meyerson, Mark D. "Aragonese and Catalan Jewish Converts at the Time of Expulsion." *Jewish History* 6 (1992): 131–49.

———. *A Jewish Renaissance in Fifteenth-Century Spain.* Princeton, N.J., 2004.

———. *Jews in an Iberian Frontier Kingdom: Society, Economy, and Politics in Morvedre, 1248–1391.* Leiden, 2004.

———. *The Muslims of Valencia in the Age of Fernando and Isabel.* Berkeley, Calif., 1991.

———. "Samuel of Granada and the Dominican Inquisitor: Jewish Magic and Jewish Heresy in Post-1391 Valencia." In *Friars and Jews in the Middle Ages and Renaissance*, edited by Steven J. McMichael et al., 161–90. Leiden, 2004.

———. "Seeking the Messiah: *Converso* Messianism in Post-1453 Valencia." In *The Conversos and Moriscos in Late Medieval Spain and Beyond*, edited by K. Ingram, 51–82. Leiden, 2009.

———. "Victims and Players: The Attack of the Union of Valencia on the Jews of Morvedre." In *Religion, Text, and Society in Medieval Spain and Northern Europe: Essays in Honor of J. N. Hillgarth*, edited by T. Burman et al., 70–102. Toronto, 2002.

Millas Vallicrosa, José María. "Un tratado anónimo de polémica contra los judíos." *Sefarad* 12 (1953): 3–34.

Miret i Sans, Joaquín. *Itinerari de Jaume I el Conqueridor.* Barcelona, 1918.

———. "Le Massacre des juifs de Montclús en 1320: Episode de l'entrée des Pastoureaux dans l'Aragon." *Revue des Études Juives* 53 (1907): 255–66.

———. "Les médecins juifs de Pierre, Roi D'Aragon." *Revue des Études Juives* 57 (1909): 268–78.

———. "El procés de les hosties contra'ls jueus d'Osca en 1377." *Anuari de l'Institut d'estudis catalans* 4 (1911): 59–80.

Mitre Fernández, Emilio. *Los judíos de Castilla en tiempo de Enrique III: El pogrom de 1391.* Valladolid, 1994.

Moore, Robert I. *The Formation of a Persecuting Society: Authority and Deviance in Western Europe, 950–1250.* New York, 1987.

Morera Llaurado, Enrique. *Tarragona cristiana.* Tarragona, 1954.

Morrison, Karl F. *Conversion and Text: The Cases of Augustine of Hippo, Herman-Judah, and Constantine Tsatsos.* Charlottesville, Va., 1992.

———. *Understanding Conversion.* Charlottesville, Va., 1992.

Netanyahu, Benzion. *The Marranos of Spain, from the Late 14th to the Early 16th Century, According to Contemporary Hebrew Sources.* Ithaca, N.Y., 1999.

———. *The Origins of the Inquisition in Fifteenth Century Spain.* New York, 1995. Reprint, New York, 2001.

Newman, Abraham. *The Jews in Spain.* 2 vols. Philadelphia, 1942.

Newman, Louis I. *Jewish Influence on Christian Reform Movements.* New York, 1925.

Nirenberg, David. *Communities of Violence: Persecution of Minorities in the Middle Ages.* Princeton, N.J., 1996.

———. "Conversion, Sex, and Segregation: Jews and Christians in Medieval Spain." *American Historical Review* 107 (2002): 1065–93.

———. "A Female Rabbi in Fourteenth-Century Zaragoza?" *Sefarad* 51 (1991): 179–82.

———. "Figures of Thought and Figures of Flesh: 'Jews' and 'Judaism' in Late-Medieval Spanish Poetry and Politics." *Speculum* 81 (2006): 398–426.

———. "Love between Muslim and Jew in Medieval Spain: A Triangular Affair." In *Jews, Muslims, and Christians in and around the Crown of Aragon: Essays in Honour of Professor Elena Lourie,* edited by Harvey J. Hames, 127–55. Leiden, 2004.

———. "Mass Conversion and Genealogical Mentalities: Jews and Christians in Fifteenth-Century Spain." *Past and Present* 174 (2002): 3–41.

———. "Was there Race before Modernity? The Example of 'Jewish' Blood in Late Medieval Spain." In *The Origins of Racism in the West,* edited by Miriam Eliav-Feldon et al., 232–64. Cambridge, 2009.

Novak, David. "The Treatment of Islam and Muslims in the Legal Writings of Maimonides." In *Studies in Islamic and Judaic Traditions,* edited by W. Brinner and S. Ricks, 233–50. Atlanta, 1986.

Omont, Henri. "Mémorial de l'inquisition d'Aragon à la fin du XIVᵉ siècle." *Bibliothèque de l'École des Chartres* 66 (1905): 261–68.

Orfali Levi, Moisés. "Rabbi Selomo ibn Aderet y la controversia judeo-cristiana." *Sefarad* 39 (1979): 111–20.

Pakter, Walter. *Medieval Canon Law and the Jews.* Ebelsbach, 1988.

Palès-Gobilliard, Annette. "L'inquisition et les juifs: Le cas de Jacques Fournier." In *Juifs et judaïsme de Languedoc,* edited by Bernard Blumenkranz et al., 97–114. Toulouse, 1977.

Pegg, Mark. *The Corruption of Angels: The Great Inquisition of 1245–1246.* Princeton, N.J., 2001.

Perarnau i Espelt, Josep. "L'autodifesa nella parola di tre ebrei davanti all-inquisitore." In *La parola all-accusato,* edited by Jean-Claude Maire Vigueur et al., 74–84. Palermo, 1991.

———. "Documents de tema inquisitorial del bisbe de Barcelona, fra Ferrer d'Abella (1334–1344)." *Revista Catalana de Teologia* 5 (1980): 443–78.

———. "El procés inquisitorial barceloní contra els jueus Janto Almuli, la seva muller Jamila i Jucef de Quatorze (1341–1342)." *Revista Catalana de Teologia* 4 (1979): 309–53.

———. "Sobre un procés inquisitorial fet per Galceran Sacosta, bisbe de Vic." *Ausa* 9 (1980): 83–85.

———. "El *Tractatus brevis super iurisdictione inquisitorum contra infideles fidem catholicam agitantes* de Nicolau Eimeric." *Arxiu de Textos Catalans Antics* 1 (1982): 79–126.

Perles, Joseph. *Rabbi Salomo ben Abraham ben Adereth: Sein Leben und seine Schriften.* Breslau, 1863.

Peters, Edward. *Inquisition.* Berkeley, Calif., 1989.

———. "*Quoniam abundavit iniquitas:* Dominicans as Inquisitors, Inquisitors as Dominicans." *Catholic Historical Review* 91 (2005): 105–21.

———. *Torture.* Philadelphia, 1996.

Piles Ros, Leopoldo. "Los judíos valencianos y la autoridad real." *Sefarad* 8 (1948): 78–96.

Pons i Pastor, Antonio. "El converso Aragonés Nicolás de Gracia." *Argensola* 13 (1953): 45–50.

———. "Los judíos del Reino de Mallorca durante los siglos XIII y XIV." *Hispania, Revista Española de Historia* 16 (1956): 352, 552–53.

———. *Los judíos del Reino de Mallorca durante los siglos XIII y XIV.* 2 vols. Mallorca, 1984.

Puig i Oliver, Jaume. "Documents relatius a la inquisició del 'Registrum Litterarum' de l'Arxiu Diocesà de Girona (s. XIV)." *Arxiu de Textos Catalans Antics* 17 (1998): 381–462.

———. "Nicolás Eymerich, un inquisidor discutido." In *Praedicatores, Inquisitores: The Dominicans and the Medieval Inquisition: Acts of the First International Seminar on the Dominicans and the Inquisition,* edited by Wolfram Hoyer, 545–93. Rome, 2004.

———. "El pagament dels inquisidors a la Corona d'Aragó, segles XIII i XIV." *Arxiu de Textos Catalans Antics* 22 (2003): 175–222.

———. "El *Tractatus de haeresi et de infidelium incredulitate et de horum criminum iudice,* de Felip Ribot, O. Carm. edició i estudi." *Arxiu de Textos Catalans Antics* 1 (1982): 127–90.

Pujol i Canelles, Miquel. *La conversió dels jueus de Castelló d'Empúries.* Castelló d'Empúries, 1997.

Rabinowitz, Louis. *The Social Life of the Jews of Northern France in the XII–XIV Centuries as Reflected in the Rabbinical Literature of the Period.* New York, 1972.

Ray, Jonathan. "The Jews between Church and State in Reconquest Iberia." *Viator* 38 (2007): 155–65.

———. *The Sephardic Frontier: The Reconquista and the Jewish Community in Medieval Iberia.* New York, 2006.

Regev, Shaul. "The Attitude towards the *Conversos* in 15th–16th Century Jewish Thought." *Revue des Études Juives* 156 (1997): 117–34.

Régné, Jean. "Rapports entre l'inquisition et les juifs d'après le mémorial de l'inquisiteur d'Aragon (fin du XIVᵉ siècle)." *Revue des Études Juives* 53 (1906): 232–33.

Reinach, Solomon. "L'inquisition et les juifs." *Revue des Études Juives* 40 (1900): xlix–lxiv.

Reiner, Avraham. "L'attitude envers les prosélytes en Allemagne et en France du XIe au XIIIe siècle." *Revue des Études Juives* 167 (2008): 99–119.

Révah, Israel. "Les marranes." *Revue des Études Juives* 118–19 (1959–60): 29–77.

Rich Abad, Anna. *La comunitat jueva de Barcelona entre 1348 i 1391 a través de la documentació notarial.* Barcelona, 1999.

Riera i Melis, Antoni. "La aparición de las corporaciones de oficio en Cataluña, 1200–1350." In *Cofradías, gremios y solidaridades en la Europa medieval: XIX Semana de estudios medievales*, 285–318. Pamplona, 1993.

Riera i Sans, Jaume. "Els avalots del 1391 a Girona." In *Jornades d'història dels jueus a Catalunya*, 95–159. Girona, 1987.

———. "El baptisme de Rabí Ishaq ben Seset Perfet." *Calls* 1 (1986): 43–52.

———. "La conflictivitat de l'alimentació dels jueus medievals (segles XII–XV)." In *Alimentació i societat a la Catalunya medieval. Anuario de Estudios Medievales* 20 (1988): 295–99.

———. "Estrangers participants als avalots contra les jueries de la Corona d'Aragó el 1391." *Anuario de Estudios Medievales* 10 (1980): 577–83.

———. *Fam i fe: L'entrada dels Pastorells (juliol de 1320).* Lleida, 2004.

———. "Jafuda Alatzar: Jueu de Valencia." *Revista d'Història Medieval* 4 (1993): 65–100.

———. "Les llicències reials per predicar als jueus i als sarraïns (segles XIII–XIV)." *Calls* 2 (1987): 113–43.

———. "Les obres catalanes de Mosse Natan (segle XIV)." In *Miscel.lània Pere Bohigas*, 3 vols. Badalona, 1981–83.

———. *Els poders publics i les sinagogues segles XIII–XV.* Girona, 2006.

———. "Un procés inquisitorial contra els jueus de Montblanc per un llibre de Maimònides." *Aplec de Treballs* 8 (1987): 59–73.

———. "Los tumultos contra las juderías de la Corona de Aragón en 1391." *Cuadernos de Historia: Anejos de la Revista Hispania* 8 (1977): 213–25.

Rivkin, Ellis. "The Utilization of Non-Jewish Sources for the Reconstruction of Jewish History." *Jewish Quarterly Review* 48 (1957): 183–203.

Roach, Andrew P. "Penance and the Making of the Inquisition in Languedoc." *Journal of Ecclesiastical History* 52 (2001): 409–33.

Robert, Ulysse. *Les signes d'infamie au moyen âge: Juifs, sarrasins, hérétiques, lépreux cagots et filles publiques.* Paris, 1891.

Robles, Laureano. *Escritores dominicos de la Corona de Aragón.* Salamanca, 1972.

Romano, David. "Análisis de los repertorios documentales de Jacobs y Régné." *Sefarad* 14 (1954): 247–64.

———. "Conversión de judíos al Islam (Corona de Aragón 1280 y 1284)." *Sefarad* 36 (1976): 333–37.

———. "Los funcionarios judíos de Pedro el Grande de Aragón." *Boletín de la Real Academia de Buenas Letras de Barcelona* 33 (1969–70): 5–41.

———. "Los hermanos Abenmenassé al servicio de Pedro el Grande de Aragón." In *Homenaje a Millás Vallicrosa*, 2:243–92. Barcelona, 1956.

———. "Judíos escribanos y trujamanes de árabe en la Corona de Aragón (reinados de Jaime I a Jaime II)." *Sefarad* 38 (1978): 71–105.

———. "Els jueus en temps de Pere el Cerimoniós." In *Pere el Cerimoniós i la seva època*, 123–29. Barcelona, 1989.

———. "Les juifs de la Couronne d'Aragon avant 1391." *Revue des Études Juives* 141 (1982): 169–82.

Roth, Norman. "The Civic Status of the Jew in Medieval Spain." In *Iberia and the Mediterranean World of the Middle Ages: Studies in Honor of Robert I. Burns*, edited by P. E. Chevedden et al., 2:139–61. Leiden, 1965.

———. *Jews, Visigoths, and Muslims in Medieval Spain: Cooperation and Conflict.* Leiden, 1994.

Rubin, Miri. *Gentile Tales: The Narrative Assault on Late Medieval Jews.* Philadelphia, 1999.

Rubió Balaguer, Jordi. "Metges y cirurgians juheus." *Estudis Universitaris Catalans* 3 (1909): 489–97.

Rubió i Lluch, Antoni. "Notes sobre la ciencia oriental a Catalunya en el XIV^{en} sigle." *Estudis Universitaris Catalans* 3 (1909): 394–98.

Russell, Jeffrey B., ed. *Religious Dissent in the Middle Ages.* New York and London, 1971.

Saltman, Avrom. "Hermann's *Opusculum de conversione sua:* Truth or Fiction?" *Revue des Études Juives* 147 (1988): 31–56.

Sánchez Albornoz, Claudio. *España: Un enigma histórico.* 2 vols. Buenos Aires, 1956.

Sánchez Real, José. "La judería de Tarragona." *Sefarad* 11 (1951): 339–48.

Saperstein, Marc. "A Sermon on the *Akedah* from the Generation of the Expulsion and Its Implications for 1391." In *Exile and Diaspora: Studies in the History of the Jewish People Presented to Professor Haim Beinart*, 103–24. Madrid, 1991.

Saraiva, António. *The Marrano Factory: The Portuguese Inquisition and Its New Christians 1536–1765.* Leiden, 2001.

Sarret i Arbós, Joaquim. *Jueus a Manresa.* Manresa, 1917.

Schäfer, Peter. "The Ideal of Piety of the Ashkenazi *Hasidim* and its Roots in Jewish Tradition." *Jewish History* 4 (1990): 9–23.

Schmitt, Jean-Claude. *La conversion d'Hermann le juif: Autobiographie, histoire et fiction.* Paris, 2003.

Scholem, Gershom. "Le centre kabbalistique de Gérone." In *Les origines de la Kabbale*, translated by Jean Loewenson, 387–500. Paris, 1966.

———. *Origins of the Kabbalah.* Princeton, N.J., and Philadelphia, 1987.

Septimus, Bernard. *Hispano-Jewish Culture in Transition: The Career and Controversies of Ramah.* Cambridge, Mass., 1982.

———. "Kings, Angels or Beggars: Tax Law and Spirituality in a Hispano-Jewish Responsum." In *Studies in Medieval Jewish History and Literature*, edited by Isadore Twersky, 309–36. Cambridge, Mass., 1984.

———. "Open Rebuke and Concealed Love: Nachmanides and the Andalusian Tradition." In *Rabbi Moses Nachmanides: Explorations in His Religious and Literary Virtuosity*, edited by Isadore Twersky, 11–34. Cambridge, Mass., 1983.

———. Piety and Power in Thirteenth-Century Catalonia." In *Studies in Medieval Jewish History and Literature*, edited by Isadore Twersky, 197–230. Cambridge, Mass., 1979.

Shamir, Yehuda. *Rabbi Moses Ha-Kohen of Tordesillas and His Book 'Ezer ha-Emunah.* Leiden, 1975.

Shatzmiller, Joseph. "Christian 'Excommunication' of Jews: Some Further Clarifications." In *Shlomo Simonsohn Jubilee Volume: Studies on the History of the Jews in the Middle Ages and Renaissance Period*, edited by Daniel Carpi, 245–55. Tel Aviv, 1993.

———. "Converts and Judaizers in the Early Fourteenth Century." *Harvard Theological Review* 74 (1981): 63–77.

———. "L'inquisition et les juifs de Provence au XIIIᵉ s." In *Histoire de la Provence et civilization médiévale: Études dédiées à la mémoire d'Edouard Baratier*, 327–38. Provence Historique 23. Marseille, 1973.

———. "Jewish Converts to Christianity in Medieval Europe, 1200–1500." In *Cross Cultural Convergences in the Crusader Period: Essays Presented to Aryeh Grabois on His Sixty-Fifth Birthday*, edited by Michael Goodich et al., 297– 318. New York, 1995.

———. *Jews, Medicine and Medieval Society.* Berkeley and Los Angeles, 1994.

———. "Jews 'Separated from the Communion of the Faithful in Christ' in the Middle Ages." In *Studies in Medieval Jewish History and Literature*, edited by Isidore Twersky, 307–14. Cambridge, Mass., 1979.

———. "Paulus Christiani: Un aspect de son activité anti-juive." In *Hommage à Georges Vajda: Études d'histoire et de pensée juives*, edited by Gérard Nahon and Charles Touati, 203–17. Louvain, 1980.

———. *Recherches sur la communauté juive de Manosque au moyen âge.* Paris, 1973.

Shepkaru, Shmuel. "To Die for God: Martyrs' Heaven in Hebrew and Latin Crusade Narratives." *Speculum* 77 (2002): 311–41.

Shneidman, Jerome Lee. "Jews as Royal Bailiffs in Thirteenth-Century Aragon." *Historia Judaica* 19 (1957): 55–66.

———. "Jews in the Royal Administration of Thirteenth-Century Aragon." *Historia Judaica* 21 (1959): 37–52

———. *The Rise of the Aragonese-Catalan Empire, 1200–1350.* 2 vols. New York, 1970.

Shrock, Avraham. *Rabbi Jonah ben Abraham of Gerona.* London, 1948.

Sicroff, Albert A. *Los estatutos de limpieza de sangre: Controversias entre los siglos XV y XVII.* Madrid, 1979.

Sierra Valentí, Eduard. "Captivus de sarraïns: Llicències per a demanar caritat dels bisbes de Girona (1376–1415)." *Anuario de Estudios Medievales* 38 (2008): 385–428.

Silver, Daniel Jeremy. *Maimonidean Criticism and the Maimonidean Controversy: 1180–1240.* Leiden, 1965.

Simonsohn, Shlomo. *The Apostolic See and the Jews: History.* Toronto, 1991.

Soifer, Maya. "Beyond *Convivencia:* Critical Reflections on the Historiography of Interfaith Relations in Christian Spain." *Journal of Medieval Iberian Studies* (2009): 19–35.

———. "'*You Say That the Messiah Has Come . . .*': The Ceuta Disputation (1179) and Its Place in the Christian Anti-Jewish Polemics of the High Middle Ages." *Journal of Medieval History* (2005): 287–307.

Soldevila, Ferran. *Jaume I, Pere el Gran.* Barcelona, 1955.

Soloveitchik, Haym. "*Halakhah*, Hermeneutics and Martyrdom in Medieval Ashkenaz." *Jewish Quarterly Review* 94 (2004): 77–108.

———. "Three Themes in the *Sefer Hasidim*." *Association for Jewish Studies Review* 1 (1976): 311–57.

Sonne, Isaiah. "On Baer and His Philosophy of Jewish History." *Jewish Social Studies* 9 (1947): 61–80.

Stacey, Robert C. "The Conversion of Jews to Christianity in Thirteenth-Century England." *Speculum* 67 (1992): 263–83.

Starr, Joshua. "The Mass Conversion of Jews in Southern Italy (1290–1293)." *Speculum* 21 (1946): 203–11.

Stow, Kenneth. *Alienated Minority: The Jews of Medieval Latin Europe.* Cambridge, 1992.

———. "Conversion, Apostasy, and Apprehensiveness: Emicho of Flonheim and the Fear of Jews in the Twelfth Century." *Speculum* 76 (2001): 911–33.

———. "Jacob of Venice and the Jewish Settlement in Venice in the Thirteenth Century." In *Community and Culture*, edited by N. Waldman, 228–32. Philadelphia, 1987.

———. "A Tale of Uncertainties: Converts in the Roman Ghetto." In *Studies on the History of the Jews in the Middle Ages and Renaissance Period: Shlomo Simonsohn Jubilee Volume*, edited by Daniel Carpi et al., 257–66. Tel Aviv, 1993.

———. *Popes, Church and Jews in the Middle Ages: Confrontation and Response.* Burlington, Vt., 2007.

Strayer, Joseph R. *The Albigensian Crusades.* New York, 1971. Reprint, Ann Arbor, Mich., 1992.

Szpiech, Ryan. " 'Is He Still Israel?' Abner of Burgos on Conversion and Identity in Medieval Castile." Paper delivered at the Tauber Institute for the Study of European Jewry at Brandeis University, November 12, 2009.

Talbot, Charles H., ed. *The Anglo-Saxon Missionaries in Germany.* New York, 1954.

Tartakoff, Paola. "Christian Kings and Jewish Conversion in the Medieval Crown of Aragon." *Journal of Medieval Iberian Studies* 3 (2011): 27–39.

———. "Jewish Women and Apostasy in the Medieval Crown of Aragon, c. 1300–1391." *Jewish History* 24 (2010): 7–32.

———. "The *Toledot Yeshu* and the Jewish-Christian Conflict in the Medieval Crown of Aragon." In *Toledot Yeshu ("The Life Story of Jesus") Revisited*, edited by Peter Schaefer et al., 297–309. Berlin, 2011.

Torres y Amat, Ignasi, et al., eds. *Diccionario de escritores catalanes.* Barcelona, 1836.

Trachtenberg, Joshua. *The Devil and the Jews: The Medieval Conception of the Jew and Its Relation to Modern Antisemitism.* New York, 1943.

Utterback, Christine. " 'Conversi' Revert: Voluntary and Forced Return to Judaism in the Early Fourteenth Century." *Church History* 64 (1995): 16–28.

Vargas, Michael. "How a 'Brood of Vipers' Survived the Black Death: Recovery and Dysfunction in the Fourteenth-Century Dominican Order." *Speculum* 86 (2011): 688–714.

Vernet, Juan. "Un embajador judío de Jaime II, Selomo b. Menassé." *Sefarad* 12 (1952): 125–54.

Vidal, J. M. "Procès d'inquisition contre Adhemar de Mosset." *Analecta Gallicana, Revue d'Histoire de l'Église de France* (1910): 555–89, 682–99, 711–24.

Vidal Beltran, Eliseo. *Valencia en la época de Juan I.* Valencia 1974.

Viera, David. "The Evolution of Francesc Eiximenis's Attitudes toward Judaism." In *Friars and Jews in the Middle Ages and Renaissance*, edited by Steven J. McMichael et al., 147–59. Leiden, 2004.

Vincent, Nicholas. "Jews, Poitevins, and the Bishop of Winchester, 1231–1234." In *Christianity and Judaism: Papers Read at the 1991 Summer Meeting and the 1992 Winter Meeting of the Ecclesiastical History Society*, edited by Diana Wood, 119–32. Cambridge, Mass., 1992.

Vincke, Johannes. *Zur Vorgeschichte der Spanischen Inquisition: Die Inquisition in Aragon, Katalonien, Mallorca und Valencia während des 13. und 14. Jahrhunderts.* Bonn, 1941.

Vose, Robin. *Dominicans, Muslims and Jews in the Medieval Crown of Aragon.* Cambridge, 2009.

Winer, Rebecca Lynn. "Conscripting the Breast: Lactation, Slavery and Salvation in the Realms of Aragon and Kingdom of Majorca, c. 1250–1300." *Journal of Medieval History* 34 (2008): 164–84.

———. "Family, Community, and Motherhood: Caring for Fatherless Children in the Jewish Community of Thirteenth-Century Perpignan." *Jewish History* 16 (2002): 15–48.

———. *Women, Wealth, and Community in Perpignan, c. 1250–1300: Christians, Jews, and Enslaved Muslims in a Medieval Mediterranean Town.* Burlington, Vt., 2006.

Winroth, Anders. *The Making of Gratian's Decretum.* Cambridge, 2000.

Wolff, Philippe. "The 1391 Pogrom in Spain: Social Crisis or Not?" *Past and Present* 50 (1971): 4–18.

Yerushalmi, Yosef H. "The Inquisition and the Jews of France in the Time of Bernard Gui." *Harvard Theological Review* 63 (1970): 317–76.

———. *From Spanish Court to Italian Ghetto: A Study in Seventeenth-Century Marranism and Jewish Apologetics.* New York, 1971.

Yuval, Israel. *Two Nations in Your Womb: Perceptions of Jews and Christians in Late Antiquity and the Middle Ages.* Berkeley, Calif., 2006.

———. "Vengeance and Damnation, Blood and Defamation: From Jewish Martyrdom to Blood Libel Accusations" (in Hebrew). *Zion* 58 (1993): 33–90.

Zeitlin, Solomon. "*Mumar* and *Meshumad.*" *Jewish Quarterly Review* 54 (1963): 84–86.

Ziegler, Joseph. "Reflections on the Jewry Oath in the Middle Ages." In *Christianity and Judaism: Papers Read at the 1991 Summer Meeting and the 1992 Winter Meeting of the Ecclesiastical History Society*, edited by Diana Wood, 209–20. Oxford, 1992.

Index

Apostates from Judaism are listed by their Christian names, when known, with their Jewish names, when known, following in parentheses.

Acknowledgments

This book could not have been written without the support of many extraordinary people and institutions. Robin Vose first suggested that I explore the inquisitorial trials that form its backbone. Caroline Walker Bynum, Benjamin Gampel, Adam J. Kosto, and the late Yosef Hayim Yerushalmi provided invaluable guidance as I began my research, and they remained the most generous of mentors thereafter.

While working in archives in Aragon, Catalonia, and Valencia—with the support of the Center for Israel and Jewish Studies, the Fulbright Program, and the Memorial Foundation for Jewish Culture—I incurred further debts of gratitude. María Teresa Hernández y Velasco and Laureano Hernández y Fernández opened their home to me and became like family. Pere Benito i Monclús was an incredible host and has not ceased sharing his erudition as a medievalist. At the Arxiu de la Corona de Aragon, Jaume Riera i Sans discussed medieval Jewish conversion at length and brought key sources to my attention. José María Magdalena i Nom de Deu welcomed me into his paleography seminar at the Universitat de Barcelona, and Gemma Escribà i Bonastre graciously shared her knowledge of medieval sources. Thanks are due also to José María Martí Bonet and Eduard Ribera at the Arxiu Diocesà de Barcelona; Josep Baucells i Reig at the Arxiu de la Catedral de Barcelona; the staff of the Biblioteca de Catalunya; Mossèn Miquel S. Gros i Pujol, Ramon Ordeig i Mata, and Rafel Ginebra i Molins at the Arxiu Episcopal de Vic; and Albert Serrat at the Arxiu Diocesà de Girona.

At Rutgers University, I am especially grateful to Rudy Bell, Alastair Bellany, Indrani Chaterjee, Paul Clemens, Belinda Davis, Leslie Fishbein, Ziva Galili, Sumit Guha, Paul Hanebrink, Jennifer Jones, Toby Jones, Temma Kaplan, Samantha Kelly, Leah Kronenberg, Jim Masschaele, Sara Milstein, Gary Rendsburg, Peter Silver, Hilit Surowitz-Israel, Camila Townsend, Azzan Yadin-Israel, and Yael Zerubavel for their warm collegiality; Mike Siegel for his patience and skill in creating the maps for this book; Jonathan Gribetz, Karl Morrison, and Jeffrey Shandler for making valuable suggestions on portions of the manuscript; and Nancy Sinkoff for her incisive comments on a draft of the entire book. Thanks are due also to Arlene Goldstein, who has helped in countless ways, and to my students, who have challenged me to think broadly about history and to ponder always the relation of the past to the present.

A fellowship from the National Endowment for the Humanities allowed me to return to Spain to conduct further archival research and devote the 2009–10 academic year to writing. During that time, Elisheva Baumgarten, Joel Colomer, Yosef Kaplan, Sara Meirowitz, Steven Schoenig, Haym Soloveitchik, and Kenneth Stow provided key assistance. I also had the opportunity to present part of my research at a conference at Princeton University on the *Toledot Yeshu,* where I benefited from the stimulating questions of Yaacov Deutsch, Galit Hasan-Rokem, Sarit Kattan-Gribetz, Ora Limor, Elisha Russ-Fishbane, Peter Schäfer, and Israel Yuval.

The first draft of this manuscript crystallized in the fall of 2010 at the Herbert D. Katz Center for Advanced Judaic Studies at the University of Pennsylvania, decisively shaped by the thoughtful comments of colleagues, staff, and visitors, including Anne Oravetz Albert, David Berger, Elisheva Carlebach, Javier Castaño, Natalie Dohrmann, Theodor Dunkelgrün, Netanel Fisher, Talya Fishman, Sarah Gracombe, Elliot Horowitz, Robert Jütte, Ephraim Kanarfogel, Jonathan Karp, Arthur Kiron, Pawel Maciejko, Barbara Meyer, David Nirenberg, David Ruderman, Ellie Schainker, Yechiel Schur, Jeffrey Shoulson, and Claude Stuczynski.

I am grateful to Miriam Bodian, who provided early encouragement and, together with Mark D. Meyerson, helped direct the manuscript toward the University of Pennsylvania Press; to the anonymous readers for their excellent suggestions; and to Jerry Singerman, Caroline Winschel, Erica Ginsburg, and the rest of the staff at the University of Pennsylvania Press for ushering this book through the publication process with care.

On a more personal note, I am indebted to Michael Gerber, who convinced me to undertake the academic study of Jewish history; Shai Held, who taught me to wrestle with texts; Thomas N. Bisson, James Hankins, and Louis Miller, who served as mentors at Harvard; Luis Girón-Negrón and Bernard Septimus, who formally introduced me to the history of the Jews of medieval Spain; and to many other friends and teachers, including Pamela Abood Buzalka, Yaacob Dweck, Akiva Herzfeld, Miriam Goldstein, and Ilana Kurshan. I am grateful to my parents, who instilled in me a love of learning; to my parents-in-law, for their enthusiastic support; and to my siblings, Daniela and Joseph.

The present work owes much also to my sons, Isaac and Jonah. Born as it came into being, they have made life sweet and put all things in perspective. Finally, to Daniel, no words can express my gratitude.